THE SECRET LIVES OF *Words*

THE SECRET LIVES OF *Words*

Paul West

HARCOURT, INC. • *New York*   *San Diego*   *London*

Copyright © 2000 by Paul West

All rights reserved. No part of this publication may be
reproduced or transmitted in any form or by any means, electronic
or mechanical, including photocopy, recording, or any
information storage and retrieval system, without permission in
writing from the publisher.

Requests for permission to make copies of any part of the work
should be mailed to the following address:
Permissions Department, Harcourt, Inc., 6277 Sea Harbor Drive,
Orlando, Florida 32887-6777.

Library of Congress Cataloging-in-Publication Data
West, Paul, 1930–
The secret lives of words / Paul West.
p. cm.
ISBN 0-15-100466-8
1. English language—Etymology—Dictionaries. I. Title.

PE1580.W54 2000
422′.03—dc21   99-052623

Designed by Lydia D'moch
Text set in Deepdene
Printed in the United States of America
First edition
ACEDB

Ah, but I love to draw beautiful words, like trumpets of light.... I adore you, words who are sensitive to our sufferings, words in red and lemon yellow, words in the steel-blue color of certain insects, words with the scent of vibrant silks, subtle words of fragrant roses and seaweed, prickly words of sky-blue wasps, words with powerful snouts, words of spotless ermine, words spat out by the sands of the sea, words greener than the Cyrene fleece, discreet words whispered by fishes in the pink ears of shells, bitter words, words of fleurs-de-lis and Flemish cornflowers, sweet words with a pictorial ring, plaintive words of horses being beaten, evil words, festive words, tornado and storm-tossed words, windy words, reedy words, the wise words of children, rainy, tearful words, words without rhyme or reason, I love you! I love you!

—James Ensor

Language, at least, may give up the secrets of life and death, leading us through the maze to the original Word as monster or angel.

—Janet Frame

Contents

The etymology may sometimes be dubious, but the dubiology is always etymous.

Preface

I wonder: Have you ever, on leaving one room for another, and without a backward glance, flicked off behind you a light that wasn't on, thus managing to install in your wake a patch of clutching, nagging brightness that a few yards farther on you feel impelled to return to and deal with? If you are paying the light bill, you return; if not, then maybe not, allowing light to squander itself in that unused room while a tiny worm of guilt begins to spin in your skull.

That is how I sometimes feel about words, moving ahead after scanting them, but at the same time dazzled by an abandoned glory that deserved better. Using a word for some pragmatic purpose is one thing; attending to its history and private life is quite another, requiring of us a tolerance and patience we have not been schooled in.

What follows is a short homage to words, and the devious route they have taken in coming usefully to us—some four hundred in particular, most of whom I propose to treat as honored guests, invited in (or out) for a drink, a handshake, and, in some cases, an exchange of blue movies.

Words we take for granted, but a year without them would perhaps bring home to us what a precious, complex heritage they are, making us unique on the planet. Indeed, it would only be in words that we could express our amazement at having such a treasury within reach. If we don't respect or treasure words for their sheer usefulness, we are hardly likely to marvel at them for their extraordinary life story; they come to us, not new-minted at the local supermarket, but hand-me-down remnants of ancient mutterings, over the centuries mauled and muddled, misused and misheard, twisted and new-fangled, yet somehow surviving their origins and incessant use. Able to use language to talk about itself, we might miss the vast story of human experience that has not only informed words—filled them with meanings—but shaped them as well. Molière's Monsieur Jourdain in *The Bourgeois Gentleman* exclaims with surprise that he has been speaking prose for years without knowing it. Well, we ourselves, using how many million words a year, have been spouting history and fiction, biology and anatomy, obscenity and understatement, without knowing it. How hard it is, if you are reviewing with any skill at all the next twenty words you are going to use in a conversation, to ponder their intimate history, if you even know it; but taking time to study them in this fashion becomes a salute to distant ancestors and a delight in viewing ourselves at our most human. Sadly, all words seem much the same to many people, like checkers, and they feel about them much as I do about Vivaldi's *Four Seasons*: all sound like Winter.

I still enjoy the image of my plumber who, with tin snips in sealant-caked hands, first heard the story of the word *gasket*. "An unstanched wench," I told him. "*Garcette* in French, meaning a boy-girl, suggests an intact virgin who nonetheless leaks." "*Of course* she does," he said, and he took *gasket* home to create trouble with among his wife and twelve children.

The word's etymology is muddled, to be sure, but etymology is muddle, and where you look for reason you often find bias. A gasket seals or improves a seal. The word's essence, to others if not plumbers, is obscure, and it may, in the lascivious dark of prehistory, have to do with female orgasm or with menstruation. This is not the place to explore the matter further, but let us note the word's undeniable sexist flavor. When you come right down to it, boys leak as much as girls, do they not, thanks to glands discovered by a Dr. Cowper in the seventeenth century? We are a Leakey species, pun intended.

I try to fix exactly when my fascination with words—and their bizarre history—began: perhaps when I started studying French and Latin, awed that there were other labels for things just as effective as English ones, and with knotty rules policing them (the constabulary of vocabulary). Sure, words have unique sound, shape, repute, but they also have uncanny insides, some of which we can ferret out, some of which will be always lost (although a BBC TV program once attempted to improvise fake etymologies). In our throats the history of the race reveals itself, sometimes cryptically, sometimes not. Over the years, I have kept word books, mainly words to be explored, and recently I have collected mostly common words that belong together.

I introduce a grateful album, a personal sampling of history-laden words, in which humanity can be seen plain, groping and hoping, somehow fudging together a manipulable language early or late. Some words, as we know and appreciate, are newcomers, yet authoritative, while others like loaves from an Alpine bakery have cloud in their dough. This is hardly a bedtime book, but one to wake you up and maybe to worry you, give you nightmares. It would also, I trust, renew our respect for slapdash human ingenuity and the bizarre twists we permit our minds to take.

I hope to have communicated the thrill of finding yet another word, and then another, full of lore, and kept alive the gusto of first celebrating my precious and semiprecious finds. Words are uniquely human, the silk of our so-called civilization, and worthy now and then of prolonged scrutiny as we blink at thousands of years (sometimes) compressed into one or two syllables, each one an emblem utterable in a breath. Perhaps the most stirring, and moving, transition in a word is the one that happens when, under the Indo-European word *dheigh-* (kneader of clay or dough), we find Anglo-Saxon *hlaefdige*, for mistress of a household, gradually drifting about until it begins also to mean all kinds of shaping, fashioning, and creating, from feint to fiction, in the end, perhaps because the provident lady of the house has kneaded enough dough to make a wall of loaves, blooming into the extraordinary metaphor found in Avestan: *pairi-daeza*, the wall of paradise originally built from mud or clay, and then from bread made by a female shielding her family from the world.

There is more to be said about this startling transformation, in which words that seem apart from one another surrender credentials that prove them siblings. This, I suggest, is the excitement of poring over the small print of glossaries and allowing the social ambit of a word to infect our modern apprehension of it. That fiction, say, never mind bread, is a unique passage to a safe paradise is a thought a novelist might treasure. When I told a seminar of fiction-writing MFA students about this, they were stunned, half suspecting I'd fudged up the whole idea—a tribute to the power of fiction. But they soon got the point and went away, if not ennobled, at least amazed by the picaresque motions of words in the hinterlands of prehistory. These motions make our reading twitch with almost invincible nostalgia.

One of the optional ways of reading, perhaps not of writing, is to try to keep in mind a word's vehicular status at the same time as appreciating its tenor. There are dead millions behind these scratchmarks we call words, possibly of no consequence to us until we realize that, if civilization survives, our own barkings and scrawlings will one day become merely anonymous touches in the onward surge of speech. Why is it, I wonder, that humans care so much about the biography of the words they use. Is it because we hate *proactive*, fresh from the factory? Or that, precariously situated in time, we yearn for something that has endured, and survived death? Perhaps, in using words informedly, we feel an honorable bigotry about them, freakish and erratic as their development has often been. What makes us unique has a love-story tattooed on its back.

II Two of the most interesting forays into the domain of words do much the same thing in wholly different ways. In *The Structure of Complex Words* (1951), William Empson, with near-mathematical rigor, explores certain salient words: "wit" in Alexander Pope's *Essay on Criticism*, "sense" in Wordsworth's *The Prelude*, "all" in Milton's *Paradise Lost*, "fool" in *King Lear*, and others. It is an arresting proposal conducted under almost sybilline auspices far from those of C. S. Lewis's *Studies in Words* (1960), which also examines "wit" and "sense," though in a more general fashion, but also "free" and "sad." The overlap looks bigger than it is. Lewis, in his down-home way, as distinct from Empson's mandarin, allows himself to concede the following:

> After hearing one chapter of this book when it was still a lecture, a man remarked to me "You have made me afraid to say anything at all." I know what he meant. Prolonged thought about the words which we ordinarily use to think with can produce a momentary aphasia. I think it is to be welcomed. It is well we should become aware of what we are doing when we speak, of the ancient, fragile, and (well used) immensely potent instruments that words are.

This makes sense to me, especially the part about what's ancient, a dimension that may indeed give us sustained pause as it hits us, perhaps for the first time, how many millions have used earlier versions of the very word we are preparing to use. A glance at such a hypothetical version of it as the Indo-European may deter us with its often unpronounceable-looking consonantal combinations and its dashes, asterisks, and numbers carefully situated in the place of the "2" in x^2. (One wonders that the mathematically inclined Empson never turned his attention to Indo-European.) *bhergh-*[2] means "high"; with derivatives referring to hills and hill-forts. Here, indeed, conjecturally speaking, because Indo-European is a conjured-up language, inevitable no doubt but without a literature, is the source, thinly disguised, of the *berg* in *iceberg*. I don't think we should quite come to a perplexing halt when we realize something such, or feel embarrassed; but we might feel awed, grateful, inspired, in the weirdest ingenious way cared for by our ancestors, who made it easy for us to refer to a floating massif of ice. Language is here to enable us, not to paralyze. It won't stop us dead when we discover, if we do, that a lot of botanical Latin, so-called, is in fact Latinized Greek. Such is one of the more abstruse recognitions that work with words may eventually lead us to.

Fortunately there are easier and more entertaining ways of demonstrating the double, multiple identity of words, the depths and distances they have come from, the hazards they have endured, the good luck they have sometimes had. It is as simple as saying, in a spirit of eminent roll-call as after a fierce battle: Abacus means dust. An admiral is an Emir. Amethyst means not drunk. April is Aphrodite. Asbestos is a table napkin. Assassins take hashish. Atishoo echoes *à tes souhaits*, the French equivalent of *Gesundheit!* or *God bless you!* An atom is uncuttable (at least it was before Fermi). Aubergine means anti-fart. An avocado is a testicle. A bidet is a small horse. Gorblimey means God blind me. Bungalows are Bengali. Character means branding-iron. A cliché is a frying noise. A cloud is a hill. A companion is one who eats bread with you. A doozie is a Duesenberg. Exuberant means big-breasted. Feisty is a word for a farting dog. And frangipani is all about an Italian count who, hating the reek of leather, had his gloves perfumed and so won the interest of pastry chefs, who named an almond-custard dessert after him that smelled, like his gloves, of red jasmine.

See how easy it might be to lose the modern sense of *abacus*, *admiral*, *amethyst*, and *April*, and the rest, initially confounded by the historical freakishness of it all, then just about submerged in what seem underground meanings that if they linger might even twist your response to the word in our own time. It would be possible to take a passage of Homer or Cervantes, say, and then write out the buried meanings of words used therein, perhaps trying valiantly to rig the whole thing together with the original sentence structure. I call this etymological reading, a kind of mining, a descent toward the center of language's earth. There is no need to read in this way, but it is hard to resist, say, battening on to the biography of a word whose vicissitudes astound us when, all our lives, we had formed rather staid responses to *abacus*, *admiral*, *amethyst*, and *April*, four lovely words to be sure.

It would even be possible, and maybe fun, to construct a sentence in which four such words, chosen at random (or forced upon you thus) figured in dramatic fashion, with slight rearrangements. Say, to begin with, since we have no verb at our disposal, *Abacus in hand, the admiral said an amethyst contained all of April.* Only to realize, we ourselves, that what this to an extent means is something on the lines of: *Hands full of dust, the Emir, far from drunk, plied Aphrodite....*Leave that unfinished. I once even went so far as to create a character in a novel (an unpublished one that actually yielded several short stories instead) who wrote poems in Indo-European, and everybody thought he was bonkers, but all the time he was on the look-out for the vital someone who would understand him.

Well, you don't *have* to dabble in Indo-European, or do a sinister kind of X-ray upon your abacus, admiral, amethyst, and April. The words await your pleasure in whatever way you want to use or enjoy them; but to each there is a cone of reverberation that aims across the ages and almost seems to amplify the mere-ness of the word, which means a cone with blunt end past-ward and point toward us, who think we have the art of reference taped and tied down. We don't, and perhaps we shouldn't.

I wonder what impact it would have on society if all speak-ers and writers used words with an acute and chronic sense of everything the words had been, so that, with each word, there came an umbra and a penumbra: the word we used, *abacus*, say, in bright modern sunlight, but its ancestors—Hebrew *abaq*, Greek *abax*—looming personably in a series of interacting devi-ous shadows. Perhaps we would develop a new, educated stam-mer after realizing that, for the Greeks, in this instance, *abax* was a drawing-board coated with sand or dust, on which to draw, write, or make calculations. You see how one kind of table eventually became another, abstract yet with moveable parts; the dust became the beads, the balls, the counting frame. Having said that, I surmise that someone will remember it and, the next time she sees an abacus, will have (I hope) a richer awareness of it, as if it had an extra dimension. Perhaps an aba-cus that both is and is not dust will have almost as pungent an impact on our senses as John Donne's famous line "A bracelet of bright hair about the bone," having within it a comparable sense of historical motion. Each to his own. I can only confess that, since I started delving into the words I used, some twenty years ago, I have had that uneasy feeling of something gaining on me, something examining me from far away, mocking me for being so bottled up in the twentieth century. Kierkegaard's lovely phrase, "happy above seventy thousand fathoms," comes to mind.

That is how I feel now, having come to know something about the lives lived by a fraction of the words I use. It's im-possible to know enough, but even a smattering alters your re-sponse to a kitchen or a garden, not to mention a classic of literature. One swims, of course, in the top two feet, or even less, but aware of the deeps beneath, if there are such. Swimming in the top layer of language is good enough indeed, but swimming there with some inkling of what's below puts all we say and write in a colossal context. It is only a matter of being aware of it, of knowledge for the sake of knowledge, to be sure, but also of our being here, the frail remainder of those Indo-Europeans who left almost nothing behind except an enticing blank like the missing-man formation flown by a squadron after a pilot's death. So far as we can reconstruct their language, they had a special word for speaking to the deity: *meldh*, and another, *wekwomtext*, for poet. Clearly they were folk of palpable seriousness and grace. We, the more or less known, are their descendants, and to some extent their rivals, blotting them out with neologisms and brilliant slang.

I am talking E. M. Forster talk, I suppose, recommending "Only connect" before it is too late, something nearly impossible to do with the so-called Indo-Europeans (how vague and amorphous a name), but feasible with other tribes, whose dialect we might regard as having been purified. The challenge is hardly that of the spacefarer, but rather that of the lingua-farer, occupied not so much with quaint little novelties that lurch up from a studied word as with what R. W. Chambers used to call the continuity of English prose, his academic term for something vaster I call the discontinuity of Western words. None of your streamlined series of marques here, with all branchings and variants meticulously labeled in subsets, but *lingua saeva*—fierce language—developing and faltering all the time, the result not unlike what goes on in the design shops of aircraft companies, where the numbers follow no even beat, and the offshoots come to have a maze of successive applications (e.g., PA-32R-301SP). That sort of thing, which also happens to aero-engines. Modifications crowd in, demanding a title, or an allusion at least, and for a moment, perhaps for ever if the designers don't clean up their act, mere appellation threatens to blur altogether and everyone is happy to settle at the last for something vivid and uncluttered such as "Citation" (seemingly), "Skyknife," or "Airhawk." Thus the descent from number mummery to verbal cliché, but, heaven help us, we have to call things *something*, and often just numbering them isn't enough, as the RAF found when, during the Second World War, they had to give numbered U.S. planes such names as Tomahawk, Maryland, Baltimore, Harvard, Yale, Hudson, Liberator, Airacobra, Thunderbolt, Mustang, Dakota, and so on.

III I have come too far perhaps, but the son of a pianist and an engineer is no doubt entitled to do so, and the distances behind the words are unthinkable, literally beyond us, whereas fifty years since a war is a mere trice. I sometimes regale myself with an image of the hell-bent reader not content with tracking the words being read who stretches out to the etymology of the words in the definitions the etymology provides, and then to the etymology of those words, and so endlessly on, accosting infinity as if it were a parlor game. I do not think we have to go so far, though if we do we come back, if ever, to a reassuring straitjacket, numbingly converted to and mutilated by the march of the centuries, those heedless diagrams. A little taste of such infinite voracity goes far enough, giving us the elastic, stratified, dwindling-power of words, receding from us at a speed so slow we cannot apprehend it (a sound change occupying a century!). A shift from the thirteenth to the seventeenth can occupy a few lines only, but we miss the creaking, gravid heave of the wheel, the obtuse slow motion of time. I think words and their naked history can acquaint us with some of this push.

My own approach to words, indeed to their iceberg nature, has grown from delighted mystification to near-voluptuous savoring of the illicit, almost as if, in a bright and pragmatic context, something criminal were brewing: a touch of gangsterism amid the rectitudes. Tracking and plumbing words, I confess I watched certain commanding entities or concepts come forth, a prancing troupe from the heart of hardbound definition; inflations, explosions, balloonings, inexplicable switches, the kind of misrule that Sir John Falstaff personifies, and all in the midst of a medium prized for its rigid accuracy.

If this be the Dionysian view of language, much as there was G. Wilson Knight's Dionysian view of Shakespeare, then so be it. I never saw so many words having a lost weekend (or couple of centuries), a whole era out on the town in uncouth disguise (small-horse bidet; lumps of asbestos chucked into the fire to cleanse them for further duty as table napkins among ancient Athenians; a cloud that becomes a hill). Carnival of the animals maybe, but one run by Wells's Doctor Moreau, with inexplicable dysgenic changes thrust upon them or wrung out of their vulnerable genes. A free-for-all. Theory used to have it that language emerged from the rational observation of phenomena and mind, in the end settling down into a perfect match of concept and word. Certainly, on the level of pious hopes exercised, that remains an element in the creation of language, but the process overall is one of preposterous flukes with the educated lagging far behind the people as a whole. One recalls T. S. Eliot's idea, amid the valiant but exasperating study *Notes Towards a Definition of Culture*, that culture is whatever the people do. So, too, language, a rough farrago hard to reform, even with Sir Humphry Davy on one end arguing for *aluminum* (and impressing only America) and the Royal Society on the other arguing for "aluminium" as having a more "classical" sound. If you discover a metal, as Davy did, then surely you have some right to name it.

So I felt I was an Aladdin rubbing the linguistic lamp in the shadows, and out came running the most extraordinary motley of engaging phantoms, who have kept me beguiled ever since, even in the throes of trying to compose immaculate sentences: no stain, somewhat original. I almost became afraid to use a word whose origin, and misadventures, I didn't know. On one level,

I almost had to teach myself *assassin, avocado, character, cliché;* on another, a sub-level, *hashish, testicle, branding iron, frying noise.* It was like trying to believe the world is both flat and round; and it was never a matter of reassuring myself with the responsible view that said, yes, all this other stuff—the replete baggage of history, epiglottis, and cussedness—is really beside the point for the modern reader. Etymology doesn't interfere. It already has.

The study of the secret, private lives of words, their hinterland and vicissitudes, sometimes recalls the good-natured music of the Swede Franz Berwald, whose voluminous mild agitations get interrupted now and then by incidents of sheer melodious delicacy, as if the sun had suddenly come through, perhaps changing your view of the entire composition. Yet he does not, cannot, develop this haunting phrase, so little so that it seems an idyllic intrusion, begging to be taken on and exploited, yet left in embryonic deliciousness and only fleetingly echoed farther on. This is to say that the history of words will not always ravish us with joy and delight, but an occasional shaft of golden light comes keenly through. Even movies for cognoscenti might emerge from, say, one tenth of these little histories, in which fey counts mingle with bull-headed explorers, taut-lipped scientists such as Davy cross swords with the Earl of Sandwich, and pucker-mouthed Greeks, who use asbestos as a table napkin, take dinner with colleagues who sport an amethyst to prove their sobriety. Certainly, without becoming a concrete poet who dotes on the contours of typography, one can become a devotee of words, the seeming raw materials we take for granted: passive and perfect. Indeed, whoever attempts to do etymology ends up doing the social history of the word, checking the underwear of the mind.

While my matter-of-fact, efficient fellow-novelists invest in svelte electronic machinery that counts up for them and churns out flawlessly printed and corrected copies, I soldier on at mere typewriters, correcting with scissors and paste, the result being an origami palimpsest I have to apologize for when I lug the resulting manuscript to the copy shop. My pages always take twice as long, having to be hand-fed. That is exactly the point, of course; I don't like to get too far from the word, either from its sleek modern model or from its tarted-up old impersonations. Could I get closer? Of course. I could print things out big, glue the words to thin plywood, and using a fretwork saw cut them out, glorying in the lightweight rib as I held it, and its meanings, in my hand, balanced like a big dry moth. I imagine not many of my colleagues and friends need this artisan's approach to words. Indeed, those who know only what words are *for* can hardly know what words *are*. I cannot find it within me to see them only as manipulable counters, though they are that; they seem, quite often, a parade of gorgeous animals muttering by, a caravan slouching off to Gutenberg or some equally imaginary place.

Behold some of my favorites, including words that have caught my attention without endearing themselves, and the roughneck lives others have led between the Indo-Europeans of the imagined abyss and the latest abomination of the MBAs. Sometimes, in our quest to appreciate the fruits of civilization, we have almost no recourse, assisted little by reason, habit, or system. We have only the faint subterfuges of untutored eloquence, gleaned from a cave, and if we get anywhere at all in our quest it is as if the words themselves had volunteered to help: spastic miscreants born to disguise and deformity.

 To the cry, *Who do you think you are?*, which we have all heard in the heat of someone's indignation, I tend not to answer, hoping to be who I seem to be. Who I would like to be, if not a novelist (or a composer of symphonies), is the faultless etymologist who, when asked, *Why do we call a fillet of steak a fillet?* or *What's the story of asbestos?*, can say,

I'll tell you. And on he goes, sweeping the verbal past with his exhaustive glass, glancing through revolutions at the scaffold and on the fashion runway, rebellions by peasant and bourgeois, vast changes in climate, new techniques of manufacturing, strange fruit imported from Siam, a new generation of industrial slaves imported from Bechuanaland, ructions at court and quiet scientists inventing and naming substances hitherto unheard of—penetrating all this to elicit the successive cores of words, never at a loss, but always able to delineate magic filaments that connect the word with social ferment, with other words even. He is never adrift in mere philology. I envy him, never having put in as much time in this as he, whose life has become overwhelming finite connections, in which everything, just about, is related to everything else, as in a supreme web.

That enviable, almost superhuman scholarly vision escapes me, but not altogether as, time and again, after I have looked something up, I sigh, "Of course: *fillet* from string, *filet* in French, *asbestos* being Greek for "inextinguishable," like the mythic stone that, once set fire to, could not be put out. The sensation of knowing more, as miscellaneous knowledge fans out over an ever-wider area, relating your slips of the tongue to the human verbal enterprise at large, is stupendous, the kind of noble aggrandisement the great Victorians Pater, Arnold, and Ruskin said came from attachment to a great religion, or indeed any body of major thought. Chronic connectedness while babbling in the current idiom sums it up. We have all been M. Jourdains in our time, with a foot every now and then crashing through the crust into something ancient and ignored, yet propulsive and definitive through centuries. To be fully languaged would entail knowing all the languages and their histories. Only a few manage that while the rest of us pick away at the feast.

You end haunted, unable to pass up a word, bound to go look it up, consider it for admission to your little black book.

You live with dictionaries by your side. You end up reading them, indifferent to the violent and nonsensical juxtapositions they foster. By the same token, you begin to worry about the way the tyrannical alphabet shapes such a book as this, burying aesthetic contrast in haphazard clash (if you were wholly in control, you would put the one-line entry on *Zipangu*, Marco Polo's word for Japan, next to the long entry about the absurd). Yet you can't, and this makes you more of a slave than ever, not merely a mnemonic one, but a passive one who must forgo the whole idea of momentum and transition in the interests of ABZ.

In any case, I live in a house where we use paper plates so we can scribble down bright ideas that occur even as we eat. When guests give us good ideas, we cannot write them down on the china, and so resort to little notebooks and pencils cached in the bathrooms. All people make love to their callings, but when your avocation seems to make love to you, requiring your attention to history, skeleton, and tissue, you feel put upon, dogged by the Greek concept *etumon*, meaning true, real, actual, as in *etymology*—etymology being study of the true word. The famous curse visited upon the intelligent reader is always to read with pencil in hand; the fate of the etymological reader is worse, requiring a phalanx of reference books in hand, swifter than the Internet and better informed. To some, this may seem too antiquarian, yet the only alternative is to read obliviously, severed from all previous usage. Etymological reading may be indeed the nemesis of attentive reading, inducing a strange absent-mindedness that turns out to be a too-much-mindedness, the reader too crammed with data to follow the writer's trajectory. *Leave me alone*, I hear the anti-etymological reader howling, *let me read in peace*. And in blindness, indifference, crass contemporaneity too. Are these alternatives anyway? Only to someone under duress. An alert, searching, inquisitive reader will always, I suspect, feel the urge to burrow backward as he/she strives forward guided by this or that author's dialect of now, but eminently tugged at, got at, tempted away, made to dream ancient dreams on modern occasions (indeed, I steal the phrase from an old ally, Philip Rahv, and his lovely anthology of that name, the phrase ever evocative). There was more to Count Frangipani's gloves than we will ever know: That is the novelist in me speaking, and vowing to fill the gap as I have filled in other gaps for Milton, Count von Stauffenberg, Jack the Ripper, and Lord Byron's doctor. Tempted, one gets in too deep and then yearns to drown.

My venerable old red-haired Anglo-Saxon professor, who once invited me to specialize in philology (I recoiled in horror then), would enter the lecture hall, soft-shod in sandals that contained bare feet, with a green jug of his special water, from which he poured a little and drank before beginning something crushingly esoteric: "The man in the street thinks the Ojibway word for secrecy is *achogna*, but he is wrong, it is *ahatuhatuhu!*" We all roared, little knowing how much he knew how little we knew. So, one tries to make amends and catch up, confounded by the history of everything, not just the worn and wonderful.

Rather than make this an assembly of mere entries, I have sometimes resorted to personal reminiscence, of the word-in-the-life, so to speak, tempted into this by some awareness of how people speak and write, not with absolute, impersonal correctness, but idiosyncratically and subjectively slanted. One's chat, say, over seventy years, becomes a monument of improvisational accost, one's written words a different form of that. In a similar spirit, the reader is invited to take from the information supplied the most gratifying pieces of a word's hidden life (say the first time the Old English word for *hill* became the word for cloud). Imagine the first week of that landscape change! Over time, my hands have become sore and sprained from wielding large reference books not available in CD ROM: a snag of the trade. Indeed, they have suffered more than I, with bindings split and sundered.

On reading through, or rather dipping as I hope the reader will, I discover certain motifs to which I recur, mainly because I was doing something else with them at the time of writing: *Macbeth*, aviation, legal parlance, but also because, for instance, if you have an English childhood you probably cannot have an American one (alas); my childhood surrounded me with words and piano music, and I have never got over it. I grew up playing cricket and soccer. I am forever exploring the names of my medications (are they arbitrary? sometimes not). Latin grammar, Yiddish and slang, idioms of Australia and South Africa fascinate me and would provide another book. Oddly, I have here written little about classical music, an art form I envy and strive to know better. The book begins with *abacus* and ends with *zymurgist*, a slightly contrived accident joining two powders: dust and yeast. Or, indeed, dust to dust.

Having mentioned C. S. Lewis, I cite him again only because he found time to write to me while he was composing *A Grief Observed*, his heart-rending cry of indignation at the death of his American wife, Joy. After that short, mesmerizingly happy marriage, he could not face the universe:

> I look up at the night sky. Is anything more certain than that in all those vast times and spaces, if I were allowed to search them, I should nowhere find her face, her voice, her touch? She died. She is dead. Is the word so difficult to learn?

It is painful to see the expert on such words as *sense, wit, free,* and most of all *sad,* grappling with a mere monosyllable that numbs the mind of all who study it.

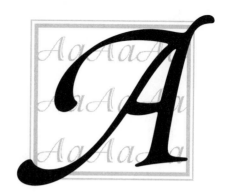

ABACUS

Some claim that this word contains the click of the balls in the frame. The word, from Hebrew *abaq*, meaning "dust," arrived in Greek to denote a drawing board coated with dust or sand, in either of which you drew with a finger or a stick. Greek *abax* eventually came to mean *table* as well, both in the literal and mathematical senses, but it was as the word for a dust- or sand-covered board that English in the fourteenth century adopted *abacus* from Latin. Three centuries later, the word came to mean the counting frame familiar to us now, followed by the concept of a frame with balls. It has nothing to do with the Bahamian islands of Abaco.

ABLATIVE ABSOLUTE

The ablative absolute has awed many who have not grasped its feeble nature. Or perhaps just the sound of certain words (*sarcophagus*, *Druid*) frightens people; I once affronted a Toronto university audience by using "entelechy." What we have here is (surgically) something cut away, removed, and this is the sense of the grammar too (not always made clear by definitions that harp on separation, cause, circumstance, and time). The essence of the ablative absolute is that something has been thoroughly subordinated to the rest of the sentence. So, if you write *Regibus expulsis, leges respublica condit*, you are saying "The kings having been expelled, the republic sets up laws," subduing the import of the first phrase as if it didn't matter. Utter removal. Often, there is some impatience, or a "Thank-God-that's-over" feeling about the ablative absolute; Julius Caesar often begins a sentence rather hurriedly and blandly saying "These things having been done," and he has cleared the ground; the silhouette of whatever was there standing above it has been felled, brought low, made piffle. Perfunctory opens the cave to splendors. A fellow-author shows me the following: "Standing in a blustery Antarctic wind, while a vast city-state of penguins milled noisily about me, I was surprised...." A copy editor has changed this to: "Standing in the blustery Antarctic wind, a vast city-state of penguins milling noisily around me, I...." Notice how the fudged-up ablative absolute unprefaced by a "with" opens the gate for a technical misidentification of the noun phrase which previously had a verb. I don't find this an improvement, and suggest it happens only because not enough readers are sensitive to such things as dangling modifiers, whatever they protest. To grammar, in other words, in a country whose favorite pseudo-grammatical link is the word "and," the copula that blurs causation and relationship.

ABOMINABLE

Misanthropes have meddled with this one, to no one's credit. In Latin, *abominari*, the passive infinitive, meant to shun as evil omen—its gist *away with the evil omen*, *ab-* signifying "away." Hence the adjective *abominabilis*, capable or worthy of being shunned, moving easily into Old French and into English. From the fourteenth to the seventeenth centuries, willful minds saw in *abominable* a reference to *homo, hominis,* intending a departure from humankind and therefore bestial, unnatural. Thus came about the misspelling *abhominable,* as salient a piece of wishful spurning as language has seen. In this way, the word, however spelled, developed an intenser blame, scotching the omen or undesirable trait in an overall condemnation that equated nasty with inhuman. Someone with abominable manners or body odor thus became a reject from the species, satanic and null.

ABRACADABRA

This magical incantation became English and encountered English prosody, probably via French, from the Greek *abrasadabra* (English *c* came from Greek's *s* written as a *c*). This is third-century A.D. material, perhaps a cabbalistic word of the Basilidian sect, Gnostics of Alexandria, who worshiped a deity called *Abraxas.* Merely to recite this formula was to bring into play magical powers that could avert disease or disaster (compare with *mumbo-jumbo*). Sometimes, when a conjuror is operating, *presto* or *hey presto* will follow *abracadabra,* to underline the moment of prestidigital revelation. English borrowed *presto,* for "quick," in the sixteenth century, deriving from Latin *praesto,* "at hand." Properly monitored (or minotaured), Abraxas delivered the good without delay.

ABSINTHE

Meet Artemisia absinthium, Absinthe, Absinthium, Green Ginger, Madderwort, otherwise known as wormwood, gray-green and nearly shrublike, declared unsafe by the U.S. Drug and Food Administration. Supposedly, *wormwood* promotes menstruation, heals drunkenness, works as a tonic, stimulates appetite, fights intestinal worms (an anthelmintic), fixes gout, kidney stones, and jaundice, makes a fine compress, is antiseptic, and a good strewing herb to hide bad odors and repel vermin. Absinthe, however, ruined nervous systems and caused mental rot, and was banned in both the U.S.A. and France in the early twentieth century, used today only to flavor vermouth (a little bitterer) and to provide a drab garden background for more colorful blooms. It remains green and aromatic, and legendary, with its licorice flavor and literary associations from the "Decadent" 1890s, when green was the in-color, from green flowers to green complexions. The Greek or Mediterranean word was *apsinthion*.

ABSORB

Words of drinking and swallowing are sibilant or popping. *s* and *sh*, *b* and *p* are common, as in Arabic *surab*, for instance, which confers *syrup* upon us. *Absorb* is another, with the prefix *ab* (away) on top of *sorbere*, to swallow or suck up (not socially). Try to say the Indo-European template word *srobh*, if you can, which has behind the scenes both *sorbere* and Greek *rofein* (slurp up). Such gobstopper juice-sluices join us to some very ancient ancestors, yet site us not that far from Adolf Hitler lowering his chin to the lip of his plate and shoveling the meal toward him with horizontal zeal.

ABSURD

We do not hear as much of the Absurd as we used to; in cold storage in Kierkegaard and Camus, the term has lapsed from vogue, still of course evoking anything that is *surdus*, meaning irrational or senseless and so, by unkind extension, backward or deaf (*sourd* is "deaf" in French). The *ab* means "utterly," but I wonder if anything is utterly absurd. The human condition is too mixed for that. Camus defined the absurd as the gap between the mind that yearns and the world that lets it down, by which usually we intend death, the way in which the universe looks after itself and has no response to our individual fates. But to complain that the universe, so to speak, doesn't treat us as well as it does itself is to liken the human to the cosmic, and not that justifiably. Semifacetious allusions apart (yes, a human can be a white dwarf, even a red giant), you and I are quite unlike the universe: not expanding or contracting or pulsating, nor made up of clusters of galaxies strewn throughout a vacuum, nor even as constant as suns, as untidy as an open cluster, or, for that, as organized as a molecule, as inscrutably omnivorous as a black hole. Indeed, even where the universe might seem a bit absurd—with its so-called "wobbles" in the genetic code, with six ways of making one essential chemical but only one of making another chemical just as essential—it still gets by, through a predominance of successful chances.

We are not the small version of that; the universe is an absolute, which means it needs nothing but itself, whereas we humans want to be without lack, as Sartre says. You could, I suppose, work out an exact ratio of component parts, likening molecules to hypothetical planets around many, many stars, and human individuals to suns, families to clusters, clans to galaxies; but the universe, made of the same stuff as we, is what includes us, and continually reuses us. We cannot sever ourselves from it to become unobligated exceptions. All we can do is heed what we have in common with suns, as we heed what we have in common with elephants or clouds without becoming elephantine or cloudy, and cease being infatuated with metaphors that take us from the body to the body politic, from a body of thought to bodies celestial. Our special gift, it seems, is to be the universe's way of pondering (and disliking) itself, and that gift brings hazards with it, including disliking the way the universe uses us to formulate a dislike of itself it can ignore without using us at all.

Even worse, if you settle for the human microcosm vis-à-vis the cosmic microcosm, you first of all run into Beckett's nastiest aphorism and get wounded by it: "The mortal microcosm cannot forgive the relative immortality of the macrocosm." The word "relative" evinces our indignant ignorance but doesn't remind us that anyone who makes microcosms, and wants them accurate, has to reckon with this: Each microcosm adds itself to the macrocosm (it has nowhere else to go), so an accurate microcosm has to include—in little, of course—all the microcosms that have been added, are being added, will be added to the great big cosm itself. Halt everything, you say; no more microcosms added until mine's finished. Impossible: Just as the expanding edge of the universe outstrips the astronomer's telescopes, so does the constant surfeit of microcosms outstrip the micro-cosmetician who, in the very act of trying to sum up, both thwarts himself and renders others obsolete. The universe at large does funny things: Galaxies collide or deform one another; every now and then, a subatomic particle called the anti-sigma minus hyperon goes the wrong way; and, each year, in a putative room full of radium atoms, one dies, but why that particular one we have no idea. The universe does funny things within us, too, making children age at enormous speed until a ten-year-old is bald and toothless, or making a mongol here, a cretin there, or (the terms vary) sustains an incessant act of revolt, refusal, defiance, disdaining both bromides and appeals. In this way, although hemmed in by a dense, alien, almost mathematical matrix of non-stop phenomena, the mind works with what it has, watching the natural world with almost opinionless attentiveness, making the most of things rather than the best, and staying put with tenacity and acumen. We are the only models of us.

This program is easier for the creative artist than for others. If the mind is redundant vis-à-vis the cosmic imponderables, it may have a role in ministering to itself; after all, the absurd—the gulf between desire and fact—exists only in the human mind, and that may make "brainworkers" of us all.

It is enlightening to study the concepts that attach themselves to the most primitive versions of the absurd, when the Arabs thought of it, for instance, as a "deaf root," heedless of human demands or preferences. Not only deafness and discordance hem it in, but buzzing swarms around it, swirls and eddies, harsh reduplicated forms of *whisper* such as *susurrus*. Back even in Indo-European, that hypothetical necessity of a language from which other languages point away, the absurd is the harsh jangle of a universe that has no attitude toward us, expecting and promising nothing. The absurd is not a fad.

ACUTE

One of those *sharp* words that all begin with Indo-European *ak*, it makes a diacritical accent "acute," meaning that, for special phonetic quality, it insists on a raised pitch and a primary stress on that particular syllable. Thus, *épuisé*, French for *worn out*, has two acute accents and could not really be pronounced without them, or with a grave accent—acute's complementary opposite— in either place. The French do not accent their capital letters, and, the better educated they are, the more they omit accents, though never in speech. English uses no acute accent, but, to ensure pronunciation of, say, an *-ed* ending to a line of verse, uses the grave: *desirèd*, which always sounds funny.

ADIRONDACKS

The enterprising Martha Barnette in *A Garden of Words* takes time to recall in a footnote that this word was the Mohawk

Indians' "sneering epithet" for that tribe: *Hatironaks* meant "eaters of trees." En passant, she notes that, among other names of abuse, Iowa is thus named because of "a derogatory label" stuck on its Sioux inhabitants: *Ayuwha*, or "the sleepy ones" (mild stuff compared to dendrophages). And *Apache*, she records, derives from a Zuni word for "enemy."

ADMIRAL

He's an *Emir*, this man, from the Arabic taken into French as *amiral* (the *d* slipped in later, from Latin). *Amir* was a Saracen chieftain, in this case *amir-al-bahr* (remember Bahrein): chieftain of the sea. As early as the thirteenth century, the word drifted into English, complete with its Latinate *d*. Notice how *amir-al*, a noun followed by its definite article, struck foreigners as a single word; ever the opportunist, the eavesdropping *Auslander* pleases himself, swiftly converting a loan-word (and a deformation) into a permanent presence. Thus Spanish *almirante de la mar*, pinched from Arabic, soon gave rise in fifteenth-century England to Admiral of the Sea or Admiral of the Navy, a term irresistible in its onrush by 1500, with never a flake in it of *admire*, though couched to command admiration.

AGNOSTIC

Embarrassed at lacking the right label for his lack of spiritual beliefs, the Victorian biologist and skeptic T. H. Huxley (1825–1895) invented this word at a party in 1869, intending by it an "unknowing" condition, from Greek *agnostos*: not knowing. Thus Huxley announced the ultimate unknowability of God, not a bad afternoon's or evening's work at a meeting of the Metaphysical Society in a house on Clapham Common, London.

Huxley is supposed to have had in mind St. Paul's allusion to the altar of "the Unknown God." It is likely that Huxley had this word all ready sometime before he launched it on the puzzled world of believers.

AKIMBO

From Old Norse, first found in its English version in *The Tale of Beryn* (1400) as *in kenebowe*, possibly from *i keng boginn*: "bent in a curve." Meaning bowlike. The arms protrude at the side, with elbows bent. On its next appearance in English, the word is *on kenbow*, and *akimbo* arrives in the eighteenth century. We must stand like this a good deal to have a word for it from 1400 to now. Is it hands on hips or hands in pockets?

ALIAS

The more congenial, cockles-of-your-heart-warming version of *aka*, Also Known As. So we might say *alias* is *aka aka*. Alias is really Latin *alius*, meaning "otherwise." The related word *alibi*, once an adverb, now a noun, literally means somewhere else, in another place: the locative form of *alius* (other), analogous to Greek *allos*. Lawyers made much use of this word adverbially, as reported by John Arbuthnot in *Law Is a Bottomless Pit* (1727): "The prisoner had little to say in his defence; he endeavoured to prove himself Alibi." By 1700, *alibi* was a plea of absence, but not until the twentieth century an excuse. Alias is dying, *alibi* has long been infected. *Inter alia*, by the way, is a neuter plural meaning "among other things" while *inter alios* means "among other people," a masculine accusative plural sexistly including women without noting their presence in the grammar.

ALTRUISM

Deceiving word, this, not least because it has "truism" embedded in it. Also contains the French word *autrui* for "other people," culled from such phrases in French law as *le bien d'autrui* and *le droit d'autrui*. Actually, the philosopher Auguste Comte coined the word in 1830 after the example of Italian *altrui* (that which belongs to other people). Kindred words are *alias*, *else*, and *alter*. It means self-denying high-mindedness or generous self-sacrifice. Schindler of List fame was more or less an altruist; Florence Nightingale and Edith Cavell were thoroughgoing ones.

ALUMINUM

That modest chemist Sir Humphry Davy was brooding on aluminum in 1808 when he confessed in Volume 98 of the *Transactions of the Royal Society* that, had he been so fortunate as to have discovered the metallic substances he kept searching for, he would have proposed for them the names "silicium, alumium, zirconium, and glucium." Four years later, much less diffident, he suggested *aluminum*, today's American spelling, calling on Latin's *alumen*, related to *aluta*, Latin for dried skins softened by being treated with alum; for shoes, purses, and, says Ovid, an ornamental face patch. When the British decided to use *aluminium* as their spelling, *The Quarterly Review* (1812) judged Davy's spelling to have "a less classical sound." *Alum*, by the way, refers to any of various double sulfates of a trivalent metal, and is much used in industry to clarify, harden, and purify; medicinally as an astringent and styptic. In my childhood I found out that alum was used to stiffen the paper cones used in old-fashioned radios, still by the British called *wirelesses*, no doubt because of the more classical sound. *Bauxite*, the ore from which Davy's aluminum came, was first found at *Les Baux* in Southern France, but is still plentiful in Jamaica.

AMAZE

It used to be much more severe, Old English *amasian* meaning to stupefy or stun, most probably by striking on the head. Swedish *masa* is to be sluggish, but Norwegian *masast* means to become unconscious. Our modern sense of *astonish* is a late sixteenth-century refinement pioneered by Shakespeare himself in *Venus and Adonis* (1592): "Crystal eyes, whose full perfection all the world amazes." Minus its initial *a*, the word long before Shakespeare had come to be used about that stand-up puzzle, the *maze*.

AMETHYST

Do you still like this stone despite the scruffy samples offered by TV marketing? It may have magical properties still. Against drunkenness and hangover, the ancients prescribed wearing a wreath of myrtle leaves, and cabbage for breakfast (high in vitamins C and K), which would soon clear the head (although an old Greek proverb gives the lie to this: *Cabbage served twice means death—Dis kramve thanatos*). Even better was the purplish-blue gem whose name was itself allegorical: *a*, meaning *not*, and *methystos, drunk*. Merely to sport this stone was proof enough; it gave its reputation over to you in spite of all the evidence. It is from this word that we get our *methyl*. *Methu* was Greek for *wine* and *methuskein* for intoxicate. *Lithos amethustos* meant "anti-intoxicant stone." Presumably you wore the stone before you began to tipple.

AMOK

We still need this word, thanks to ungovernable behavior in the streets. It comes to us from seventeenth-century Malaya, where *amoq* meant "fighting frenziedly." The word had already, in the previous century, gone into Portuguese, becoming *amouco*—a homicidally crazed Malay, of whom there must have been many, to require a word. *Amok*, often pronounced amuck, has branched out since then (*running amok* is nearly metaphorical now). A crazed accountant running *amok* in Macy's with a surgical rubber hammer would almost qualify.

AMPERSAND

&? An exercise for the symbolic logician? Hardly: This is the sign meaning "*and per se and*," which phrase isn't much help even when you know it means "and by itself and." This sign and only this sign means "and." Can it mean that? Or does it hark back to old grammar books in which it was printed last at the end of the alphabet, and the name of this sign or character is "*and*"? Or was it once a way of writing Latin *et*? With much curlicue and twist? After all, the quaint pseudo-word "*ye*," meaning "*the*," has stuck around for ever, on tea shops and old curiosity shops, and it was merely an earlier culture's way of scrawling "*the*." In my childhood, during which my father read *The Daily Express*, I became accustomed to the newspaper's own emblem: a Crusader with his shield against his side.

ANTIMACASSAR

This cloth covered the backs of chairs from the nineteenth century on to protect them from greasy hair, unwashed or overpomaded or both. The oil was Macassar, a proprietary brand made by Rowland and Son, supposedly from ingredients found in Makassar, part of the island Sulawesi, once Celebes, in Indonesia. Some folk still have antimacassars in their possession, but the need seems not to have survived World War One, not that men began using less oily hair creams, although there was a distinct shift in men's pomade from the brilliantines of yesteryear to less perfumed lotions such as Brylcreem, easily squeezed from a tube and stably perched on the palm. Brylcreem left the hair feeling tight and rigid, with no need of antimacassar behind the recliner's head. Another name for Makassar was Mangkasara, hardly commercially concise.

APRIL

Aphrodite shortened, *Apru* was an Etruscan borrowing from Greek *Aphro*, the goddess of love. In French this became *Avril* (sometimes a girl's name). The fourth month, April, was the Roman month of Venus. They did not come up with the term "April fool," which appeared in the late seventeenth century, signifying, most probably, someone besotted with hormones, cranially affected by the season, whereas our contemporary narrowed usage denotes someone duped and easily so on the first.

APRON

This is one of those words that come about when someone misinterprets the combination of indefinite article plus noun: *a napron* had already become *an apron* by the fifteenth century, a bounce-off from French *naperon* deriving from *nape* ("cloth"), the source of our *napkin*. Oddly, the word *nape* originated with Latin *mappa* ("towel," "napkin"), whence our word *map*. Other words undergoing this consonantal swing to the left are *adder* and *umpire*, a fate denied such a combination as *an anaconda* and *an eft*, for obvious reasons.

ARGOSY

Those who think grandly about words without finding out about them like to relate argosy to the good ship Argo aboard which Jason with his Argonauts sailed in quest of the Golden Fleece. It happens that the two words are quite unrelated, *argosy* having come from Italian *ragusea*, big merchant ship or, more picturesquely, vessel from Ragusa, the seaport on the Dalmatian coast now called Dubrovnik. A spray of spellings appeared in the sixteenth and seventeenth centuries (*arguze, rhaguse, argosea, ragusye*) until *argosy* won out, to become the title of an early twentieth-century men's magazine.

ASBESTOS

Asbestos is old, our wisdom about it new. Hard as it is to believe, both Greece and Rome made table napkins from this stuff; when they got grubby, Greece and Rome, instead of washing them, set them in the fire, then tugged them out again, their whiteness new-minted. The same substance they used as lamp wick, as in the Roman Temple of Athena, where a constant light hovered over the fireproof yet absorbent stem. Greek for this magical fiber was *amiantos lithos* or "undefiled stone," an appellation that went nowhere because Pliny the Elder, a man of estimable social heft, gave it a clever name of his own: *asbestos*, from *a-*, meaning not, and *sbestos*, quenchable. It was as if Shakespeare, with anachronistic spin, had decided to call petrol gasoline. We nowadays go in fear of this undefiled stone, and the image of high-born Greeks and Romans mopping their chops and lips with some deadly wicklike substance gives one pause.

Was there not, once upon a time in the twentieth century, a cult of charcoal not for drawing masters but for indigestion sufferers, who, urged to consume pills of burned wood, vaunted blobs of "purity," did themselves untold damage for reasons now familiar to us from smoked and burned food, not good for us at all, but brimming with carcinogens?

ASSASSIN

During the Crusades, a sect of Muslim fanatics dedicated to the murder of Christians and others kept themselves worked up by taking hashish (cannabis). Hence *hashshash*, for hashish-eater, the plural of which word, *hashshashin*, struck the incurious British as a singular, and thus the word abides, indicating murder for idea or ideology rather than passional crime. The cult began eight hundred years ago under the guidance of an East Indian sheik epically called "The Old Man of the Mountains." The point of eating or smoking hemp was that Mohammedans were teetotallers slow to pious frenzy, at least until they had partaken and met Christian Crusaders en route to the Holy Land.

ATISHOO

Excluded from dictionaries, this imitative word corresponds oddly with French *à tes souhaits, ataysoo-eh*, their version of *God bless*. It even sounds like it, though *à tes souhaits* follows the sneeze. Is this overlap a mere fluke, or has somebody really been listening?

ATOM

What a journey! This word means "undividable" and was assigned in the Middle Ages not merely to the smallest part of matter but also to the smallest imaginable bit of time (an hour contained 22,560 atoms). Democritus and Epicurus were fond of the word, as were their followers in the Middle Ages; when, in the nineteenth century, chemists sought a term for a nucleus surrounded by electrons, *atom* was to hand, even hanging on to its bomb when, in the next century, the uncuttable atom was cut or split. Relatives are *tome* and *anatomy*.

AUBERGINE

To etymologists, this is known as the "anti-fart vegetable," from Sanskrit *vatinganah* (compare Persian *badingan* and Arabic *al-badindjan*). The Moors took it into Spain and Portugal, where it yielded Portuguese *beringela* and Catalan *al-berginia*. Clearly, for good reasons, it was on people's minds. The French came up with *aubergine*, but the British, ignoring the plant's shape, let *eggplant* sink into abeyance while Americans retained it.

AUBURN

Here's a mess. Latin *alba* means white, and *alburnus*, derived from it, means fair-haired, literally "white-like." Then *alburnus* passed into Old French and Middle English as *auburne* only to become confused with the French word for brown, *brune*. This was how *auburne* could come to mean brown-like. So the blondes of ancient Rome, beloved of patrician clubmen, it is said, became redheads. Here is a case of a word getting lost after being kidnapped.

AUTORESPONDER

This gadget dishes out mindless and unresponsive "answers" to letters that constituents send to politicians. Can the dumbing-down of America be done with a blunter hand than this? I am reminded of Mr. Knott, the deity parody in Beckett's *Watt*, who has no needs but needs that fact witnessed. Here is Congressman Bunting's bunting:

> Thank you for contacting me.
>
> If you live in my congressional district, please be assured that any message you send me over the Internet will be brought to my attention. Be sure to include your mailing address. Thank you again for your interest.

And here is part of the White House blarney:

> The White House home page provides, among other things, a single point of access to virtually all government information available on the Internet. Children especially enjoy the 'White House for Kids' feature—look for your tour guides, Socks and Buddy, the First Pets.

Somebody should collect these things and expose them as trophies from the Wax Museum.

AVOCADO

Succulent avocado comes from a Latin-American Indian word for testicle. The Nahuatls called the fruit *ahuacatl* because of its shape, but the Conquistadors turned it into *aguacate*, not a far cry, only to allow it to mingle with a more familiar noun, *avocado* ("advocate" in Spanish). English acquired the word in the late seventeenth century and, ringing new changes, transformed it into the *alligator pear*, a name still current.

BALM

This was the name for yeast in my childhood: not Jane Austen's balm of friendship for "the pangs of disappointed love," nor any balsam or resin, or ointment or iodine rub, nor lemon balm or bees' balm used to varnish the insides of cells before the laying in them of eggs. No, this was clammy, dank stuff, soft enough to mold as you walked, clutching the triangular twist of paper as best you could, appointed to a grave mission: "fetch a penn'oth of balm" (a pennyworth). It came from a big earthenware pot, an earthenware embryo, perhaps, and it made bread rise. It amused my sister that, when I went off to Burton's for this treat, I was "going balmy" (or barmy—one bunch of end-of-the-century cricket fans dubs itself the Barmy Army). Had this word anything to do with sultry summer air? I think so, knowing now it's not the teat, it's the tumidity that gets you. Tasting balm, I winced, not enjoying its sickly, rotten flavor, glad to surrender it to my mother, the neat packet's sharp lines pristine, the little covering flap still in place over the triangle's top. Perhaps it would make me rise too. This was leaven. I saw pure magic as my mother kneaded and baked. I inhaled the oven aroma and bit corners off hot loaves.

BARBARIAN

Cawfee, say Brooklynites when they mean coffee. If we were ancient Greeks we might think them barbarians for saying it thus;
a barbarian to the Greek was someone whose speech, unlike
Greek, sounded like an uncouth babble, or "barbar," source of
the xenophobic Greek word "barbaros," which covered all elo-
cutional crudity. Not only that: In its journey to us, giving us
barbarous from Latin *barbarus,* the word brought with it Latin
balbus, "stammering," in Spanish *bobo* (fool) and English *booby.*
Something heroic seems to have hitched a ride along with this
word, providing Italian with *bravo* (from *brabus*) and, by way of
French, our *brave.* The foreign yob, bewildering with his barbaric yawp and pitiful stammer, extorted a little admiration now
and then, even a Bronx cheer, for persisting in the effort to talk
at all when clearly he was not wanted.

BARNACLE

Once a kind of goose, *Branta leucopsis* grew on trees or logs,
attached to either by its beak and being born from within a
fruit. Or it gestated inside tiny shellfish stuck to timber or
rocks by the seashore. By the end of the sixteenth century, the
goose had disappeared and the word had removed itself to the
shellfish. Not much more is known beyond the original word's
being *bernak* (it gained the suffix *-le* while the goose was waning), from Medieval Latin *bernaca.* Now officially the white-
eyed.

BASTARD

A nasty word that has lost its force in the hurly-burly of modern
sex. It looks back to Old French's phrase *fils de bast,* literally

"packsaddle son," which is to say one conceived in the saddle or on an impromptu bed of a packsaddle pillow. The etymology is Greek *bastazein* (to carry), Latin *bastum* (packsaddle), emerging in late Middle English as *bat* (hence *batman*, who fetches and carries, mends and brews, for an officer). The familiar use of this word in generalized, unresearched abuse dates from the early nineteenth century, but the much later, punning use, *baystard*, for the offspring of a turkey-baster pregnancy, dates from the late twentieth century, when all sexual bets were off, and almost unimaginable obscenities became commonplace, virtually anesthetizing the popular imagination. White House fellatio, resorted to as casually as a cigarette, elasticizes any sense of shock that may have survived from the pious Sixties: anything can consort with anything else, and decorum, so called, goes a-begging. In the end, perhaps we are more shocked to learn that the art critic John Ruskin never consummated his marriage because he had never suspected that his wife had pubic hair and for having it was a freak being punished.

BAT

Old English has *batt*, "cudgel," but whence we do not know, although Gaulish has *andabata*, "gladiator," perhaps related to Russian *bat*, "cudgel," and English *battle*. Surely this is a French gift, from *batte*—*battre* (to beat). Bat the creature comes from Middle English *backe*, stolen from Old Swedish *natbakka*, "night bat," and may be a distortion of an earlier word, *-blaka*, from Old Norse *lethrblaka*, "leather-flapper." This, of course, matches other names such as German *fledermaus*, "fluttermouse," and English *flittermouse*. This last hung on in dialects into the twentieth century. The flitting, fluttering effect seems accurate, but the words for it begin in the sixteenth century, before which, strangely enough, there seemed no word at all, which cannot be. The one word that did duty for *bat* was *hreremus,* "rearmouse," also surviving dialectically into our own day. The image of the bat as a crippled master of arts in black regalia, crawling slowly forward, has not caught on. Nor that of flying crucifixions.

BEVERAGE

From Latin *bibere,* to drink, whence *imbibe, bibulous, beer,* and *bibber.* Old French had *bevrage* and Vulgar Latin *biberaticum,* "something to drink." Newcomers to the United States may form the initial impression that beverage is a dodge to avoid using the word "drink," which has alcoholical overtones. Or is it a way of emphasizing the non-liquorous quality of tea, coffee, Coke, or whatever? Personally I have never asked anyone if they would like a beverage, which sounds stilted, and I have no inhibitions about the word *drink,* elastic-minded enough to allow all of its associations to flourish in the same verbal orbit. However, some people do use the word as a jussive, meaning they are not offering, or even contemplating, alcohol, and some genuinely use it as a generic for all drink. Imagine the Bogartian actor crawling out of his umpteenth sand dune after a dry week, or Lawrence of Arabia arriving at Shepherd's Hotel bar in Cairo after crossing Sinai, and requesting "a beverage." *Soft* is better these days.

BIDET

You straddle this little horse in order to bathe your genitals and posterior, from French "small horse," from Old French *bider,* to trot.

BIG BERTHA

Huge cannon used by World War One Germans. The name is a translation of *dicke Bertha*, "fat Bertha," nickname of Bertha Krupp von Bohlen und Halbach (1886–1957), proprietress of the Krupp Works, where the cannon was made.

BISHOP

In the north of England, if you char something cooking, you may excuse yourself by saying "the bishop has put his foot into it." Early in the sixteenth century, William Tindale wrote that "If the porage be burned...or the meate ouer rosted, we say the bishop hath put his foote into the potte, or the bishop hath played the cooke, because the bishops burn who they lust and whosoever displeaseth them." Both John Milton and Jonathan Swift used this expression. All very well to adduce it when accounting for such sayings as "You've put your foot in it," but one has to wonder why the foot, and why into the fire. Were these bishops in the habit of kicking back into the blaze any fallen embers? Or is the whole thing more masochistic, with bishops first testing the martyr-purifying blaze, then playing chicken with themselves by thrusting a shod foot into the base of the bonfire? We remember Lucius Scaevola who, captured by Lars Porsena, shoved his right hand into an altar fire and turned it to charcoal, to prove his grit. Do we see bishops tampering with the fire at its outskirts, literally putting in the boot, a practice not limited to thugs and muggers?

BIT

Widely used, from morsel to a small role, *bit* lives up to its perfunctory name, coming from Old English *bita*, meaning a piece bitten off. One Usage panel, perhaps heedful of the word's matter-of-fact ancestry, deplores the word's use for distinctive activity or behavior ("do the Palm Beach bit") while condoning *bit part*.

BIZARRE

Bizarra is Basque for *beard*, converted by Spanish and Portuguese into a word for "handsome" or "brave" (if you had a beard, you were an Adonis). This is a dangerous concept, surely. Perhaps that is why *bizarre* was forced sideways into meaning "peculiar"; we do not really know, but it is possible that not enough bearded men were either handsome or brave but wimpy or dorky, and so the word had nowhere to go, especially if the disappointing barbed ones were thought freakish.

BLARNEY

Repeatedly Queen Elizabeth I's deputy, Carew, asked Cormac MacDermott Carthy, Lord of Blarney, to relinquish the traditional system by which the Irish clans chose their chieftain, and to defer to the Crown. But, while appearing to consent, Carthy kept putting things off "with fair words and soft speech," until the queen said, "This is all Blarney. What he says he never means." So this is a royal invention, *blarney* coming to mean amiable chat calculated to deceive, sometimes empty and inflated rhetoric. Dr. David W. Madden, Professor of Irish Literature at Sacramento State University, recalling his student days, remembers an examiner asking him, "How did Swift come to Ireland?" "I went into all this blarney," Dr. Madden says, "about his grandmother, his education, his appointment as Dean of St. Patrick's Cathedral, etc. With each response, he'd frown a little more deeply, until finally I said the unthinkable: 'I guess I don't know.' 'By boat,' he cried. Now, there's a true Irish exam!"

BLESS

Unique to English, originally meaning "mark with blood" (as with the fox's brush when hunting). We must remember that holy rituals at sacred altars in the time of Sir Thomas More involved animal sacrifice. There was once a prehistoric Germanic word, *Blothisojan*, derived from the word for blood, *blotham*, but only English acknowledged and assimilated it. So Old English has *bletsian*, by the thirteenth century *blesse*. Connotations of joy and euphoria, going back to at least the year 1000, arrived perhaps from such a word as *bliss* (origin of *blithe*). When we sneeze, others bathe us in blood.

BLIGHTY

More familiar from the song "Take Me Back to Dear Old Blighty" than from the heartsick nostalgia of soldiers craving homeland, this is the word invented in British India to denote England, Britain, the white cliffs of Dover, the tenements of Manchester. The word is from Hindi *bilayati*, meaning "foreign" or "European." Not a far stretch as far as sound goes, the word comes actually from Arabic *wilyat*, for "country" or "district" and so joins the crudely eclectic lexicon of military Arabic that extends from *bint* (woman) to *charp* (sleep), *shufti* (look-see) to *inshallah* (God willing). This Arabic word recalls the verb *waliya*, meaning "rule," and is bound to lapse into disuse now that the Blighties have nowhere to feel nostalgic from. Has there yet appeared a word that means craving the old empire? Dylan

Thomas in *Under Milk Wood* coined *Llareggub* from *Buggerall* (meaning "nothing"). Can *Ythgilb* be far behind? *Ythgilb* seems oddly Swiftian to me. Perhaps it is the Irish rather than the Welsh revenge.

BLIMEY!

Sometimes preceded by *Cor*, not for "heart" but for God, this mild British expletive means either "Blind me" or "By my Lord," depending on how serious you are. "Bless me" has also been suggested. *Gorblimey* can be heard, too, *Gor* more openly representing God.

BLIMP

Smugly jingoistic and addled ultraconservative British colonel invented by cartoonist David Low (1891–1963), depicted in London's *Evening Standard* and popularized by Roger Livesay in a broadly drawn movie. Colonel Blimp's fatness and relative immobility has little to do with the non-rigid buoyant aircraft called *blimp*, which comes probably from "Type B + limp." Their shapes, however, are akin.

BLIZZARD

In 1881, after a savage winter, *The New York Nation* observed that "The hard weather has called into use a word which promises to become a national Americanism, namely *blizzard*. It designates a storm (of snow and wind) which we cannot resist away from shelter." This was a blow, a loud noise, or sudden blast, coined perhaps from the dialect word *blizzer*, meaning flash of lightning (itself partly onomatopoeic, evoking *fizzer* and *sizzle* to convey the idea of a sudden volley, a cold wind filled with fine snow). The word generated *blizzard head*, for a female TV performer with hair so blond as to demand special lighting to prevent a halo or flare from showing up.

BLOODY

Notorious as both an expletive and a specific since the seventeenth century ("What bloody man is that?" when Banquo appears, *Macbeth*), it is more interesting than blood itself, from Germanic *blotham*, while Greek has its *haim-* and Latin its *sanguis*. Its use many billion times over shows how often other words failed someone as not intense enough, or not enough at hand. I have heard drunks in remote Derbyshire pubs howling, "I'll bloody well bloody you, you bloody lot, you bloody buggering bloodies." The fourth word is a timely and appropriate verb, little that this inarticulate fellow knew it. Highly educated people under stress use it, in a formal, almost directorial sense that might have suited Greek tragedy, but only in Britain, I think; in the United States, its use denotes something treasurably curious about someone or something, as if the person or thing had suddenly been backed by silver paper. In this sense it may approximate "extraordinary." Spelled out in full, it says *By Our Lady*.

BLURB

It is 1907 and the Retail Booksellers Association is hosting a dinner for Gelett Burgess, whose new book, *Are You a Bromide?*, adorns each diner's place. A little weary of extravagant flap copy, Mr. Burgess has concocted an airhead for the jacket, her name Belinda Blurb, pictured "blurbing a blurb to end all blurbs." *Blurb* he coined as a joke. Not only did *blurb* stick; so did *bromide* (for a thing or person exasperating or just tedious, soporific). Mr. Burgess should be lured into coming back.

A publisher will sometimes ask the author to compose a blurb (self-portrait in a complex mirror?), and he or she, in a mood of indignant self-protection, will perhaps oblige. I have done it on occasion though I hate writing paraphrase, so my blurbs are usually uninformative. What came out as a near-blurb for *this* very book, or at least a huckster's pitch, began as a subtitle and read as follows:

> OR
> Wit, nerve, luck and lewdness, dogged smarts and stealthy grandeur, mayhem and melody, the bread of paradise and the nettles of hell, minds like tadpoles or outboard motors, misunderstanding, slander, plagiarism, myth, mummery, and the blithe subterfuges of untutored eloquence, in a grateful album.

This then became:

> OR
> Souvenirs of Untutored Eloquence in a grateful album after long amazement.

You can see which phrase I was determined to keep in, but it went the way of flesh, now sneaked in by the back door. And the original, working title, *Who Put the Bread in Paradise?*, sneaks in too. Somewhere in Latin there must be a tag about going to the stake for certain phrases. Behold the stylist *in flagrante*. Even if one's dearest exclusions have to end up engraved on a gravestone. Is there anywhere, I wonder, a book of blurbs, as there is one of bad reviews, penned by Belinda of course.

BOLO

It used to be, in the 1920s, a wobbly marksman, or a punch that looped over an extended course usually to the heart, named perhaps for the long, ponderous knife of the Philippines. Its more recent application is from the police: *Be On Look Out*, no doubt in the interests of speed. Besides, what policeman worth his salt would be caught napping with a four-word English phrase when he could have a macho-sounding acronym for four letters?

BOONDOGGLE

Coined in 1925 by R. H. Link, American scoutmaster, for the plaited leather cord worn around the neck by Boy Scouts. From pointless doohickey, the term advanced to cover trivial and wasteful labor. An over-trimmed Boy Scout defined a doodling drone.

BOSH

When did someone last put you down by exclaiming this, a way of pungently saying "rubbish" or "twaddle"? It's Turkish, originally made popular (or at least common) in English in the early nineteenth century by the now-forgotten oriental novelettes of James Morier, who larded his romances with bits of Turkish. The word is more likely these days to evoke the painter Hieronymus Bosch, though certain military officers of advanced age can be heard puffing it at one another in the smoking rooms of their recessive clubs.

James Justinian Morier (c. 1780–1849) can be worth looking at, especially for *The Adventures of Hajji Baba of Ispahan* (1824); not only did the novel decide foreign notions of Persia but, translated into Persian in the early twentieth century, it pioneered the modern Persian novel of social critique. Morier was on the British Embassy staff in Teheran from 1809 to 1815. He was *born* in Smyrna, Turkey.

BOSOM

From the Sanskrit *bhasman*, "blowing," this word has a bellows in its past, much as *breast* harks back to Middle High German *briustern*, meaning "to swell up." The implications seem crude, as with *exuberant*, and have a male emphasis.

BOTTLE

I grew up among people always saying that something was "not much bottle," meaning it wasn't much good, not what it was cracked up to be. Why *bottle*, I never knew, not even aware that a bottle was a small barrel (Medieval Latin *butticula*, diminutive of *buttis* for cask, entering English by way of Old French *botele*). The servant who gave you wine with your meal, at least in medieval times, was a *buticularius*, in Old French *bouteillier*, giving us our *butler*. Perhaps *not much bottle* began as a comment on the butler, whose duties also included taking care of the wine cellar. *Bottle* has come some way since then, firmly establishing itself in the twentieth century to mean "courage, guts, nerve," as in, "He doesn't have the bottle for that." Perhaps the bottle, as the source of "Dutch courage," has become dominant in that sense, which, of course, implies an enfeebled view of moral bravery as depicted in the rhyming slang expressions *bottle and glass* (meaning "class"). Or the image is sleazier, from male prostitution, its rhyming version *bottle and glass*, too, but meaning *arse* (British for *ass*, since *glass* will be said as *glarss*). *Bottle* is no longer the certainty it was when the Milk Marketing Board announced "Milk Delivers Bottle," and it may not survive, any more than its French equivalent, *cran*.

BOUDOIR

Do you pout? Then go to your boudoir, where, like any French lady, you may pout—*bouder*—to your heart's content. There must have been a lot of pouting, and with it, of course, a lot of sulking, fretting, frowning, and the rest. Is the boudoir, now regarded as the summit of elegant luxury, a euphemistic *purdah*? *Bouder* in Modern French is to sulk or be sullen.

BRIDAL

From two Old English words, *bryd* (bride) and *ealu* (ale), together forming *bride-ale* drunk at weddings, *bridal* only gets into trouble when linked to *bridegroom*, so-called. The correct term was *bridegoom*, meaning a bride-man (from Anglo-Saxon *guma*), but confusion set in and the bride was accidentally destined to walk the aisle with a man who grooms horses. Lady Macbeth got it right, vowing, "I'll gild the faces of the grooms withal," these actual grooms in the stables where the unruly and symbolic horses clattered about all night, and not young husbands.

BUFF

What a load this word has to carry. If you are a buff, you're an expert, a maven, maybe even a specialised fanatic, but if you're alive in the nineteenth century you are a volunteer fireman in New York State, so named for the color of your coat. The word wafted outward to denote someone who liked to watch fires, and so to devotees in general. Buff for naked is a kindred word (pale leather resembling skin), but *buff* for *shine* may not be (I just saw a photographer snapping naked black models among the Masai and spraying their skin with some aerosol to make it shinier). The British regiment nicknamed the Buffs must be cousins to those New York firefighters. The tunic facings of this old third regiment of the line (later the East Kent Regiment) were made from buffalo hide, supposedly, but more often from cowhide dressed with oil and having a fuzzy surface of dull whitish yellow.

BUGGER

Western Europe regarded Bulgarians as heretics for belonging to the Eastern Orthodox Church, which is how Latin *Bulgarus* got stuck onto just about any heretic, most of all to the Albigenses, a Catharistic sect in Southern France. Old French *bougre* and Middle Dutch *bugger* gave English a word it uses too much, from heretics given to anal intercourse, a hearty generic equivalent to "fellow" (women never use the word thus), and an extraordinary object or person, to *bugger up* (ruin or confuse), and a piece of solid nose mucus. What word could retain its dignity amid such use and misuse? Any rationale seems to be that, once the word has mired deep in heresy, it is fit for any unfortunate purpose. So, *bugger off* is almost no more than a cry; one wonders how it is to be taken, certainly with a shredded echo of extinct heresy, to which all other crimes belong. You have to be careful with this word, especially if referring to the movie *The Conversation*, say, in which Gene Hackman plays what *TV Guide* was careful to specify a famous *bugger*, i.e., installs electronic surveillance devices. The word has nothing to do with *vulgar* or *vulgarian*.

Bill Cox, in *Plane and Pilot*, exemplifies the grudgingly affectionate use: "It's still possible to fly in thunderstorm season as long as you give the woolly buggers a wide horizontal or vertical berth."

BUNGALOW

It means "Bengali," the Hindi word *Bangla* (as in *Bangladesh*). English helped itself to the Gujarati version (*bangalo*) for a house in the Bengali style, first a simple, lightly constructed thing not meant to last, but in the long run definitive for having only one story and a wide porch, as not only in India and Bangladesh, but also in California and Florida. Some bungalows qualify for the term although having one and a half stories. English bungalows look different, in the main being stuccoed.

BUPKISS

Every now and then a word crops up to whose sound and physiognomy we respond more than to what it means. This is one, on everybody's lips (in the U.S., anyway), but scarce in dictionaries. Other such words may be *cummerbund, dinkum, flamingo. Bupkiss* is more blatant and personable than many of its neighbors; deriving from the Russian for a few beans, it has come to mean not that but literally nothing. When people say *bupkiss*, they usually mean zero, and they do so with a proud, declaratory air as if revealing an Eastern European mystery. Or, in the journey from beans to nothing and onward to beans metaphysical, we take a hint from Donne and envision a bracelet of beans about the bone. Also possible that mistaken etymology has grafted itself here, evoking a bum-kiss, and all that goes with it, what German prostitutes used to give GIs after World War Two ended. Here is a zerophilic word on the way up in a mercantile society. Now, these things being so, why must a bum-kiss or anilinctus amount to nothing? It is patently *something*, though to some the last trump of nihilism and so, no matter how repeatable, the blueprint for *nada*. To most speakers (who *writes* this word?), the bum-kiss is a superficial, chubby thing akin to a *potch* or a footballer's pat. Mispronouncing Polish *bob-kisc-* (bunch of beans) may summon up an old saying about something not amounting to a hill of beans; but aren't the beans different? Most folk seem pleased that Mother English has gifted them with so lively a word for nothing.

How quaint that speakers of English with no training in philology, phonology, or linguistics happily hear in *bupkiss* a word as remote as *bumkiss*. Heedless of language families, and all such fancy taxonomy, they hear what they want to hear, siting much of their heart's desire on mere percussion, raciness, and verbal physiognomy. The language is the people's, and, so long as they keep it vivid although unruly, who cares? Those of us who write can hardly afford to squander their impetuous bravura.

BUREAU

This is as if the green baize that covers the pool- or billiards-table had supplanted the table proper, so one would be unable to lift the baize. In Old French, *burel*, a coarse woollen material used to cover writing desks, gradually mutated into *bureau*, and so the writing desk changed its name, the word eventually coming to denote the room in which the bureau would be found—office or department. *Bureau-cracy* was waiting in the wings, of course ("rule of the writing desk"). It is common, amid the rough and fumble of language, to find the tail becoming the dog; after all, this is the governing spirit of bureaucracy: What is minor becomes monolith.

The bureau (the desk) should be painted red, at least according to Greek etymology, since Greek *purrhos*, "red," comes from *pur* for fire (compare English *pyrotechnic* and *pyre*). In Latin, the word's initial *p* became a *b*, hence *burel*, from Latin *burrus*, becoming French *bure* for dark brown. Our burel was a dark brown cloth blotter for spilled inks and beaker stains.

BUTTERFLY

Why? Does the butterfly land on uncovered butter or milk in kitchen or dairy and eat its heart out? The German name seems to vindicate this folktale, calling the butterfly "milk-thief" (*Milchdieb*). Another suggestion is that the butterfly, at least the common cabbage white, has wings the color of butter or milk, or indeed buttermilk. Or is it the creamy look of butterfly excrement that names the fly? Milk the idea a bit further and you find that Monarchs live on milkweed, which secretes a digitalis-like toxin that actually protects Monarchs from predatory birds.

BUXOM

Once upon a time, a buxom girl ("buxom and bonny," as the phrase had it) was pliant, pleasant, and obedient; her adjective came from *buhsum*, from *bugan*, meaning "to bend." In a word, yielding. Later, *buxom* came to mean "gay and jolly," then, even later, "healthy and vigorous." The girl was to be distinguished from a bendable piece of wood by her easy-going and obliging qualities; she became plump, and large-breasted (compare *exuberant*) only in our own time, the word having traveled all the way from the twelfth century. The word *bonny* often linked with *buxom* has an unfortunate effect, seeming to pay tribute to good looks without quite summoning up pretty, beautiful, handsome, gorgeous, et cetera. In my native Derbyshire, a girl extolled as bonny knew she had been snubbed about her looks and went away grieving. "She's a bonny lass, all right" is a species of curse. A bonny lad was usually rather stout.

CAB

When V. S. Pritchett entitled his autobiography *A Cab at the Door* (1968), he was not thinking of "cab" as short for the nineteenth-century *cabriolet*, the light horse-drawn carriage Italians called *capriolo* from *capriolare* ("to jump up in the air"). *Capreolus*, Latin, meant *goat* (hence English *caper* and *Capricorn*), and Italian *capriolo* meant "roebuck." What is all this jumping about? The vehicle's suspension was so springy it jumped up and down as it advanced. *Cabriole*, for leg, an eighteenth-century word, comes from here, meaning "like the front leg of a prancing animal." Probably a goat.

CAD

Here is a word that performed a double parabola, in one instance beginning as the Latin for head, *caput*, which diminished into *capitellum*, for "little head," then slunk into Provençal as *capdet*, meaning "chief," and so into French proper as *cadet*, word for a younger son or an officer. When the word reached Scotland, it began to mean an errand boy or gopher, abruptly, because of all that golf, mutating into *caddie*, who carries golfers' bags. In England, *cadet* soon became the in-word for a college layabout or, in sports, an amateur coach who did odd jobs such as mowing the grass or painting white lines on the field of play. In Oxford, for instance, he ran afoul of the standard split between town and gown: pretending to be of gown, he was indelibly of town, eventually called a *cad*, a parasitic slob. In the United States, cadet came to mean *pimp* alongside all the virtuous-seeming cadets in the country's military academies. Here is a word that splintered and fell, narrowly redeemed only by the military.

Cyril, our part-time college groundsman, just about qualified as a cad. He boasted non-stop of his sexual encounters, season in, season out, and I vividly recall the time he told me how he had managed to rope some unfortunate female to a rather wide gurney, but a cricketer or rugger-player showed up at the last moment with a question. "Ay," Cyril told me [I lived in a nearby house owned by the college], "I had hers all ready, you see, and mine too. It were awful." After that I always listened for sounds of female distress as I neared the pavilion but never heard any. Perhaps Cyril had given up sex, I thought, or practiced it elsewhere, out in the countryside, a lonely cocksman bound to fail.

CARDIGAN

Named for the cantankerous and pushy James Thomas Brudenell (1797–1868), seventh Earl of Cardigan who, while a major in the British Army, led the disastrous charge of the Light Brigade during the Crimean War. He it was who thought up, for his own military comfort as he bought his way up the ranks of senior officers to general, the worsted jacket called *cardigan*, which women regard as a toasty woollen jacket with sleeves and a button-through front often worn open. This garment of his brought him greater fame than Tennyson's luminous, incantatory poem celebrating the gallant Six Hundred who rode into Balaclava's valley of cannon and death.

Other members of the English aristocracy have given their names to articles of clothing, Lord Chesterfield to an overcoat (as well as a cigarette and a sofa), Lord Raglan also to a coat, loose-fitting with sleeves that run all the way to the neck. Perhaps nowadays only the sleeves—*raglan sleeves*—retain his name, which nonetheless lives on against the hinterland of his marriage to the daughter of the Duke of Wellington, whose name attaches itself to waterproof boots (slang versions, *welloes, wellies*) and a twin-engined bomber (slang version: *Wimpey*).

CARDINALIZE

A French verb, meaning to plunge crustaceans into boiling liquid, so turning them the color of cardinals' vestments. For *pears cardinal* you poach the fruit in vanilla syrup, then top with kirsch-flavored raspberry sauce and almonds. *Red mullet* belongs in the same zone of influence.

CASTANET

I am grateful to this word for recalling to me the word *knacker*, not for commonly denoting testicle (as it often does in impolite speech), but for its other meaning: "chestnut." The *knackers* I played with were twin pieces of slate the size of shoehorns, which clattered if jiggled loosely between middle finger and forefinger and thumb. You could build up an impressive speed that actually reminded people of—yes, *castanets*, so named because they reminded the Spanish of chestnuts: *castaneta* comes from *castaña*, from Latin *castanea*, for chestnuts and rattling chestnut shells.

CASTLE

Used in the *Anglo-Saxon Chronicle* only nine years after the Battle of Hastings, *castle* was one of the earliest words adopted by the British from their Norman conquerors. Hailing from Latin *castellum* (diminutive of *castrum*, "fort"), by way of Norman *castel*, it reminds us that Old English also acquired *castrum* as *ceaster*, still present in such place-names as Doncaster and Winchester. From Old French's *chastel* (a version of *castel*) came the word *château* (circumflex accent marking the lost "s"). *Castle* itself appears, of course, in such names as Newcastle and Sir John Old-castle, the martyred nobleman on whom Shakespeare modeled Falstaff.

CASTOR

There are two *castors*, one being an oily, brown substance taken from glands near the beaver's anus, used in medicine and perfume. Castor oil, with which millions of children have been threatened, is a substitute for this substance, culled from a tropical plant. It was a beaver business in the fourteenth century (*castor* meant *beaver*, as in Castor and Pollux), and after, but one of plant extraction by the 1700s. The other *castor* comes from the verb *cast* and was often spelled *caster*, meaning to sprinkle or throw sugar (this kind of sugar was common in the nineteenth century). It also meant a small wheel you steered a boat with, *cast* meaning to turn or veer, as in George Nares's *Seamanship* of 1882, in which he writes: "Prepare for casting to port." As *ricin*, a lethal poison extracted from the beans of *ricinus communis*, the castor oil plant of Africa and Asia, *castor* took its place among the horrors of modern power-politics when a Bulgarian diplomat, crossing London Bridge, was pricked in the calf by an umbrella spike containing a pellet made by the KGB. He died soon after, without ever realizing that in London an umbrella carried by a bowler-hatted gentleman assassin is commonplace. Since then, *ricin* has been used in other killings, a children's laxative writ large as a hitman's toy.

CATHARSIS

When I was a student, this word, touted by Aristotle, who knew everything but nothing else, puzzled me non-stop. Did it mean *purge* or *purify*? Purge seemed to me wholesale, too much of an absolute, akin to laxative, whereas purify (put to the fire) was to burn off what was extraneous—after all, one of the many meanings attributed to Greek *catharos* is "unalloyed." So, after *catharsis*, there was always something left, something pure, all itself. That struck me as the right answer and gave the shocking denouements, and comeuppances, of Greek tragedy, a refined dimension. The idea of atoning, present in all these *kathar-* words, isn't a blank, doesn't leave a blank, and a person who has atoned has something worthwhile left. Simply, what Eliot in his essay on *Hamlet* calls "some stuff that the writer could not drag to light, contemplate, or manipulate into art," has been cleaned away, which is no doubt what tragedy by proxy does.

CEDILLA

Yes, the underwater five, from obsolete Spanish *cedilla*, diminutive of *ceda*, the Spanish *zee*, from late Latin *zeta* so named because a small *z* was once used to make a hard *c* sibilant. It goes beneath, as in garçon, which would otherwise be said as *garkon*. The *cedilla* has a quite important destiny in Turkish and Rumanian too.

CHAMPION

Where I grew up, this was a frequent exclamation at something adjudged superb; restrained people going over the brink would say *champion* in a quiet, almost confiding way when they wanted to make you trust them more than ever. The word used to mean to defy or challenge, and still does retain its combative sense in *defend* or *promote*. Actually the key derivation is from *champ*, French for *field*, most often a battlefield, more distantly from West Germanic *kampjo*, meaning *warrior*, filched from *kamp* for battlefield and, ultimately, Latin *campus* (field). The word remains noun or verb, but nostalgia and a smattering of French keep it as an adjective for me: the slightly uncouth attribution of absolute delight.

CHARACTER

How odd to find this epitome of moral integrity descending from Greek *kharakter*, which meant a branding iron, from *kharassein* (to sharpen or brand) and *kharax*, a pointed stake. Perhaps the outstanding should be delineated thus, not by brand-name but by incision, the trouble with this idea being that individuality flies out the window. To brand is to group, not to brand is to leave all kinds of questions open to guess and inference. It would be more usual to brand the person without character, as we do, even in spoken idiom (branded a traitor). Was Vlad the Impaler branding his victims internally when he sat them on pointed stakes, or just trying to be Greek? The possessive facet of branding seems to have nothing to do with personal caliber at all.

CHARISMA

The Greek and the English are just the same, though the drifts vary, from Greek "grace, gift of grace" to our own irresistible attractiveness. I don't think we go much for grace but rather for erotic magnetism, which the Greeks themselves never slighted; the Greek concept is nobler, more ethereal, perhaps implying something godlike grafted on. You have to be a little superstitious for that. The Greek neuter noun implies repeated acts of charm, or bouts of it, which is worldly enough, but reflecting something from beyond, better than human, as when Homer calls Odysseus *dios* for *godlike*. Repeated acts of charm sounds like your standard politician or anchor person (those plutocrats from the poorer colleges), but the emphasis of the Greek is on the gift given, as always by the gods, in no way an act of Horatio Alger and self-help, but something conferred during that *enthusiasm*—possession, however briefly, by a god—I have thought about under that heading (see). *Charisma* has made a firm place for itself in English, but it should not be made to spin.

CHARM

Has come down in the world, from magical allure as depicted in Shakespeare to mere trinkets on an arm. The word began as Latin *carmen*, for "song," when incantation really sang and moved worlds, and Old French *charme*. The Greeks had a word, *charis*, for this enchantment by the gorgeous, but it got no farther than a perfume of the Sixties—nobody knew how to say it. The charms worn in the Middle Ages as talismans lost their power to the bourgeoisie and *brummagem* of the mid-nineteenth century, when progress replaced magic.

The other side of charm's coin is that, in fourteenth-century

England, a girl called charming was almost certainly destined for the ducking stool, the rack, or the stake. Was she a witch? One sixteenth-century sentence says it all: "The serpent stoppeth his eares with hir taile, to the end that she may not heare the *charmes* and sorceries of the inchanter." When charm really counted, it could get you killed; when it became "a lucky charm," it had no effect at all on bad luck.

CHESS

If you warn a chess opponent by saying "Check" or guard your king, you are talking old Persian and using their word *shah* for king. This word came down to us mutated into Old French *eschec*, Middle English *chek*, and eventually came also to mean a hindrance, a halt, a restraint. Our word *chess* is actually the same word, from *ches* from Old French *eschecs*, just like "check." It is merely the plural form. Chess is made up of checks. When, at the end, you say "checkmate," you are still speaking Persian, this time *shah-mat*: the king is dead, or checkmate. Long live the loan-word.

CHOWDER

Milky thick or red thin, its name comes from the pot it was cooked in. We are in Brittany, in Northern France, where a returning fisherman drops a portion of his catch into the *pot-au-feu*, the cauldron forever on the fire, the perpetual result from this common pot of fish and biscuit, *la chaudière*, being a fishy stew that varies little from week to week. In no time it has reached St. John's, Newfoundland, and that non-province's outports, and then the eastern United States where, indeed with broken biscuit supplied in cellophane wrappers, it becomes *chowder*: hotpot sludge of appetizing fume. In the old days, in which chowder firmed up its identity, the clam was optional.

CIRCUMFLEX

Not your everyday word, not in English, certainly, in French it warns of a missing "*s*" (*maistre* has become *maître*), say, and literally does what its etymology specifies: it bends around the gap and holds the two severed parts together, as from *circum* (around) + *flectere* (bend). It literally bends itself around the breach; the past participle is *circumflexus*—a bending around. Teaching me, Miss Roberts introduced it as a little roof, and I began to like French. Jean Genet, the French novelist and playwright, has no circumflex on his surname, but the Parisian correspondent Genêt (alias Janet Flanner) does, perhaps to distinguish herself from him (with the result that you tend to think of her as Genest). A child's question caps this diacritical tile: Does the circumflex accent-roof house the dot on *i*? Or do you omit it?

CITABRIA

High-wing, braced aerobatic monoplane with tailwheel, two-seater, manufactured by Champion (Bellanca). The airplane's name is "airbatic" (a form of "aerobatic") backwards. Aerobatic backwards would have been *Citaborea*, not much different. One wonders about the slight lift afforded the owner when he gloats over the name, knowing the secret, as if an outside loop turned into an inside one. Was it worth any effort at all?

CLICHÉ

This is the word that hisses at you between tenched cleeth for being trite (word that means worn-out) and for using trite phrases. It used to be a printer's term for a stereotype plate, which is to say, a metal plate made from a papier-mâché mold. The print on the surface was thus transferred to the metal. Supposedly, the word imitates the frying noise made when the mold enters the molten metal. *Clicher* in French meant "stereotype," and the later *cliché* indicts a hackneyed expression—one that has been repeatedly used from a single metal plate. The explanation gains credence from being attributed to Firmin Didot, an eminent French printer, inventor, and namer of the stereotype process. *Stereo-*, by the way, is Greek for solid. It might be just to think of M. Didot as the inventor of the *cliché* rather than of the stereotype plate; its nineteenth-century sound may have gone from us, but the cliché, like all words with a rebuke in them, remains with us, unlikely to depart.

CLINGFILM

Americans call this Saran Wrap, a manufacturer's word without any of the sensuous suggestiveness of British *clingfilm*, which sheathes your nudity and isn't shy about saying so. Saran Wrap has turned people on, to be sure, but not the name, whereas *clingfilm* has in it something of abandoned Dido and soft-centered pornography. Perhaps the first and best clingfilm is the pericardium.

CLOUD

The Old English word for cloud was *weolcen*, whence the poeticism for sky, *welkin*. *Clud* was Old English for hill or mass of rock (a huge *clod*, perhaps), but in the thirteenth century, because cumulus clouds looked like lumps of ground, the word slowly acquired the new meaning, given over to something much less substantial. This etymology fleshes out, long before Shakespeare's time, the phenomenology Hamlet proposes to Polonius (III.ii. 400):

> Hamlet. Do you see yonder cloud that's almost in shape of a camel?
>
> Polonius. By the mass, and 'tis like a camel indeed.
>
> Hamlet. Methinks it is like a weasel.
>
> Polonius. It is backed like a weasel.
>
> Hamlet. Or like a whale?
>
> Polonius. Very like a whale.

Hamlet here is not only plaguing the old buffer, he is making a serious philosophical point that later on is going to interest Maurice Merleau-Ponty and has already warped the advance of *clud* in English. It is delightful to watch English making a U-turn thus, reattributing a word on stronger evidence as more cloudlike, fleecier. A similar accuracy informs the word twilight, *twi-* signaling the *two* faces of it: the two half-lights that compose the day, dawn and dusk. (*The Airman's Information Manual* specifies even finer registrations of natural effects, such as "The End of Civil Evening Twilight.")

CLOUD ON TITLE

A legal term: An outstanding claim or encumbrance which, if valid, would affect or impair the title of the person who owns a particular estate, and on its face has that effect, but can be shown by extrinsic proof to be invalid or inapplicable to the estate in question. A conveyance, mortgage, judgment, or tax-levy may all, in proper cases, constitute a cloud on title. To remove a cloud on title, you bring an action to Quiet Title.

COBWEB

I once heard someone wondering why a spider's web was called a *cobweb*, then snootily put down by someone else who said it just possibly might have something to do with the Middle English word for spider's being *cop*. This unusual word has meant lump of coal, loaf, male swan, horse, nut, and ear of maize, all these meanings derived from the concept "head." A Middle English *cop* was a head, and a spider was mostly head (compare Latin *caput*, head). Actually, *cop* is short for *attercop*, an Old English word that had vanished by the seventeenth century, its meaning "poison head," only to be reintroduced as a living relic by the Anglo-Saxon scholar and fiction writer J. R. R. Tolkien in *The Hobbit* (1937), a novel written for his children, then reissued to the world at large, where it appealed to students. Having reviewed this frolic and been subsequently denounced by the Hobbit Society (weird messages shoved under my door "Mr. West, Frodo lives!"), I feel the same honorable bigotry about Hobbits as before. Feeble twaddle, I called it, wondering why a competent professor of Anglo-Saxon should meddle in such stuff, even as an emeritus doodle aimed at airheads.

COCCYX

One of those words that nobody can spell but does not hesitate to use, especially after having sat down hard. The Greek physician Galen thought this small tapered bone at the bottom of our spine looked like a cuckoo's beak and so named it *kokkus*, Greek for cuckoo, which came into English unchanged from Latin *coccyx*. Clearly this Galen was an ace observer, akin to Scotland's D'Arcy Wentworth Thompson, whose treatise *On Growth and Form* remains a readable and utterly persuasive classic; he sees shape analogies everywhere, as a holist might.

COLD FEET

In the play *Volpone* (1605), Ben Jonson, that agile social Proteus, refers to the "Lombard proverb," when Volpone garbed as a mountebank doctor tells why he has put his bank in an obscure corner rather than in the midst of the Piazza of St. Mark: "I am not, as your Lombard proverb saith, cold on my feet; or content to part with my commodities at a cheaper rate than I am accustomed: look not for it." In other words, he is not hard up and need not sell his goods at inferior prices. In Lombardy, to have cold feet (*Avegh minga frecc i pee*) still means to be without money. A card player, "skint" or penniless, will say his feet are cold, an idiom that can also mean to back away from a bind. To us, it means *dare not*. To shrink from something.

COMEDO

Here's an after-dinner unsavory, both the Roman verb "eat up" for gluttons, and also ours for what the *Oxford English Dictionary* says is "a small worm-like yellowish black-topped pasty mass which can in some persons be made, by pressure, to exude from hair follicles. They are found on the cheeks, forehead, and nose." Roman *comedo* advanced to cover all the attributes of gluttony, even the worms that will at last devour us, of which this black-head is a model. Whitehead too. Either kind of cylindrical ex-pellate may be called a "maggot-pimple" or "whelk." Nothing to do with comedy, in Greek *komos*, an event for music and danc-ing. One wonders about the medical profession, still in pursuit of a lingua franca at least as obscure as Cockney rhyming slang, yet eager for clinical good taste as well, preferring *comedo* to *black-head*, *coryza* to *common cold*.

COMPANION

A startling and rather beautiful word, this, once you peel it open; used almost as a leitmotif in Ignazio Silone's novel *Bread and Wine*. It means whom you break or share bread with: *com* plus *panis*, and it branches off into such words as *compaignie* and *company*. It also lurks in the nautical term "companion-way," meaning a stairway on or to a ship, deriving here from *com-pania*—"what you eat with your bread"—and easily becoming, at full stretch on the ladder of ideas, provisions, storeroom, gangway up to storeroom, quarterdeck, any stairway on board. It's an odd decline, when the holy ritual of the breaking of bread becomes a stairway to the storeroom. Anyone deploring this descent should read Silone's novel, in which the word *cumpaanii* (companions) recurs with almost obsessive tenderness. So versatile a term ac-quires dignity because, whether applied to a lifelong companion who has taken bread with you daily for decades or someone who lunches with you once, it refers you back to the miracle and mys-tery of the act, the planet that provides edible grains for us to harvest. Its burden is need witnessed by the Other.

COMPOSE

This is what composers do, and self-disciplined people who try not to flutter. All it means is *to put together*, from Latin *componere*, *composui, compositum* (source of our *composite* and *position*) and French *composer*. From it come many common words such as *compound, component,* and *compost* (it used to mean stewed fruit, like *compote*). The trouble with this verb is that few want it to do its work, preferring *comprise,* which they constantly misuse, as in *comprised of* when they mean *composed of. Comprise* has to do with something taken, seized in war, from the French *prendre,* but while we can say "The Union comprises fifty states" we cannot say "Fifty states comprise the Union," for clearly the parts cannot contain the whole except in a deviously metaphysical sense. We can, however, logically say "Fifty states *compose* the Union," because *to compose* is to make up. Alas for English, though: Most people, even the educated ones, tend to say "comprised of" (which is as nonsensical as saying "contained of") when they mean *composed of,* maybe because the former sounds more impressive, more bureaucratic, overlaps less with a word kept apart for those who write music. Once again, what the people do will prevail.

CONEY ISLAND WHITEFISH

Used condom washed ashore, symptom of a healthy civilization or, perhaps like Auden's orange rotting on the mantelpiece in his Oxford rooms, a badge of decadence. The initially appetitive taint of this fish may sicken some unacquainted with its terrestrial avatars. Surely as complex an icon as can be. A Coney Island of the flesh.

CONKERS

If you ever played this game as a child, striking a baked horse chestnut on a length of string against another one held by your opponent, and he against yours, you probably never recorded it in letter or diary as *conquering*, which is how the nineteenth century wrote it. The game began with snail shells (*conker* from *conch*, perhaps, and Greek *konkhe*), but the simpler derivation seems that Victorian image of conquest: the meek shall inherit the earth, and the strong shall inherit the meek. Conkers may be read as a dry run for the game of Empire.

CONSIDER

I once used this as the first word in a novel of mine about astronomy; only scientist readers spotted the etymology in the imperative-invitation, remarking that *consider* used to mean "set alongside the stars." The intensive prefix *cum* accompanied *sidus* for star. Ancient astrologers such as Roman practitioners of divination coined this word, but more recent astrologers fix on planets. Tracking the courses of stars soon weakened into observing them, and that into observing in general, and in no time observing has become "remarking," not in the sense of "notice" but in that of "saying," in which case it joins the abominable modern "I was" and "I went," both referring to speech. If you don't tie words down, they drift away like astronauts. The sense "have an opinion about" came in in the sixteenth century from French, but "considerable" came straight from Latin. That other sense, "an appreciable amount," began in the seventeenth century, but all these rather abstract formulas pale beside the old impetus to test things out alongside the stars. Perhaps the word is so popular in different ways—considerate, an unconsidered act, considerable weight, just consider, consider absent—because the etymology no longer counts, alas. Nowadays it has a bureaucratic flavor whereas it used to be a prelude to stargazing.

In Roman times, when augurs told the future by studying the flight of birds, nobody worried about the difference between "compare to" and "compare with." In our own day, when the augur has quite vanished from such a word as *inaugurate*, "compare to" suggests an unequal comparison, "compare with" an equal one. Both expressions come into play when we *consider*, trying all against the stars, the quotidian and ephemeral against the heedless and the almost permanent. I think John Milton, inventing *pandemonium* in *Paradise Lost* (demons everywhere), was exploiting this disproportionate sense: even demons count for little against the constellations, the part of the universe called *sider* or starry.

CONSOLAN

A low-frequency, long-distance navigation aid used mainly for transoceanic flight. One sometimes wonders if, winnowing and embellishing the jargon books of the aviation community, there isn't some rather forlorn, introverted, lyrical pariah who comes up with such words as *Consolan* or Civil Evening Twilight, Sublimation, Wind Shadow, Radiosonde, Pilotage, Perceptive Learning (!), Geographic Rain, Mammatocumulus ("Cloud showing pendulous, sac-like protuberances"), Isallobas, Graveyard Spiral, Glory, Frost Smoke, French Landing, Flying the Wet Beam, Flicker Vertigo, Falling Leaf, Dynafuel, DeadStick, Cracking of Oils, Cone of Silence, Cone of Confusion, Comfort Chart, Chubasco, Mother-of-Pearl Clouds, Clearance Delivery, Calms of Cancer, Burble Point, and on and on. A separate language, sometimes of enormous, poignant appeal. Perhaps, like surgery, it has so many agreed-upon terms for what might go wrong. Premonitions of disaster haunt the argot.

COVENTRY

If you were a Royalist prisoner of the Puritans in the English Civil War, you were sent to the city of Coventry so as to ostracize or banish you. Since then the metaphor of sending someone to Coventry, once a feature of life in English private (i.e., public) schools, has fallen into abeyance, and the person claiming such exclusion from human intercourse sounds a bit histrionic. One wonders to what extent this quasi-punishment was carried out; after all, nobody was supposed to speak to you, least of all in Coventry, which could surely begin with a lower case letter, being a state or condition like exile. Clearly, if you were sent to Coventry, no one in London would be talking to you; but what of your guards en route, and of people in Coventry proper? The city was virtually obliterated in World War Two by Nazi bombers, which fate in an odd way consummated the metaphor, supplementing ostracism with death by bombardment. Note the British practice of calling any settlement with a cathedral a city. Lest we forget, the soccer team of Coventry is called Coventry City.

COZAAR

Trade name for Losartan potassium, an ACE inhibitor (Angiotensin Converting Enzyme) I enjoy calling "Cortázar" for an Argentine writer I admire, and who in his publicity pictures looked eternally young until he started taking male hormones, when he began to wither hornily like the rest of us. Doctors do not get this allusion. Cozaar replaced a drug that made you cough a lot, *Vasotec*, derived from the venom of the pit viper, a classification including *bothrops atrox* and others. When my doctor counseled me to take this drug, I agreed only because of its origin: turning the wiles of the pit viper to my advantage appealed to the novelist in me. *Cozaar,* causing no cough, does the same job as *Vasotec,* dilating the blood vessels to reduce blood pressure. We have come a long way, the pit viper and I. Anyway, Vasotec always sounded like a Czech long-distance runner (shades of Zatopek?).

CRICKET

Incessantly slandered by those who never played or seriously observed it, cricket happens to be one of the most dangerous games played on the planet (see the American-football headgear the batsmen wear, and the padding). Cricket abounds in rules, each set specific to the type of game being played: only 600 balls bowled, so many hours, league cricket, county cricket, Test cricket (usually a match at this level is scheduled to last five days). A kind of double baseball, with two bowlers and two batters operating alternately, cricket can be slow or hectic. One of my prized possessions is a commercial tape of a Test match in which the camera catches my brother-in-law sitting peace-fully alone and reading poetry during the game. At its fastest bowled, the ball will reach ninety miles an hour, at which speed the batsman has two seconds in which to decide what to do with it. People have been killed and maimed at this game, although its image to the innocent is of torpid, indolent, dreary introversion, which can happen. Players make extraordinary efforts to abide by a morality of Byzantine complexity. Americans increasingly use the phrase "not cricket," meaning unethical, ungentlemanly, and presumably that meaning will last (an icon of ghostly rectitude), while the game gets more and more strident, like the spectators, and the old style of long cream flannels and long-sleeved shirts gives way to a colorful *mêlée* of jump suits and a white, not a red, ball. Rock music now forces its way into New Zealand cricket, though not during actual play, and gymnastic antics once confined to Antigua (and a bizarre anorexic contortionist named Gravy) now accompany a parade of masks, plastic inflatable suits, and fancy dress that belongs in a Venetian carnival. Supposedly, with blacks now playing for South Africa (where there used to be a color bar as once in U.S. baseball) and no longer separate gates in the pavilion for "gentlemen" and mere "players," cricket is turning into the demotic, holistic game it should always have been, as distinct from the snobby ritual it sometimes dwindled into being. Maybe so. But in some ways it was always classless, especially in the North of England and in the kind of village cricket presented with affectionate relish by Charles Dickens in *The Pickwick Papers* (1836–37). It used to be said that fretwork patterns, done in green on white, used the most soothing colors, just as cricket was white on green. Cricket these days is less soothing than it used to be, more of a gladiatorial gala with few holds barred and as much bad temper on show as in hockey. Perhaps only in Denmark, France, Philadelphia, and Santa Monica does it remain its old self, smooth and fastidiously tricky, the legendary demi-paradise of flanneled fools and muddied oafs.

If cricket continues to use the white ball, the game is going to change a good deal: This ball with its polyurethane lacquer finish, to keep it from becoming grimy, swings about in the air more than the old red ball that was finished with buck's fat. Such a shift as this brings cricket's other problems into tight, physical focus, not the least of which is that the white ball tends to splinter bats; it's harder. Perhaps there will come along a pink ball with its own virtues and snags. Cricket has become worldly and, in a curious new way, professional—the old word still used for players who get paid, though not that much, as distinct from amateurs who do not. The game needs both. Recent experience prompts me to cite the delicious otherworldliness of being able to get same-day scores and reports on the Internet, from all over the world. One's living room (or study) is now the cricket pavilion.

CROSSWORDIO

This is how Winnie Klotz, the Metropolitan Opera's house photographer, italianizes everything. Does she then, as she may well, say her name as Klotzio? The mind reels at *Lady Macbethio of Mtsenskio*, *Gotterdämmerungio*, and the rest.

CRUD

Where does the appetite for, the drift toward metathesis— reversing letter order—begin? Did people get tired of saying *wops*, for instance, in preference to *wasp*? This word is really *curd*, as in lemon curd or curds and whey. All the way from dried semen to a 1920s Army blurt for venereal disease, it has come to mean almost any undesignated ailment, eruption, expectorate, as well as a scruffy person, or anything loathsome. Coagulated milk, says one dictionary, and why not? It goes back to Middle English, when it was *curd* replacing *crud*. One sixteenth-century derivative is *curdle*. Perhaps Gaelic *gruth* figures in its past. No doubt there are cycles: First, before the fifteenth century, *crud*, then *curd*, now *crud* again. Surely we need both, *crud* especially, considering our passion for undifferentiated dismissal.

CRUEL

The theater of cruelty had brief enough vogue, leaving people vaguely surprised that *cruelty* and *crudity* were siblings. *Cruel* comes from Latin *crudelis*, from *crudus*, itself meaning both "cruel" and "raw" or "bloody." How curly the advance of language often is, as here deriving from two words that meant the same. Both those words come from an Indo-European base that also gave us English *raw*, Greek *kreas* ("flesh," as in *pancreas* and *creosote*, and even Old Slavic *kruvi*, meaning "blood"). The word had a wide span, *crude* coming direct from Latin in the fourteenth century, and ancient *kruvi* reminding us in the present century of the Russianate word *krovvy* that Anthony Burgess used for blood in his least favorite novel, *A Clockwork Orange*.

CUMMERBUND

This wide pleated sash, part of male formal address (overdress perhaps), used to be a loin-band, loin-cloth, or breech clout, from Hindi *kamarband* (*kamar* [loins] + *band*). Often of resplendent satin, the cummerbund has an antique, quasi-diplomatic aura, a vast improvement on its unsanitary predecessors, and has been used most effectively to camouflage middle-aged spread: "Why, no, this's all fabric."

CURFEW

In Europe of the Middle Ages, certain settlements rang a bell at some hour of the evening, demanding that street fires be put out or covered. This applied to lights as well and was the *couvre feu*, meaning "cover fire." Curfew has not altered much in its parabolical descent to us. Curfew, whether in old Dodge City or Kosovo, has widened its meaning to include all outdoor activity; under some curfews, the penalty for being even out of doors has been death. One may speculate about sadistic tyrants preferring the vision of a deserted city or town without realizing that its other face is a pack of seething dissidents under lock and key. In Nazi times, even open cities such as Rome were subject to curfew and other strictures.

CURRANT

Debauched Corinth, actually, where delicious grapes came from in the Middle Ages: small and dried, in Old French called *raisins de Corinthe*, evolving into *corauntz* (imagine that) and *coraunce*. By the sixteenth century, *coraunce* had understandably come to be regarded as a plural, introducing a new singular, at first *coren*, then in the next century *currant*. By mistake, also in the late sixteenth century, the name got transferred to such fruit as the red-and-black currant, an assumption having been made by one of those invisible but taste-creating majorities that the delectable grape of Corinth, the currant, came from them. This kind of shuffle does damage to the notions of those who believe language is logical, for a logical species. Instead, one sees humans blundering about in the penumbra, guessing at what came from where and using language's apparent finality to clinch a rumor. If language is translated epistemology, then bananas are boomerangs. In the North of England, currants are pronounce "*kerrens*," root of some odd spellings. Currants figured in the first absurdist poem (a village romp) I ever heard:

> One summer's day in winter,
> The snow was raining fast.
> Three bare-footed lads with clogs on
> Stood sitting on the grass,
> Went to the pictures that night
> Bought three full seats at the back,
> Ate some plain cake with currants in

PAUL WEST

And when they'd eaten it
They gave it them back.

Language's power to contradict itself, and change history, works
on all levels. The contradictions in those lines evoke the weird
changes that power of naming brings about.

CURRY

Curry lovers, not of *currycomb* and *curry favor*, but of the spiced
sauce called *kari* in Tamil, will not relish the word's bland history. But they may well enjoy the fact that *curry favor* derives
from an Old French phrase *estriller favel* or *torcher favel*, which
means to groom a chestnut horse, an expression for reasons unknown denoting hypocrisy. Presumably the reference is to calcu-
lating behavior, with English *ready* coming out of the prehistoric
Germanic thicket *garaethjan*. There is almost a suggestion that, as
in Lady Macbeth's speech about the impending arrival of
Duncan ("he that's coming must be provided for"), almost any
act of preparation entails the disingenuous, which somewhat
robs good manners of their base in charity and assigns them to
cunning.

CURTAIL

Once upon a time a curtal was a horse with a docked tail, appropriated in the sixteenth century from the French *courtault*
(court means short). Behind both *court* and English *curt* lies
Latin *curtus* for "cut off," ancestor of both *short* and *shear*. All
these words get at the same thing with a similar sound evolved
from Indo-European *ker*. In the late sixteenth century the noun
became a verb and thus ministered to a whole host of new

objects, not tails at all, such as committee meetings and nefarious activities. A curtal friar wore a short cloak.

CUSHION

Cushion holds some kind of a record, having mutated more than almost any other word; the Oxford English Dictionary cites nearly seventy different spellings, few of which we need rehearse here. *Cushion* and *quilt* are the same word, actually, from Latin *culcita*, mattress, cousin to Sanskrit *kurcas*, bundle, and both words came into English by devious paths. In Gallo-Roman (the Latin language of France between the fifth and ninth centuries), *culcita*, the feathery bolster spoken of by Plautus and Cicero (*culcita plumea*), ended up as Old French *coissin*, then turned into Middle English *quisshon* and *cushin*. By the seventeenth century, *cushion* had arrived, and came to stay.

The verb *to cushion* has prompted some curious uses, so perhaps it too will have numerous metamorphoses, mostly having to do with redundant prepositions, as in *cushion from* (which seems to mean from the impact of), whereas *cushion against* is normal, and the transitive verb *cushion* (cushion the blow) does all the work needed. One suspects that people insert useless prepositions for something to say while having a think, not wanting to get to the nub of things too fast, as with those who with grandiose redundancy say "during the course of" when they mean *during. Cushion* will outlive them all.

One day at the check-out counter in a fabric store, I encountered a woman with a bundle of various fabrics under her arm, all ready to make what she called a *quillow*. Now the etymology of *pillow* is a straight line from Latin *pulvinus* to prehistoric West Germanic *pulwin* and Dutch *peluw*, but we have no idea of how *pulvinus* came to be. Never mind: This woman in her guided way was going to put cushion and quilt back together again, as they almost were in the sedate Latin bosom of *culcita*. True, she was not going to make a cushion-quilt but a pillow-quilt (or a quilt-cushion but a quilt-pillow), but it might have been a *quushion*. She was close to etymology's erratic heart, the word-manger of habitual repose.

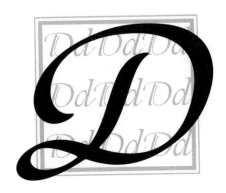

DAFFODIL

Initially, from the sixteenth century, *affodil* meant a plant of the amaryllis family, the acquired *d* coming wrongly from Dutch *de affodil*. The plant's botanical name, *Narcissus pseudonarcissus*, suggests an element of double-dealing amply borne out by the Greek word *narke*, meaning *numbness*; in fact, the bulb contains toxic alkaloids that can paralyze the nervous system and cause death. This is the flower the Greeks thought bloomed in the afterlife. Once, physicians and apothecaries used both bulbs and flowers to treat hysteria and epilepsy and to induce vomiting. Nowadays we make a tea or syrup from the flowers for breathing troubles. This was the unlucky Lent Lily that gypsies hawked in old London in the early spring, its bloomtime. Daffodil is a corruption of *asphodel*. *Asph* became *aff* because, in medieval manuscripts, *s* resembled *f*. The daffodil bulb is often mistaken for an onion and can kill. It is often to be found, one herbalist notes, growing in abandoned gardens, the two-faced flower, waiting to numb amateur Wordsworths.

DAMASK

This irresistible, exhausted word in its varying incarnations occupies an entire column in the dictionary, from the ornamentation with wavy patterns of Damascus-steel blades (*damascene*) and gold arabesques on a Kurdish flintlock, to Turkish pottery made with a clear glaze over a white engobe and decorated under the glaze in rich colors, and *Damascus barrel*, a shotgun barrel for use with blackpowder cartridges usually made with strips or rods of iron or steel coiled in a spiral to form a tube and with a speckled or mottled pattern often running at right angles to the bore. Ignore the exquisite damask rose for a moment to study damask weave, that firm lustrous fabric done with warp-faced and filling-faced satins for figure and ground respectively on the one side and with reversed effect on the other, made on jacquard looms, mostly of linen, cotton, silk, rayon, or combinations of these fibers. Used for interior decoration, household linen, and clothing. One account of damask rose is a found poem in its own right: "A grayish red that is bluer than *bois de rose*, bluer, lighter, and stronger than blush rose, and bluer and deeper than Pompeian red or appleblossom." *Damask* also means to deface a book with scribble or to make a seal invalid by hitting it once with a hammer.

DANDELION

Mohegans took dandelion tea as a tonic, while others made a tea from the root against heartburn. Brought into the New World by European settlers, it was later introduced into the Midwest to provide food for bees. It also feeds people, in a salad or cooked, rich in vitamins A and C. The blossoms make a wine and the roots, ground roasted and brewed, make a kind of coffee. The English make a drink called dandelion and burdock.

As a diuretic it has achieved the vivid French name *pissenlit*, piss-in-bed. It is good for the liver. The dandelion was so useful, in fact, to apothecaries that its specific name, *Taraxacum officinale*, denotes "of the workshop," the shop in question being that of the apothecary, forerunner of today's licensed pharmacist. Other "officially" sanctioned and saved plants include balm and eyebright. The dandelion's leaves are "lion-toothed," although some feel the simile refers to the long taproot. Its local and regional names are legion, from *clock, farmer's clocks*, to *schoolboy's clock, tell-time*, and *time flower*, all citing the tradition of blowing away the tufted seeds (the number of puffs required tells the hour).

DAUB

It is said that, if you are daubing, you are not painting well. Of old, to *daub* was to apply whitewash to plaster, from Latin *dealbare*, to whiten (*de*, thorough, *albus*, white). The verb entered French and became *dauber*, and so *daub* in English. Something *slapdash* (etymology unknown) enters into *daub* and suggests the amateur; it's a denigratory term (from Latin *denigrare*, to blacken, a verb that contains a mystery word, *niger* for black, of unknown origin). In the beginning, *denigrate* was literal ("This lotion will denigrate the hairs of hoary heads," Richard Tomlinson, *Renodaeus' Medicinal Dispensatory*, 1657). Since then it has become a metaphorical word for belittle or defame.

DEAD-CAT BOUNCE

This phrase from Wall Street envisions a market drop followed by a faint revival. It might have been a swing number from Count Basie or Benny Goodman. One wonders who does the fieldwork on behalf of the metaphor. Or is it all cerebral?

DEBUT

A debutante is one who is starting out on a social career, making her preliminary bows, and like a player at billiards she is making the first stroke in a game. French *debuter* means exactly that, *but* signifying goal or target (cf. *but* and *butte*, for target). *Debut* also occurs in archery, giving someone the right to shoot first.

DECIMATE

In Tacitus and Suetonius, and in Caesar's army, *decumo* or *decimo* meant "I take a tenth, one man in every ten, for death or punishment." Perhaps to us the word sounds so gruesome, a bit like macerate or obliterate, that we have upped the cull into nine out of ten. When there was a mutiny in the Roman army, one in ten soldiers were put to death. An appropriate fate for nowadays is to take nine out of every ten ungrammatical speakers and do the same. What we have here, in spite of experts and learned scholiasts, is the populist sweep of language and idiom toward a wholly unacademic ideal: the language of the people, heedless of precepts and what things used to mean. So *transpire*, which should mean *become known*, often signifies "happen." Lacking some equivalent of the French Academy, we can do little about it. And who would heed the pronouncements, if any, of the American Academy and Institute of Arts and Letters, whose doings the nation eminently neglects?

DEINOSIS

A mouthful, not least for those ancient Athenians who used this word for the habit of seeing things at their worst. Greek *deinos* means venerable, frightful, awful and *deinoō* to exaggerate.

Certainly such dreadful things happen in Greek tragedy, but they show up too in the fiction of Samuel Beckett, whose *deinosis* always struck me as the most articulate, potent account of what we can barely stand. For twenty years I taught a seminar on his novels and stories to a brave group that included one Canadian, who regularly disappeared to the washroom to douse his head in cold water. We used black candles, and a small wind-up skull that toured the table. My students wrote to Beckett, who sent them gifts, mostly French editions of his books, inscribed, and they would appear at class open-mouthed, wreathed in smiles, holding the gift aloft. The question they all asked was: "Why doesn't he kill himself?" That was what the *deinosis* did to them. I doubt if I could have managed the course without the word, which came to seem even more appalling than the condition it described. This *dein-*, by the way, is the beginning of *dinosaur*, the dreadful lizard.

DEPOSE

What does a deposed monarch sit upon? An overthrown. The joke is little relevant these days, when we hear continually of someone's being *deposed*: getting them to make a statement about something, on oath. Nothing exposes the vagaries of language more than this double value of the word, or of the Latin prefix: from *down from* and *after* to *on account of*, *wherefore*, and *according to*. Look it up and you will find, in the dictionary's necessarily complete account of a dead language, the prefix's use by Vergil, Cicero, Horace, Lucretius, Livy, and others. Latin has two distinct ways with what for us cramps itself into one verb: depose—*remove from office*—is *loco movere* or *abrogare homini magistratum*, while to make a witness set something down (like the man in the Eliot poem obsessively murmuring "Set down this, set down this") is *testari* or *testificari*, the good old habit of swearing on your testicles. So, when someone nowadays gets deposed, we might hear overtones of overthrown, or when someone gets removed from office we might hear overtones of being legally transcribed. We have learned to live with the complexity of language, with homophones and homonyms (bear–bare; bear–bear), while language is forever on the move, especially in the United States, but we cannot remain indefinitely flexible, assimilating all the echoes without losing some of the drift. Or can we? This feature of evolving speech revives the debate about language's being rigidly tied down for denotation or allowed to wander for the sake of exuberant liveliness. The French Academy may try to control things, but the British Academy and the American Academy Institute, so-called, take no interest in the disciplining of speakers or the sea-changing of words. For a while, there may be a shred of grandeur in being deposed, and on the rare occasion of an overthrow a touch of attorney's pedantry in the act. To live doubly thus may bring a new word into being in the long run.

DIABETES

Those who curse modern doctors for coining so many fancy terms (*coryza* for common cold, *hypertension* for high blood pressure, and so forth) should curtsey to the ancient Greeks, who actually came up with some words for diseases themselves. Noticing that sufferers from this ailment made water excessively (polyuria) and drank non-stop (polydipsia), they dubbed it *diabētēs*, "the siphon," a word based on Greek *dia* for "through" and *banein*, to pour, which tells all.

I have heard other theories about the word *diabetes*, one of which invokes the verb *diabainein*, meaning to cross over, which brings into view the splay-legged diabetic in piddling position, anxious not to cross over either foot with a jet of sugar water.

Banein has become confused with *bainein*, surely, pouring with going. Old texts reveal the diabetic in the stance of a pair of compasses or dividers, no doubt after the same misprision, but anyone who has traveled this way, especially with the mature onset form known as *diabetes mellitus* (honey-sweet diabetes), understands the uria-dipsia, those two ugly Norns infernally repeating their one experiment again and again. I'm a *banein* man.

DIATRIBE

Here, once, since the sixteenth century, was a useful word for a worthwhile career. *Diatribe*, from the Greek verb *diatribein* (to pass or waste time), used to mean study or discourse that *wears away* time, as in the preparation of a very long book or, from fiction, the seminar annually devoted to the question "What is Man?" in André Malraux's intellectual novel *The Walnut-Trees of Altenburg*. This is either solo pensiveness or chronic discussion. The gist of the whole process is rubbing (compare Greek *tribe*, rubbing, which yielded *tribadism*, a little-used and seemingly antagonistic word for lesbianism). The word's association with hostility and bad temper stems from the nineteenth century, which must have needed such a word with such a new slant. Alas, to see a worthy word pawnbroked thus because people's blood pressure had gone up.

DIDO

Not that Tyrian princess, founder and queen of Carthage, abandoned by Aeneas the dutiful rake, not even in belated homage and restitution, with her name brought back to life by computer freaks, but short for "dreck in, dreck out." A product can be no better than its component parts. Compare with GIGO ("garbage in,

PAUL WEST

garbage out") and MEGOGIGO ("mine eyes glaze over, garbage in, garbage out"). I am unsure of the chemistry implied here, and of the inexorable qualities implied; for example, if you want a fine explosion, you need procure and mix only two hypergolic chemicals, inert apart, but violently explosive when joined, as Hitler proved in World War Two with his flying bombs.

DINGY

Probably from Middle English *dung*, suggesting "dung-colored," but, if so, why not *dinghy* rather than *dinji*? Old English *dung* may well have come from Indo-European *dhengh* (hard to say these days), which means "covering" (compare the Lithuanian verb *dengti*, to cover). So *dingy* really does seem to bear the burden of material spread over the earth to hearten crops rather than mere dung. Some element of greater complexity and constructive good husbandry seems missing from the word's trajectory. Perhaps Sanskrit *droni*, for "trough" or "tub," is the missing piece or at least a clue to it.

DINKUM

As Australian as *"gdy!"* (contraction of "good-day"), this engaging word refers you to work, or a fair day's work, work fair and square, but it also means "truly" and "honestly" when it's an adverb. "Dinkum oil" is *the truth* whereas *dinky-di* means loyal (as in *true to*). We most often hear the phrase *"fair dinkum,"* which seems tautologous because *dinkum* means fair anyway. *Dinkum* has nothing to do with British *dinky*, meaning cute or small, as in their famous line of Dinky Toys (miniature cars and planes, etc.). Those intent on driving themselves mad will enjoy wondering about the word *dink*, vastly overexploited, from trim or neat, small duck-hunting boat (from *dinghy*), to cut with a die, a freshman cap, hit a tennis ball, a drop shot, and penis.

DIPHTHERIA

To my childhood ear, this disease was slinky and whispering. So was the effect on the human throat and mouth of the leathery membrane that formed during the illness, from Greek *diphthera* for hide or skin. Those whom the ambulance (the conveyance that "ambled") took away swathed in scarlet blankets never came back. The French physician Pierre Bretonneau called it *diphtheritis*, then settled for *diptherie*, borrowed by English in the 1850s during an epidemic. A colloquial name for the disease was *Boulogne sore throat*, from its first occurrence in Boulogne. The *itis* in *diphtheritis* is the suffix for *inflammation*.

DIS

You don't often find a prefix wandering about as a verb, but *dis(s)* does, severed from its moorings in *dismiss, dispose of, dispatch*, and so on. Its curt sibilance appeals to someone who has found something too worthless to waste a big verb on. In a sense what's been *dissed* has been merely prefixed. Sometimes slang for dissertation (*dissy*); not to be confused with *ditzy*. The question now is how to make *dis(s)* even curter; by dropping the vowel?

DOOZIE

A bit of a real doozie itself, this, meaning spiffy, wonderful, superior, classy, beaut, bee's knees, humdinger. In fact the word

 PAUL WEST

comes from Duesenberg, that eminently desirable motor car of the Twenties and Thirties, still seen today although rarely in motion. Super-duper lollapalooza, almost as if a Platonic form had given up the ghost and consented to appear naked among carsick mortals. Why do we have no Rollsie, no Mercie, no Lexooza?

Those who yearn for the models named Torpedo Phaeton ("the shining one," epithet of the sun) or the Torpedo Roadster will need at least a quarter of a million dollars. Otherwise, the hand-crafted lights, the chromed steel radiator shell, the gold-plated emblem, the hinged louvered hood, the stainless steel running boards, the bagwell door, the beveled crystal lenses of the instrument panel, the Wilton wool carpet, and the twin original type bugle horns will go to some other subscriber. More, perhaps, can afford the Estate Golf Car, but no one can have the one Duesenberg II Speedster (160 mph on Bonneville Salt Flats, designer Gordon Buehrig). As the boat-tail trunk recedes from us, we should heed the 1929 catalog in all its snobby vanity:

> It is a monumental answer to wealthy America's insistent demand for the best that modern engineering and artistic ability can provide...Necessarily, its appeal is to only a very few. Any masterpiece can only be appreciated by those who understand the principles on which its greatness is based. Therefore the ownership of a Duesenberg reflects discernment far above the ordinary.

But maybe the engineering company that came up with hydraulic brakes in 1917 is entitled to some honorable bigotry. They paid their Duesie.

DORMOUSE

A raw guess might explain it, summoning up the French verb *dormir*, to sleep, and it would be right. This is the sleepy or sleeping mouse, squirrel-like *glis glis*, often to be found asleep during the day or hibernating.

DOUBLE-BAGGER

It sounds like a ricochet from baseball, but is actually a cruel colloquialism popular with high-schoolers. You need one bag to hide the hideous head of the person identified and another in which to hide your own, lest you catch minimal sight of the horror. This is a teenage version of the Medusa's head, perhaps; one wonders if hangmen might emulate. Sounds as if the supermarket clerk, bundling up your groceries, is saying how hideous both you and they are, but not so, when he/she asks "Double-bagged?"

DRAWERS

Not chest of, but old word for *knickers* (see). This is something you slide off, draw or pull away from you, for whatever purpose. Perhaps from French *tirer* and *tiroir* (drawer). From the sixteenth to the nineteenth centuries, drawers did duty for knickers, "a garment pulled on." The old word survives still on the shooting range, where *Maggie's drawers*, as yet unreplaced by Maggie's knickers, indicates the concentric ring next to the erotic bull's-eye on a target.

DRUB

Drub, like *aluminum* and *paraffin*, seems to have been the work of a single individual (cf. *blurb*), keeping his ears open as he journeyed about and finally adopting a certain group of phonemes into his

PAUL WEST

own vocabulary, then launched into the world with proud humility, as by Sir Thomas Herbert (1606–1682, not the poet George Herbert or the other poet Herbert of Cherbury), who traveled in the East and published *The Relation of some yeares travail into Afrique and the greater Asia* (1634). "[The pasha]," he writes, "made the petitioner be almost drub'd to death." His word came from Arabic *dararaba*, meaning not merely "beat," but precisely the bastinado, in which the soles of the feet are thrashed to punish or torture the victim. It is not the kind of word a civilized nation ought to need, but when was a nation ever wholly civilized? Its modern uses are mild and tend to exaggerate; the drubbing is akin to what the English call having a strip torn off you or being on the mat. The punishment is mostly orally administered.

DRUDGE

Another puzzle, first recorded as a noun toward the end of the fifteenth century, the verb emerging some fifty years later. (Compare this gradual evolution of the verb with the sudden arrival in the late 1990s of *to sunset*, "wane, dwindle," which I last heard in 1998 used by NPR legal correspondent Nina Totenberg. Is this a verb we ever needed?) Middle English *drugge* may have spawned *drudge* ("to drag laboriously"), or Old English *dreogan*, meaning to work. The rest is blank.

DUDE

The dude ranch certainly still exists, perhaps no longer the butt of faintly amazed condescension; from the late 1800s the dude hovered between dandy and fop and sometimes in Western attire at those ranches. Since then, *dude* has denoted generic man or guy, but with some subtler insinuations: what I call the accusatory generic almost akin to *Monsieur* or buddy but with that overtone of arrogant familiarity. It is almost equivalent to an expression from my childhood, uncouthly uttered as "Thee wi' t'hair on" (You with the hair on), and all individuality stamped out. A *dude heaver* is a bouncer. A dude is no longer an Easterner or city person out of his element. Could he be a dud all tarted up? Etymology unknown. In American pronunciation, the *u* is never broken and sounds like *oo*, not *ee-ew*, which adds to the word's rebuke, when there is one, a hint of contempt, just as, when *dude* gets said among friends, the *oo* signals a dropping of pretense—we're all in this together, *dood*. It's an involuntary noise, a bit like *old chap, hombre, mon vieux*.

DUFF

An uneducated attempt to pronounce *dough*, this word tastily survives in plum duff, the flour pudding with raisins or currants, boiled in a cloth bag. It also endures as part of a famous Royal Air Force expression, *duff gen*, first heard during World War Two, meaning false information, either data that had been kneaded or otherwise messed about with or disinformation, looking like the real thing but useless and homogeneously bland. *Gen*, one presumes, comes from the "general" in "general information," but *duff* has extraordinary and attractive relatives elegantly summed up in a line by John Ayto: "dairy, effigy, faint, fiction, lady, paradise." See the entry under *fiction*.

DUFFEL

After its place of origin (manufacture or export), *duffel* commemorates Duffel in Belgium, a town near Antwerp. A duffel coat dates back to the seventeenth century, although nowadays more readily associated with hood and toggles (Royal Navy style) than with the rest of its cut. *Duffel*, or *duffel bag*, is a twentieth-century Americanism, at first a bag for personal gear, at very first a set of spare clothes made from duffel. *Duffel* seems halfway between camel hair and the even softer wool of a Crombie (silky yieldingness), from which many military officers' overcoats are made.

DUNCE

There is nothing so vindictive as punishing the terminal moraine left behind him by a philosopher. Three hundred years after the death of the Scottish thinker and theologian Duns Scotus (c. 1265–1308), Renaissance philosophers ridiculed those who stood by his views, and *Duns* yielded up *dunce* to the language, later made physically evident in the nineteenth century by the conical dunce's cap with which stupid-seeming schoolchildren were afflicted, standing in a corner. It is an odd historical spectacle, requiring over five hundred years to complete itself, as if the casuistical Scot had put a curse on his detractors, making them ever late (or re-tarded). Duns Scotus was one of the most ingenious thinkers of the Middle Ages, but, when his devotees opposed the Renaissance that swept Europe, they rapidly became "*duns* men" and got him a bad name.

DUNDERHEAD

Not literally, but perhaps metaphorically, a *thunder head* is akin to a numbskull, a blockhead, a dunce, though it is hard to see why a thunder head is dumb, unless it strikes us as a fidget of mute, mindless nature doing its noisy thing. Possibly, too, the head-ness of a thunderhead makes this anthropomorphic: a big black or dark-green head looming, best seen from an airplane. Bizarre-sounding siblings accompany this word, from *dunder* (lees of cane juice used to ferment in the distillation of rum) to *dunderfunk* (smashed sea biscuits or crackers mixed with molasses and baked—emergency rations while at sea). There is something almost complimentary about *dunderhead*, at least if it is a head that hears and heeds its own thunder without trying to conform.

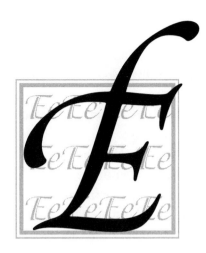

EGG ON

No, not being pelted with rotten eggs or prompted to aphrodisiac excess by the omelet of many yolks, but, as in Old Norse's *eggja*, to incite, a relative of English *edge*, as in cutting edge. So, you can be *eggja-ed on*. This is *eggment*, as an earlier English expressed being urged or prompted. Find it in Chaucer's rehearsal of an old misogynistic canard: "Thurgh wommannes eggement Mankynde was lorn" (or lost). The sharpness or pointedness felt in *edge* also makes itself plain in such words as *acid, acrid, acute, alacrity, acne,* and *oxygen,* all of which have a bite of some kind, as does the *egar* of *vinegar,* that wine turned tart. Indeed, someone being brought around from a faint with vinegar or smelling salts may be said to be being egged on. Or perhaps tickled back into alertness with an *ear* of wheat or corn at its spikiest. Oxygen, by the way, forms from the Greek for sharp (*oxus*) and the suffix *-genes,* meaning formation or creation; it is an "acid-former."

EKE

Not going strong, but *eking* out a living still, this verb had no forerunner in Old English, none that has been found anyway, so it figures as a twelfth-century arrival, akin to words in other Germanic languages such as Old Norse *auka* and Gothic *aukan*. Latin *augere*, source of English *auction* and *author*, and Greek *aukhein* witness to a prototype in Indo-European, *aug-*, source of English *wax* (grow). Originally *nickname* was an *ekename*, which *eked* you out, augmented your identity and presence on the planet; and then someone divided the phrase up wrong, attaching the *n* of *an* to the front of the word (as in *a newt*). In a sense, the term *ekename* includes not only *nicknames* but also surnames (a name over and above your other one). We cannot be surprised that *eke* used to mean *also*, an autonomous meaning now lost. When you are lying on the ultra-sound table while a technician passes the wand over your goop-coated body, you will hear, among the litany of other technical words having to do with matters vascular the word *augment*, which is a good sign; your blood is coming to the rescue, to eke you out.

ELIMINATE

Some old dictionaries include the expression "eliminate—to put out of doors," meaning to eject someone proved undesirable. Latin *eliminatus* combines *e* (out) with *limen* (threshold, doorstep), so to *eliminate* anything you put it past the threshold of your house, or your body. *Limen* also shows up in *preliminary*, what gets done before crossing the lintel. And what is a threshold? Old English *trescold* is where you tread; this word evokes the link between treading and threshing. One does not think of the doorstep as the place where threshing is held, but where else more convenient, with all the chaff kept outside for the wind to blow away? Not surprisingly, my first Latin primer was called *Limen*, a word not in the glossary. In athletics, elimination races or eliminations decide who shall be out of the running, not allowed up to the *limen* of the final, its start. Or they're what's merely expelled.

ELIXIR

In the days of the Eastern alchemists who tried to convert base metals into gold, there was an imaginary substance, a "dry powder" they thought would work the trick. This they called *al-iksir*, which entered Medieval Latin as *elixir*, then adapted from alchemical dry powder to the potion that would confer eternal life: the so-called elixir of life. Almost an old Viagra. Ponce de Leon actually combed Florida for this chemical and Faust pursued it in his laboratory. It has been suggested that a dry powder of the Greeks, *xerion* (compare *xerox*), used for treating wounds, impressed the Arabs enough to give it an Arabic name. So, from Greece to Arabia rather than vice versa, or from Greece to Arabia and then back. All these substances must have been the same powder. The last fit of the madcap idea was that of the mad scientist in his primitive laboratory in old black-and-white movies, messing about with beasts and captive humans, the mutilated and the deformed.

ENTHUSIASM

This word, given to pedants as a wind-up bathroom toy, has filled them with censure for years. It means, really, being possessed, snatched up, by a god, and so you cannot yourself *enthuse*; only gods can do that. I doubt it meant "being inspired by a god," unless inspired is being read with appreciative wideness. *Pace* Richard Baxter in *Infants' Church Membership and Baptism* (1651), who writes "Doth he think they knew it by enthusiasm or revelation from heaven?" A god may seize you, especially a Greek one, for the mere joy of capture, the raptor's rapture. In the seventeenth century, as Puritanism waxed in England, *enthousiasm* became a bad thing: excessive religiosity, not unknown in the New England of that time. The word's assignment to "eagerness" or even "excitement" arrives with the eighteenth century. Our modern "sports enthusiast" is light years from the person captured by the gods—not far from those supposedly abducted by aliens. Perhaps it is time for the word to go back to its origins. Then *enthused* will regain its passive victims, snapped up by spacefarers, gods or not.

I was intrigued to hear, and watch, a German survivor of World War Two confessing on the History Channel that Hitler "enthused" him. This was Emil Klein, for whatever reason getting it right in a language he wasn't wholly at ease with. Hitler had swept down upon him like a god and possessed him. If he had said "I was enthused," he would no doubt have meant seized, and when he said Hitler had enthused him, he might have meant awakened in him some preternatural approval; but he also meant what I in my pedantic way relish. He'd been snatched out of his usual self enough to join the Hitler Youth.

ESCAPE

This word pleases me because, before I looked it up, I had no idea of its origin, though I could see the trouble it was in from the usage note which told me 74 percent of a usage panel rejected the following idiom: *Three prisoners escaped at three o'clock.* It should be stated, they felt, what the prisoners escaped *from.* Intransitive escape, as in commercials, or legal clauses, is a fascinating thing, evoking a popular show called *Escape to Happiness.* In fact, from Vulgar Latin via French the word means *to take off your cape or cloak. Escaper.* Somewhere, in the swirl of usage, there's a hunch that clothing, even the loveliest of capes, is a hindrance to—well, one can guess.

You have done with escape once you recognize that, when the police seized a malefactor in the old days, he slipped off his cape and ran. *Es*, for out of, and *cappa*, for cape. So there are civil and criminal uses, which sometimes overlap.

ETYMOLOGY UNKNOWN

Alas that this only too frequently appearing phrase's initial letters spell EU, Greek for "pleasant," "agreeable." To be wholly confounded amid the golden terminal moraine of word history, with weird slackenings all around, as well as absurd twists and gross misunderstandings, is harsh. To come up blank only reminds us that we are lucky to know anything at all. Look how nothing of Indo-European language survived, requiring its hypothetical substitute to be a complex of algebraic-looking blurts no one can pronounce. To find this phrase glaring at you before your avid quest even begins is to be reminded of how many other matters puzzle us too; we rehearse on words for the mysteries of the cosmos, which, of course, may not even have a beginning, whereas, clearly, there was always a predecessor for a word, could we but find it. In truth, many of the words whose etymology we know turn out to be rather dull (*word*, for instance), quite without vicissitudes or bizarre shifts; it is then, perhaps in a mood of grateful resignation, that we marvel at any word's very creation amid all the other noises of the planet, forever wondering why *that* sound, *those* vowels and consonants? Meanwhile, we are left wondering by *clobber*, *gib*, *hornswoggle*, *josh*, *pang*, *piker*, *pod*, *polecat*, and *stunt*, and, among those here mentioned, *dude*, *eke*, *pump*, *rhesus*, *swivet*, and *toad*.

EUCALYPTUS

In 1788 the French botanist Charles Louis l'Héritier coined this Latin name, *eucalyptus globulus*, for a tree whose buds have a conical cover (the Greek prefix *eu-* means "well," and the past participle *kaluptos* "covered"). There would be little more to say, apart from citing the pungent, searching aroma of the oil that has spattered many a handkerchief stiffened with use; but Calypso, who managed to hide Odysseus for seven years on her island Ogygia, is an offshoot of the same verb. What the tree does for its flower buds, she did for him. Her name means "she who conceals." Can we believe that l'Héritier in no way had Odysseus in mind when he named the tree thus? Why did he have to go back to Greek when he could have used the Latin verbs *celare, occulere, occultare, abdere, abscondere? Globulus* is Latin anyway, a diminutive of *globus* ("round ball"). So why did he create a Greek-Latin phrase? In either Greek or Latin he mythicized his tree and its blooms, not in the least fixing on the slipper-shaped lip of the pinkish flower, nor on the oily aroma, but on something minor: the bud sheath. Was he thinking of Calypso after all, whose name went easily into Latin? Other aspects of this Australian tree might have caught his imagination: its rapid rate of growth, its enormous height, its heart-shaped leathery young leaves, its lance-shaped mature ones, its vast root system, which can drain any marsh and in fact was used to dry up many of Algeria's so-called "fever districts." Indeed, we know it also as the fever tree, the blue gum. Had l'Héritier detected there in its oily presence an ancient temptress ghost, from whom he had to turn away abruptly?

EUPHEMISM

Fascinating in that an important word signaling a social and cultural custom of the ancient Greeks has become a mere convenience for grammarians. *Eu* (good) + *phemi* (speak) gave *euphemismos*, originally denoting abstinence from words of ill omen at religious ceremonies, but the word has declined into the choosing of a less offensive word over a more offensive one. A pity. *Pheme* has such English relatives as *fate, fable,* and *fame.* The so-called *dysphemism,* a word we no doubt never needed, is a late-nineteenth-century trump-up based on Greek *dus* for "bad," and meaning, of course, *a bad word.* Although *eu* is all over the place in modern English (*eulogy, eugenic, euphonious, eupeptic, evangelist*), *eunuch* does not belong with them, composed from Greek *eune* for bed and *echo* (keep). The eunuch was the guardian of the bed, what Cambridge University came to call "the bedder" and Oxford "the scout."

EUREKA

It was a famous conversation when King Hiero II of Syracuse asked the Greek mathematician Archimedes (c. 287–212 B.C.) to find out if a certain goldsmith had cheated him. "I ordered a gold crown," he said, "but he may have mixed in some silver. Can you investigate?" Archimedes wasn't sure, but he said he would take a bath and, while soaking, have a think. According to Plutarch, some of the water overflowed, reminding Archimedes of the fact that pure gold would displace more water than an alloy. Elated, the mathematician leaped out of the bath crying "*heureka!*": I have found it! (the perfect indicative of *heuriskein,* "to find"). English-speaking readers tend to skip the aspirate (denoted in Greek by a tiny sign above the e (ἑ), as did Henry Fielding, the first English author to use the word as a delighted exclamation of discovery, in *Joseph Andrews* (1742): "Adams returned overjoyed cring out 'Eureka!'" All you ever have to do is set the crown in water, then separately try equal weights of gold and silver and measure the different levels. The goldsmith had indeed cheated and, it is rumored, was appropriately punished, having the exact quantity of the silver melted and poured into his mouth.

EXUBERANT

What modern woman would take offense at having this innocent-seeming word applied to her? She might even take it as a compliment to her abounding *enthusiasm* (see). In fact, it used to mean "overflowing udders," from Latin *ex-* (out) and *uber* (udder), giving *exuberans*. It seems an oddly intrusive, presumptuous, and speculative way of describing any woman who was not nude and close by, and it might have been reserved, instead, for commentary on goats, cows, and sheep.

Another puzzling word in this vein is *nonchalant*, the French meaning a woman who does not heat up or has not yet done so. *Non* plus *caleo*, to be hot, explain it. Again, one wonders at the presumption, and the failure to heed such folk wisdom as "still waters run deep." Surely this word was meant to get a rise out of a female failing to respond to male overtures. She may well have been cool, in our modern sense of neat and snazzy, or of cool demeanor, or cool in our other modern sense of well-adjusted within herself. Whatever, she's a cool customer.

One shrinks from combining these two words, suspecting an exuberant woman of being heated up, or vice versa. There is, too, the old male canard that an exuberant woman can't help herself; her bosom leads her by the nose. Here are etymologies we are glad to forget.

FECTOR

Coined by the chemist Paul Bickart, this is a handy way of designating "one who flees back to the country from which he has fled; whirlcoat...: Svetlana Alliluyeva, the daughter of Joseph Stalin, is the current record holder, a trifector." Care must be taken, however, not to confuse a *trifector* with a *trifecta*, a horse bet. How the maxim "You can't go home again" bears on the *fector* is uncertain, but it is clear that Gottried Benn's doctrine of domestic emigration transcends all fection.

FEISTY

Middle English for "farting dog," going back to the obsolete English *fist* (fart) and Latin *pedere* (break wind). The expression "hoist with one's own petard" has the same origin (in English, *petard* is a little bomb). In the sixteenth and seventeenth centuries, any mongrel or tripehound got the phrase *fisting dog*, not so much for its wind as because *fisting*, somewhat like *fucking* now, was an imprecise expletive, designed more for abuse and insult than for specific complaint. *Feisty* nowadays, of course, means either quarrelsome or vigorous, though one can almost see some kind of a link between high energy and the breaking of wind.

FICTION

Just about any dictionary will relate fiction to invention, and the Latin verb *fingĕre*, meaning "to touch, to form, to mold." *Fictus* is the past participle. In some dictionaries a bald note sends you to the Indo-European form *dheigh-*, which no one knows how to pronounce. As soon as you find it, however, you are in an extraordinary Aladdin's cave of deep and potent relationships.

You begin with kneading clay, as in mold, of course, and quickly move to bread kneader, someone who molds dough. Now it gets lively, calling up the mistress of an ancient household in the Anglo-Saxon compound noun *hlaefdige*—the loaf-molder. Skip to dough, predictable enough and quaintly backwards, until you find the Latin idea of a *figura*, a form or shape produced by kneading. Now comes a shower of like-sounding words such as figure, configure, disfigure, prefigure, and transfigure, followed by *fingĕre* along with faint, feign, feint, figment, and fiction, upon whose brink we are now trembling, still linked to touch and mold but now advancing to a wall originally made of clay or mud bricks, otherwise construed as paradise.

So, if you wish to dig beneath the surface of the word *fiction*, you discover an able lady, the mistress of her household, keeping it together by kneading dough into loaves, which, at least metaphorically, she then stacks around her into an enclosing wall or barricade to create a safe paradise. I have no doubt omitted some steps in this evolution, as you must when dealing with so hypothetical a language as Indo-European, which does not have a literature. But the drift or magic is clear: Fiction, like the lady's loaves, will save you from the world outside, yet not without keeping you in touch with things of the earth earthy. Is this an early form of the worry that fiction, capable of being so farfetched, will sever you from reality altogether? The point always has been that nothing is underived, that the most far-fetched conceit owes something to the close at hand. I don't think it preposterous to divine here the presence of Lady Fiction, akin to Boethius's Lady Philosophy, who will minister to your bodily and spiritual needs. I love the idea that fiction derives its ways from the kneading habits of the often maligned *Hausfrau*. In an ancient language known as Avestan—the eastern dialect of Old Iranian, once called Zend—a mud or clay wall enveloped paradise, and you may well wonder why; unless this happens to be a complex metaphor for the wall of loaves instead of bricks that keeps a household together and, like fiction itself, perhaps chanted by a local bard, supplants the world outside.

To go farther into this bakery-of-fiction idea, you may need to delve until you find that, in premedieval times, no one said *a loaf of bread*. You just said: A loaf, whereas the word *bread* referred to bits and pieces, so if you went ahead and asked for a loaf of bread you would be asking for a loaf of scraps. I am not sure that here, once again, we don't have something in disguise: namely that all fictions are fiction, much as Julio Cortázar said all fires are fire. It is no doubt easier to talk of the loaves of fiction—individual works—than to try to define the realm of fiction *in toto*, which all of a sudden begins to include poetry, the essay, and even, after the Last Tapes of Krapp, those of Tripp.

There is something gorgeously disturbing about a wall of loaves, unless you are a screaming pragmatic; rainproof, no; bullet-proof, of course not; but, when situated in paradise—*pairi-daeza*, as the Avestan scribes called it in the sacred writings that *have* come down to us—a carrel, an enclosed garden, a paddock for unicorns. In the presence of this walled-in paradise, I am not sure we aren't close to the notion of burying oneself in a good book, or the Victorian three-decker novel, or what used to be called the willing suspension of disbelief. Or the ivory tower, in which, reading or writing, we say to ourselves *Can life be this good? Is it real?* And, obedient as Wimbledon ball-girls, we read or write on, in love with our trance.

To get a full sense of the lady's place in the Anglo-Saxon household, you have to go to Sweden, where *matmoder* (meat-mother) remains a servant's term for the mistress of the house (the Anglo-Saxon lord was the *hlaford*, loaf-ward or guardian of the loaf).

FILLET

When my butcher grandfather made a fillet, he boned a piece of meat, rolled it up, and tied it shut with a length of thread (*filet* in French, from Latin *filium*). Nowadays you never get the thread, but you can have the fillet "*mignon*," which means dainty or exquisite. If you order "jerked" beef, you get Spanish *charqui*, which means dried and cut. *Hash* has been hatcheted to death and a chop has felt just one blow of the French ax (*hache*). Hachette is a famous French publishing house, no doubt lost for an emblem.

FLAFFY

From French *faire laugher* or *faux laver*, a false wash, or *foutu élevé*, an abortion on horseback, this is the quality of expendability raised to an exponential extreme. "Flaffy" should be pronounced with maximum disdain, heavy emphasis on the first vowel, and some time spent on it too, almost yawning. A histrionic word, this, unlike "worthless" and "jejune," although it signals what these words say, but without the imputation to the *flaffer* of base motives. The word stigmatizes the pointless product of a hopeless mind or gift, although, especially in Scotland and Canada, it almost seems to imply a quality of gentle befuddlement in the flaffer. Flaffy refers to works or products that cannot be praised for anything, not even by hired hacks out on the cutting edge of hypocrisy. Essentially the word invokes a dead work, one of the curious effects of its application being that no one ever remembers the object of the scorn, even though the scorn was merited. Thus flaffy should be seen as one of the words in our language that not only condemn but efface as well, lately dubbed "detergent adjectives," or more vulgarly, "wipe-words." Once you have been called flaffy, you are doomed to be thought irrelevant to every human enterprise thereafter. This lexicographer will provide no examples, of either works or people, of course; but the death-dealing sentence often reads: "————'s latest is totally flaffy" or "Flaff, flaff, flaff." Also **flaff** *v*: To execute something as poorly as possible, but without deliberately seeking oblivion for doing so.

FLAMINGO

Not surprisingly, this reddish-pink, leggy wading bird belongs to flame (Germanic *ing*, suffix for *belonging to*, added to what is flaming, from Latin *flamma*). The devious, obvious route of development is from Provençal through Portuguese, *flamenc* to *flamengo*, but it might just as easily have soared toward us from Latin, the gregarious firebird whose name says *flaming*.

Flamingo, by the way, has nothing to do with *flamenco*, which came from the Spanish word for "Flemish," the people of Flanders having had a name in the Middle Ages for flashy, exuberant dress; this is why to Spaniards "Flemish" meant "gipsy-like."

FLAUNT

Strange to relate, while *Webster* offers a section on this word's etymology, citing Greek *planao* (to lead astray, to wander), it makes no comment on usage at all, while the *American Heritage* says "Origin Obscure" but goes fully into Usage. You don't *have* to do both, but it helps, like the bilingual person who says he has two tongues in his head. *To flaunt* is to indulge in gratuitous swank, "to be gaudily in evidence," as John Dos Passos intends when he writes "Every great hostelry flaunted the flag of some foreign potentate." Such is the standard use of the word, the non-standard being to use it to mean *flout*, which means to *defy*. The *American Heritage*'s Usage panel condemns this use (91 percent), but you hear it all the time, so many people regarding *flaunt* as a two-purpose word at odds with itself, meaning both *show off* and *defy*. This has been increasingly the situation since the 1930s, and it is no clue to a person's degree of education to find them misusing *flaunt*. Perhaps they hear the two as the same, as *flont*. Perhaps the explanation is the simple old one of *flaunt*'s being the more plangent-sounding word for either occasion, which is no doubt why people prefer *went* to *gone*, as in "he had went." All one can do, when they flaunt their misused flaunt is to flout it: show contempt or disregard for. Etymologically speaking, *flouting* is *fluting*, a wimpish warble only.

FLOP

Is *flop* crumbling from overuse? When hoboes of the nineteenth century crashed, lay down to sleep, they called this *flopping*. "Kip, doss, flop, pound your ear," as Jack London says, "all mean to sleep." We are still familiar with the flophouse, the run-down place where you find a bed, rudimentary and perhaps squalid. Back in the late 1800s, *to flop* was to fail utterly, which entry into a fleabag might befit, although a *bellyflop*—a stomach-first dive—is a more sudden happening, as likely to split you open as not. Another use I collected from my native village, where we often played various games in the meadows belonging to local farmers. The grass in these fields was always splattered with cowdung in various stage of desiccation; in whatever state, this was always *cowflop* to us, at its driest an adequate if unstreamlined Frisbee, and, if still liquid within, a fearsome weapon to sail through the air at a rival, if your aim was good. Elsewhere, *cowflops* were *cowpats*, whose presence encouraged the growth of *cowslips* (Old English *cuslyppe*) or *cowslops*, plants whose unobserved symbiosis reposes in the maxim: You slip where it is sloppy.

Cowslip is the Old World's primrose, *Primula veris*, otherwise the marsh marigold, Virginia cowslip, and shooting star. It is interesting to juxtapose *slyppe* and *slyma* (slime, paste) with the fact that *Primula* is the name of an English margarine.

FLOUNCE

Perhaps from Norwegian *flunsa*, to hurry, or the Swedish dialect word *flunsa*, to plunge, this word, a rather sophisticated work of observation, envisions someone moving suddenly and jerkily in a seeming state of emotional turmoil: expressive departing, say, "She flounced away in a boiling swivet." To move like this draws attention to you, which is surely the desired result. It also means to struggle wildly. You can flounce out on a contract (if you know what to do). And there is an archaic use, too, unless the very word is archaic (requiring a billowy dress unless you are a horse), which is to move violently, as in slamming, splashing, or flinging. I am not sure that the novelist E. M. Forster's habit of throwing himself against the walls of his rooms in

King's College, Cambridge, when he was in a pet or fit of pique, isn't *flouncing*. He always bounced off, so the self-throw was for show all right, and made his point heavily. It takes some practice not to crack a rib thus and must surely have been rehearsed in private.

FLOWER

This is the rather engaging term of endearment meaning *my dear, honey,* or *love* in Yorkshire and Derbyshire, used mostly by working-class people, and unselfconsciously. Of course, what eases the endearment into popular use is its other meaning: Yorkshire- or Derbyshire-born, part of the mystery being that three of the English counties flaunt a rose: Yorkshire, white, Lancashire, red, Derbyshire, yellow. If you still recall the Wars of the Roses, these were they, with Derbyshire left out. A Yorkshire–Lancashire cricket match commemorates the wars.

FORLATERS

A word used mainly by people unafraid of seeming to have said *fellators*. It means scraps from one meal squirreled away in purse or pocket and kept for the next, for later.

FORLORN HOPE

This once military notion has passed through myth and folk etymology, beginning as Dutch *verloren hoop*, which means "lost troop," culminating as the phrase we know, a forlorn hope that the forlorn troop might have embodied. So this troop vanishes into crypto-history and ends up alongside the lost command.

We have to choose between a scouting party sent forward on a risky mission and the risky mission itself. *Hoop* is related to "heap." *Forlorn*, evocative of the abandoned or deserted, from Keats's "faery lands forlorn" to *la cathédrale engloutie* (the submerged cathedral), means wretched, pitiful, or desperate. It also means "lost." The combination of suicide squadron, *enfants perdus*, or *kamikazes* with the idea of the already lost can be excruciating, even though the original lost troop is less hopeful than forlorn hope. *Forlorn hope* first appears in the seventeenth century.

FORTY WINKS

Originating in the humor magazine *Punch*, this jovial synonym for "nap" has held on to its number uninflated. Referring to the thirty-nine articles that clergymen of the Church of England were required to accept since 1571, the writer in *Punch* observed (November 16, 1872): "If a...man, after reading through the Thirty-nine Articles, were to take forty winks." Since then, even more tedious catechisms have arrived, profoundly anesthetic, but forty has held fast, even against the onomatopoeic "zee," plural *zees*.

FRAG

One of war's few privileges, this, after *fragmentation grenade*, is the verb for wounding or killing an unpopular officer in one's own unit. From the Vietnam War. It was done in other wars, too, before we had a word for it. My father, a sergeant, was suspected of it in World War One, when a certain lieutenant suggested they go out into no-man's-land together just to waste some time and give him an opportunity to write my father up for a decoration. "I don't care to have an undecorated senior

NCO." My father came back unscathed and alone. The lieutenant's successor repeated the excursion, but had the same bad luck, and my father returned intact and undecorated, saying a sniper each time had fired on them. There was no third time: No officer could be found willing to take my father again into no-man's-land, lest he get fragged by whomever. Did German nighttime snipers kill officers only?

FRANGIPANI

In the sixteenth century, the Marquis Muzio Frangipani of Rome, weary of the smell of leather, devised a perfume with which to scent his gloves. Made from red jasmine, this almond-scented aroma attracted the chefs of the time, inducing them to prepare a similar-smelling custard made with crushed almonds, which they dotingly called *les gants de Frangipane*. ("the Gloves of Frangipani"), possibly deciding that *Frangipani* meant "broken bread." The marquis marinated in the creamy pastry of his almond-smelling gloves, his chiming name twice famous.

Another, less picturesque account introduces Charles Plumier, the French botanist who made voyages to the Caribbean in the seventeenth century, who gave his name to *Plumeria* (for example, the Singapore Plumeria keeps its dark green Rhododendron-like leaves the year round while others shed theirs). The stems of all varieties exude a milky juice that stains clothing. In Haiti and French Guiana, *frangipanier* means "coagulated milk." The tree is often planted near temples and burial grounds for its wonderful aroma, and is sometimes referred to as the Temple Tree. In Hawaii the blossoms go into leis to hang around the visitor's neck, and in Venezuela the tree is called *amapola*, *atapaimo*, and *tamaiba*. Broken bread, coagulated milk, almond paste in pastry, frangipane excites and sustains the imagination of those who live through and by it, coming full circle perhaps in the French adjective *fourré*, which means both fleecy-lined and lined with cream or chocolate. Merely the scent of frangipani prompts people to excess, creamy fantastication, on the verbal as well as the culinary level.

FRANGLAIS

Slang for a brand of French invaded by English. The standard example used to be *le smoking*, for smoking jacket. There seems, thus far, to be no comparable contamination in other languages: no Espanish, or Englese, no doubt because the opportune pun has not made its appearance. Webster adopts "Spanglish," however.

FRANKENSTEIN

Epitome of the creator who loses control of his creature, which ends up destroying him. The only snag, and there may be a moral or dictum here for novelists, is that too many people think the "monster"'s name is *Frankenstein*. If it had been named Shreck or Golem, it might have had a chance, but the name would have to have been comparably original, just as outrageous-sounding. When little boys used to distort their faces by tugging their lower eyelids down and shoving their noses up, to make a hideous mask, the word they would yell to further enhance the horror was "Frankenstein." Perhaps the maker was meant to merge with his creature, but there is no evidence that Mary Shelley intended any such thing. Why the very name *Frankenstein*, rather than, say, Frankincense, should seem grotesque is hard to establish; why should this particular array of vowels and consonants strike terror into small children? Mere connotation building up over the years through repeated references? Or is there something evil-sounding in the very sound -*stein*, and why? Is the vowel sequence A-E-Y inherently frightening or alarming or ST intimidating? This is 1818, long before Nazis, so the Nazi overlay on the names is unique to our own time; it's not essentially Nazi, any more than Wallenberg, say, so perhaps we can thank the movies for the name's impact.

FREEZE

Ever since Indo-European *preus* and Latin *pruina* (hoarfrost), this word has suffered only one mishap, at the hands of the police. Already on record, Japanese visitors to the U.S. have been ordered by the police to "freeze," and have not known how to do it—hands up and keep still. As a cautionary imperative, it is no doubt no more fatuous than *melt* or *pray*, but it has done more damage. How often the concisions of a crude elite elude rational folk not even on the run. In one infamous English murder case, a young man named Bentley went to the hangman for having told an accomplice on a roof, "Let him have it," meaning either *Shoot the cop* or *Let the cop have the gun.* The jury opted for the former, and the judge went along. Bentley's family kept trying to clear his name, but could not. If his death depended on a quibble in interpretation, think what a foreigner, commanded to halt, would make of the colloquial "Hold it." Hold what?

FROM

Despite its many other uses, in American speech it can also mean "about," as in *I don't know from sea urchins*, which implies an odd thing: sea urchins communicating direct. It is a quaint idiom, in

which a fake reciprocity tints a prepositionally absolute ignorance. The sense of a domain unexplored and unwanted comes
through, adding power to the speaker's bland stance.

FRONTISPIECE

Piece here has nothing to do with a piece of anything, coming instead from *spic*, a root meaning "to see," as in *spectator, conspicuous,*
and *auspices. Spicium,* added to Late Latin *frons, frontis* (face),
yielded a word meaning "judgment of character through interpretation of the face." Thus, you sample a book from this artifi-
cial "face" bound in as a page. As such judgment became less a
thing to talk about, the word drifted away to mean "front part,"
at first the façade of a building ("an indiscreet builder, who pre-
ferreth the care of his frontispiece before the maine foundation,"
Richard Brathwait, *English Gentleman,* 1630). By 1600, though,
the word's link with prefatory illustration opposite the title
page was coming into its own. *Piece,* the red herring of this travail, continued to mislead connoisseurs and spellers for some
time, with *spic* surviving in such words, among others, as *inspect*
and *spy.* When Sir Christopher Wren wrote, in a mood of par-
donable vainglory, *Si monumentum requiris circumspice* (If you need
a monument, look around you), he was using it too.

FRUIT FLY

The mountaineer of urinal troughs, this tiny bit of smut feeds
on ripening or fermenting fruit and has figured in experiments
to retard the aging process conducted by Professor Leonard
Hayflick. Its most arresting feature, however, is its Latin name,
that opens up whole entire vistas of its behavior. *Drosophila
melanogaster* is the black-bellied dew-sipper, also called the

pomace fly. I am not sure that the dew it sips in Men's Rooms is exactly that, but it seems to keep them going.

FUCK

Not much of a word, really, for all its *réclame*; it does not exist in Old English and began its career in the early sixteenth century. There was, however, a John le Fucker, recorded in 1278, revealing that the word was there previous to 1500, yet forbidden even then. No doubt it is of German origin, descending from Scotland, which argues a Scandinavian provenance. Compare with Norwegian *fukka*, "copulate," and the Swedish dialect words *focka* (copulate, hit) and *fock* (penis). Learned treatises have been compiled about this word, which seems to survive just about equally as both limbo expletive and lascivious come-on.

FURBELOW

Often pronounced with a lascivious sneer, this is actually a ruffle or flounce on a garment, or any fancy bit of ornamentation. A variant of *falbala* (from dialectal French *ferbela* for frill), it often sends verbally attuned people in the wrong direction.

FURTLER

The *furtler* gives up on the world of everyday, though perhaps coveting the realm of high society, the incessant showbiz gala, and resigns him/herself to making love with photographs of celebrities, so-called, perhaps even using life-size blow-ups with suitable orifices snipped therein with nail-scissors. Your furtler is a flatlander.

FUSELAGE

Sufficient unto the day are the malapropisms thereof, the latest offered by someone talking about the grisly end of Bonnie Thornton and Clyde Barrow amid a "fuselage" of shots. This was on the TV program *Biography*. One marvels, of course, since a fuselage, the body of an airplane from spinner to tail-light, resembles a spindle, for which the French word is *fuseau*, from Old French *fusel*, from *fus*. The most interesting fuselage in the world was that of the Vickers Wellington bomber (World War Two), designed by Barnes Wallis, who came up with the idea of a criss-cross pattern much stronger than the old notion of stringers grouped around a series of formers. This was called geodetic, from the Greek word for the division of the Earth, or reticular, from the Latin for "net." The rest is mathematical.

GAFFER

Functions in the theater alongside *juicers*, who control the electricity. Long the foreman of a stage crew, the gaffer is still that, but in film and TV a senior electrician. This is a sixteenth-century word rough-hewn from *grandfather* or *godfather*. In Britain, a *gaffer* is also a boss, overseer, or charge-hand, a master glassblower, and just about anyone in a position of authority such as a gamekeeper, land agent, or farmer. A stock joke of my childhood was that, up in Cumberland, the Wordsworth country, there were signs everywhere reading "Keep off the daffodils, Property of Gaffer Wordsworth."

GAMP

If you carry your umbrella untidily rolled or loosely tied, people in the know will think you are carrying a *gamp*, word appropriated from Sarah Gamp, the nurse with the huge cotton umbrella in Charles Dickens's *Martin Chuzzlewit* (1843–44). In both England and Australia, though, the word becomes a mere synonym for an ordinary umbrella, the word that means "a little shade," from the Italian diminutive of *ombra*. A word notable for an extreme sound change is British *brolly*, perhaps invented for children.

GAUCHE

For a while, there was a rumor that lefties did not live as long as righties, but that's been scotched. Problems remain, however, for social lefties, whose *gaucherie* keeps them at social unease, gawky, and maybe even sinister. This last word means left-handed too (as in "bend sinister," to the left). We have only to ruminate on a "left-handed compliment" or the intentions, so-called, of a leftist. Does anyone ever mention his or her "left-hand man"? Not if you wish to keep on the right side of the powers that be. I remember, with chagrin, the way my left-handed sister was pressured at school to use her other hand, until they all gave up. Myself, I am that most dangerous person of all, a shifting sinistral, which means that, if pushed, I can write with my left hand, and that when I bat I bat left-handed, doing all else with my right.

On the other hand, as it were, things on the right appear to be acceptable. Latin *dexter*, for *right*, gave us *dexterous*, for example, and *ambidextrous* (two right hands?), while French *à droit* (to the right) gave us *adroit*, the opposite of gawky or British "cack-handed." If you are left-handed, they call you a *keggie*, but there is no comparable word for a right-hander.

Go back to Old English and find the word *winestra* for "friendlier," thus implying that the trickier side of human anatomy could belie its evil reputation. Latin *sinister* itself used to have ostentatiously genial overtones, as if to ward off the evil eye; it meant "more useful," although *sinister*'s other meanings—harmful, devious, deadly—overpowered it. Deeper into Old English we find *left* or *lyft*, meaning "foolish" or "weak," not until the thirteenth century established opposite "right" as a queasy, complementary opposite. Something superstitious is at work here, including the supposition that, if you whitewash something evil, the veneer will take.

GEEZER

A friend of near-impeccable literary sophistication, indeed the editor of the poetry magazine *Parnassus*, called me to relay his young, baseball-afflicted son's new word for classical music: "geezermusic." I gratefully used the word as the title for a piece I'd just written on Samuel Beckett's short prose. The mood and connotation seemed just right: decrepit and aloof. I didn't know then, however, that *geezer* meant someone who went around disguised: a *guiser*, perhaps a fugitive word from the verbal array attending masques, masquerades, and mummery. Both *guise* and *disguise* depend on, from, prehistoric German *wison*, source of Old English *wise*, meaning "manner." Oddly, *geezer*, which sounds so brittle and windless, came in during the nineteenth century, only then escaping from show business.

GENOCIDE

Coined by the Polish-American jurist Raphael Lemkin in 1944 at the Nuremberg trials. Lemkin looked back especially to the slaughter in 1915 of one and a half million Armenians by Turks. On August 22, 1939, Adolf Hitler asked in a speech on the eve of his invading Poland, "Who today remembers the extermination of the Armenians?" Lemkin diagnosed genocide not only as an abomination but as a recurring human habit.

Strangely, the United States, which had taken a leading role in creating Lemkin's International Convention against Genocide, took forty years to ratify it. This does not say much for the Senate of a man who lost seventy-two of his seventy-four family members in the Holocaust. In the same year as he devised the term genocide, Lemkin published *Axis Rule in Occupied Europe*.

GERUND

In English often used without being named, the *gerund* (Latin *gerere*, to carry, to bear) like the present participle ends in *-ing: loving, loving*. Not in Latin: *amans, amandum*, loving, have to be loved. The gerundive means *have to* or *must*, as in the obsessive phrase with which Cato the Elder prefaced all his speeches in the senate: "(*ceterum censeo*) *delenda est Carthago*"—(as I see it) Carthage must be destroyed. The *nda* means it has to be done, a necessity sometimes rendered in a different way, with the verbs *debere* and *oportet*. It is possible to glean from Tacitean Latin the full meaning; you need say or write only *moriendum*, which means *dying has to be done*, which would make this one word an excellent motto for a suicide squad. It is typical of the Roman mind to tuck some idea into the back of a word, as it tucks *que*, meaning *and* (see Robert Louis Stevenson's title, *Virginibus Puerisque*—For Girls and Boys). The habit is concise and curt, achieving an almost apocalyptic neatness. The Romans liked to group associated thoughts together in one uninterrupted word, which tells you something about their reverence for the unit as distinct from a dozen fluttering small articles. The massiveness of Roman masonry figures in their language too.

One of the most unusual uses of the *gerund*, call it the prophetic gerundive, is that of the Oxford classical scholar, Ronald Syme, who in his oracular, abrupt way pioneered the view of history that depends on inscriptions only. Almost in contrast to this New Zealandery pragmatism, there was the counterpoint of his singular enforcing technique, enabling him to have his own way with historical figures merely by saying something such as "He would have been one of Y's supporters," where *would have been*—the knowing gerundive—lets him have his own way with history. What an amazing juxtaposition: epitaphs-on-stone vis-à-vis iron-handed guesswork got up as plausible reasoning. Actually, when he writes "He would have been" he means "He would *have to* have been"; common sense could not conceive of it otherwise. Thus he distills about him an air of conspiracy: Those who hear him, read him, belong to a plot that makes history behave. It must have been intoxicating for him to write or say "He will have been" when he knew how *jussive*—how dictatorial—that formula was. A cult figure at Oxford, whose courtiers have spread out world-wide, Syme, with his tart, rebarbative style, distracted readers from his unyielding ways. I think my old supervisor must have come under his influence in that famous Oxford school called "Literae Humaniores" (The Humaner Letters), which, saturating its disciples in Greek and Roman history, literature, and thought, won the reputation of being the training-ground for prime ministers. My supervisor used to collect Latin epitaphs and then publish them in elegant format, almost as if projecting an unwriteable history based on serendipitous graveyard fragments. They were never great poetry, these epitaphs, but clearly they were significant, and I suppose he must have thought you had only to collect up all the epitaphs in the world and contrast them to the zero of all those buried in unmarked graves to see the true texture of human doings. I mean he would have to have thought along such lines, commanded thus by *his* supervisor, *le grand* Syme. It is worth noting, by the way, that *gerund* itself is a gerund, meaning "it has to bear," "that which has to be borne."

GIMMICK

What did the world do before George Maine and Bruce Grant's *Wise-crack Dictionary 1926* identified it as a "device for making a fair game crooked"? Not until the 1940s did *gimmick* convey the sense "attention-getter." Etymology unknown, although the suggestion has been made that *gimmick* began as *gimac*, an anagram of *magic*: a magician's codeword.

GLITCH

From spaceman's argot into our everyday misadventures with equipment, especially of the electronic kind, this evocative word, from German *glitschen* and Yiddish *glitshen*, to slip, has replaced *mishap*, *fault*, and *defect*, but not *malfunction*. This amounts to a provoking disturbance that remains a minor problem.

GLITZ

From that early 1980s waft of tinsel, *glitzy*, from Yiddish *glitz* (glitter), from German *glitzern* (to sparkle), whence English *glitter* and *glister*. *Glitz*, a kind of superficial dazzle, a cheap sparkle, seeming to fuse both *Ritz* and *glamour*. "Blatantly scintillant," says Robert L. Chapman, stressing the flashy finish of it all. Perhaps *the glitterati*, formed after *literati*, are those dazzled by it or the dazzlers.

GO

Gehen (German), *gaan* (Dutch), *ga* (Swedish), *gaa* (Danish): take your pick from among the variants; this is an ancient verb, though only in the Germanic languages. In Old and Middle English the past tense was *eode*, then *yode*, but from around 1500 the past was *went* (the word so many want to be the past participle because it seems somehow more emphatic). *Went*, of course, came from *wend* as in *wend your way*. What is interesting is the verb's lack of repercussion among the Romance languages. Greek has *kikhano* for "leave" and Sanskrit *ha* and *hi* ("leave"), indebted to the Indo-European *ghei*. The odd thing now is the application of this ancient verb to speech, as in: "Watch your step," *she says*. "I can walk," I *go*. Or, if not that, someone uses the phrase "I'm like" to replace "I say" or "I go." I have even heard these samplings of speech done without a verb, as in "I'm 'I can walk.'" American speech excels at omitting *if*, as you could discover by watching the TV series *Law and Order*: "You get in the way, Mr. Mason, you're next." If, to the streetsmart, must have come to seem sissy. Between Manhattan economy and Silicon Valley archness, speakers of English in other countries have much to learn, not least the stressed *it*.

GOAT'S BEARD

If you watch baseball at all, you see that both the catcher and the home-plate umpire have on their face-masks a small flap that dangles down over the neck. This is the *goat's beard*, which protects Adam's apple.

GOBBLEDEGOOK

Still firm in the argot of resentment, for the jargon or unintelligible word-mongering of bureaucrats, since its invention by Representative Maury Maverick of Texas in 1944. Pseudo-sociological claptrap or real sociological claptrap making the sound of a turkey choking on *gook* (see p. 126).

GO BLOOEY

Or *kablooey, kerflooey, kerflooie, kerfooey*, all supposedly attempts to mimic an explosion as something ends in disaster. Why an explosion should sound thus, instead of, say, *thetthwhit* or *fnungl*, is hard to say. Those who have been close to bangs have reported no such noises, but rather a negating, subtractive hush, which of course was the abolition of all other sounds.

GOLLIWOG

This grotesque black male doll first appeared under the same name as a doll designed by Florence Upton for a series of children's books by Bertha Upton. Sometimes a golliwog has been regarded as the boogieman, other times as a descendant (somehow) of the tadpole, whose popular name *polliwog* derives from Middle English *polwygle* or head-wiggler. The *golliwog*, for much of the twentieth century, was the trademark of a popular British marmalade, though what the connection was between shredded oranges and the caricatural grinning coon on the label has not emerged.

GO MISSED

This is what you say when you are a pilot and wish to execute a missed approach—go around again. Here is part of a transcript published in *Plane and Pilot*: "About 7:54:36, the first officer asked the captain if he wanted to do a missed approach....The captain responded, 'Yeah, yeah, tell him we go missed.'" I like the pidgin conciseness, but I wonder about foreign pilots condemned to English as the lingo of the airways. Is this easy for them or hard? It's a bit like Emmanuel Kant calling up the Tower of Reason and explaining he wants to go critiqued.

If you like neo-grammar, read the sports pages. Jerry Landon of Gannett News Service, commenting on the U.S. Women's soccer victory over China, wrote as follows:

Midfielder Kristine Lilly, who had the third shootout goal, experienced her best game of the World Cup, highlighted by a spectacular header save off the line on a goal-bound header from Fan Yunjie in the first overtime. Without her guarding the near post on Liu Ying's corner kick, and staying there, China wins.

Straight narrative past until the last sentence, when we lapse into—what? The speculative present? We perch on a permanent-sounding hypothesis that keeps the game in doubt for ever.

GOOK

Once a term of contempt for Filipinos, during the 1899 insurrection, and revived for the Korean war in 1950, *gook* perhaps came from Korean *kuk*, but may also have taken its start from Filipino *gugu*, or Vicol *gugurang*, spirit familiar. Nothing to do with *glop*, *goo*, or *goop*. But there is another *gook* (sediment or schlock) approximating these words. Racist *gook* is an epithet for any person of Asiatic origin and looks.

GOOMBAH

A dear friend mentioned this word to me, but neither of us realized we were talking Italian: *goombah*, from a dialect pronounciation of Italian *compare*, companion or godfather. The word fans out widely, taking in *companion* (see), *associate*, *Hengest*, *patron*, and *mafioso*, having suffered, it seems, from decades of adenoids and postnasal drip, almost on its way to *gumbo* (indeed, one version heard is *gumbah*).

 PAUL WEST

GOSSAMER

The etymology of gossamer seems incongruous: a good time in which to catch geese for cooking and eating (goose-summer) contrasted with superfine skeins of cobweb floating on the breeze. Perhaps this is not the etymology at all, but what passes for one and is really a borrowing from German *gänsemonat* (geese-month), which celebrates warm weather in mid-Fall, what we call Indian Summer. This is when those silky filaments dangle in such plenty and tangle our eyelashes as we move about, whether in pursuit of edible, plump geese or not. Let us say a crude, peasant idea has given birth to dreams of palpable delicacy.

GOSSIP

This person used to be the sponsor at a baptism, *god* standing for God and *sip* (*sib*) for a sib-ling, used in an earlier, different sense from our "sibling rivalry." This god-person was hardly in competition with the baby being baptised. Queen Elizabeth was the *gossip* at the baptism of James VI of Scotland. After the word weakened into "boon companion," it became the tattletale of Shakespeare's time. Edith Sitwell demonstrates the word's use as "crony" when she writes "taking presents of...strawberries to the Queen and the Princess's other gossips."

GRAPE

Slang term for a fuel-handler aboard a U.S. Navy aircraft-carrier, who is required to wear a purple T-shirt. An ordnance handler or a fireman wears red, and someone involved with actual air operations—launch and recovery—yellow.

GREMLIN

If this must derive from something else, and not burst full-fledged from the innovative mouth of an inspired word-builder, let it be from Irish *gruaimin*, an irascible pigmy. In which case you have to quiz Irish members of the Royal Air Force, such as the ace Paddy Finucaine, unlikely to live long and weary of the way their Spitfires and Hurricanes went mechanically wrong on the ground or even in the air. The word seems most congruously uttered by World War Two pilots otherwise muttering about *going for a Burton* (name of a popular beer indicating someone has been shot down in the English Channel) and *wizard prang* (glorious crash you walk away from). *Piece of cake* (an easy prey to shoot down) and *roger-dodger* (pilot's affirmative echolalia) fill out the gremlin's context, although the word seems to have reached workers in aircraft factories, who found planes going wrong before they even rolled outside. The image of a mischievous imp destined to create malfunction in machinery, mayhem in carefully laid plans, obstacles in good intentions, has nothing to do with UFOs but echoes, perhaps, the imp of the perverse and the *kobolt* inhabiting cobalt. Conceivably this is the nuts-and-bolts equivalent of Aristotle's fatal human flaw, the point being, no doubt, that all attempts to make the material world obey us with unfailing exactness are doomed. Murphy's Law applies here (if a thing can go wrong, it will). There were no gremlins before 1939; in fact, the British seaplanes from which R. J. Mitchell evolved his Spitfire, shortly before his death, repeatedly carried off the prewar Schneider Trophy, and *their* machinery hardly ever failed. I suspect the most empirically justifiable source of the gremlin is the haste and shortage of parts that afflicted harried airmen trying to repair damaged fighter planes while the Nazi air armada poured in. The gremlin is the perfectionist's virus. It affected bombers and transport aircraft, too, but only fighter pilots appear to have created an argot, not yet quite lost, and leaking over into the quite separate argot of the U.S. Army Air Force.

For reasons unknown, a gremlin is also a beach bunny to be found haunting surfers; she never has a board and does not enter the water. A deterioration of *goblin*? What machinery is there in a surfboard for her to spoil?

GREYHOUND

There is no more reason for this hound to be grey than to be pink. The *grey-* means "bitch," from Old English *grieg*. The very idea of a Grieghound named for a Norwegian composer is tan-talizing and perhaps appropriate for fans of his music. Nazi Himmler idealized the greyhound (German, *Windhund*), wishing his SS men to be just as lithe and swift, which is no doubt why he force-fed them on porridge, a diet he had filched from British public schools. Not surprisingly, Greyhound buses are grey. Just imagine Bitchbuses.

GRIEVOUS

From grief, which used to mean heavy or oppressive (like *grav-ity*). Latin *gravis*, from *gravare*, to weigh upon, weigh down, traveled into Old French as *grever* (to cause to suffer, harass), whence English *grieve*. The modern sense of grievous, as in "grievous bodily harm," denotes not only pain and sorrow, but also *extreme, almost beyond belief*, which is perhaps why so many people, aching to register something almost off the scale, say "grievious," inserting that extra *i* to extend the word and thus convey pain longer. That vowel has no more place in *grievous* than *went* is the correct past participle of *go*. Yet this is how people talk, and indeed write, and language seems unable to resist, the true Internet before the Internet came.

GROTTY

From 1964, introduced to mean bizarre and somewhat tacky, originally "grotto-like" and *grottesco*, Italian, as in the phrase *pittura grottesca* for wall paintings found in old cellars or grottoes; hence the term's reign as the label for weird, which is what these found paintings mostly were, the work of unknown amateurs with a point to prove. Fantastic. English turned Old French *crotesque* into *crotescque*, sanctioning the word from the mid-eighteenth century on until it began to denote "absurd" or "ludicrous, wacky." A good word went to waste here to report the nature of something that might have been ignored. One has to wonder if *all* the work found in cellars, grottoes, crypts, vaults, catacombs *was* inferior, as the word now implies. If some of the work found in caves is any guide, some of it must have been superior and merited a better fate than lumpish dismissal.

GRUELING

Mainly linked to punishment, this is punishment's Pritikin form, deriving from Frankish *grut* and Old French *gru*, both meaning oats or oatmeal, with the diminutive *gruel*, giving Middle English *grewel*. *Gruel* is a thin, watery porridge that will, supposedly, exhaust and disable you in no time, though not if you are on the expensive diet. This is the kind of severe gastric punishment known in solitary confinement, like bread and water. The *gruel* in *grueling* has nothing to do with *cruel*, whereas *crude* does.

GUBBINS

Apart from being a derisive name for people living at the edge of Dartmoor, savage in their ways, *gubbins* often serves as a collective noun for miscellaneous impedimenta that the speaker or writer cannot be bothered to specify. As *The Sunday Times* (London, December 5, 1969) says in its color supplement, "Many machines have a vast illicit complement of rivets, nails, nuts, bolts, torches, pliers and half-eaten sandwiches...One of the modern test pilot's less enviable jobs is to fly new aircraft upside down and try to catch the gubbins as it hurtles past his face." The word has also been applied to fish-parings, trash, gadgets, thingummies, and "almost any part of the equipment of a plane." In 1940, a small wiry Scottish Highlander took charge of Britain's Special Operations Executive (SOE), located on Baker Street, London. This was Sir Colin Gubbins, who supervised the project known as Foxley, which was to kill Hitler. One wonders what effect his name had on those working for him, or if indeed he was appointed not for his several languages and his expertise in irregular warfare, but because his name embodied the desire not to be specific about secret operations, suggesting that *gubbins* might be the venereal term for everything in the world.

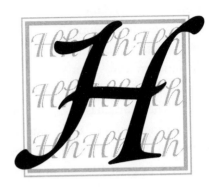

HAM

As in actor. Reasonably well-to-do actors remove their grease-paint with cold cream or "vanishing cream," but, in the nineteenth century, less prosperous actors, often black, removed it with ham fat or pork grease, thus forever relating mediocrity to ham. In her *New Dictionary of Americanisms* (1902), Sylva Clapin defines the term as "In theatrical parlance, a tenth-rate actor or variety performer." The old word for *ham* was *hamfatter*. The word has gone afield since it first irked late nineteenth-century negro minstrels, extending to ball-players, boxers, and athletes, even innocent radio operators merely for being novices. *Ham it up* is a seedy relative. It makes sense that Jewish actors used *schmaltz*, chicken fat, which is no doubt how schmaltz entered the language as a derogatory term for something excessively sentimental.

HAVE A TICKET ON ONESELF

Australian for being conceited. Empson might have enjoyed this complex phrase, suggesting as it does that he/she pays the price of admission merely to be aware of him- or herself. This person is so much in awe of him- or herself, he/she doesn't realize the show of self is free.

HEART-RENDING

All right as it stands, if you get it right, this is an effective way of tearing the heart, a sensation many might know for emotional or medical reasons. *Rend* is a powerful word, denoting anguish; but what we often hear, especially from radio presenters playing opera, is "heart-rendering," which introduces a wrong image of reduction, conversion, or melting down (fat) with heat. The melting heart is a known and acceptable image, but not in this literal combustible sense, as if it were a haunch of beef. Perhaps heart-rending will go the way of *transpire*'s correct use or *memento*'s. Is this the dumbing down of language or a natural fidget toward something more natural? Nothing can stop either.

HEINOUS

Having nothing to do with Heine or Heinz, this word is full of hate (*haine* in French) and seems doomed to be spoken as *heinious*. The first *i* seems to generate a second one out of the speaker's nervousness. Let the word serve as casual rubric for other mauled words such as "deteriate" for "deteriorate," "odiferous" for "odoriferous" (a National Public Radio expert on penguins no less), "calclate" for "calculate," and "kudoes" (as if *kudos* were crying out for plurality). Behold, in *Health* magazine for March 1999 "Another Kudo for Calcium." Let me add to this midden of malaprop "the lay of the land," "gigolo of lamb," "Cabaret Sauvignon," and what I recently jotted down as the beginnings of a helpless new gibberish: *arthur, thot, tharts, ardio, ardience,* and *Parl,* for *author, thought, thoughts, audio, audience,* and

Paul (Parl surely has a reindeer standing close by in the blizzard of phoney phonemes).

As I get older, I find myself understanding less and less of what I hear or overhear, although still raging against those who spout "during the course of that time" to mean *then*, but utterly bamboozled by an announcement that goes "Her time horizon for investing was short-term," perhaps a posy for "she was impatient." This is what happens when the semi-literate cleave to jargon like flies to dead meat. Oh, as I am always saying, for the shock of American slang, from *chin music* to *bupkiss*, *trim* to *gobsmacked*, *scuzzy* to *zone-out*. That's English.

I refuse to prolong this entry day by day, and close with the old lady who, her obituary in the local paper says, was "interned" at a certain cemetery, presumably where she is still roaming about within the barbed wire. She did not deserve it. Nor did what Geraldo Rivera said on TV ("interred in the sea") match the ghost of JFK's son, John. Far better to have an approach fix in the sky named after you, as *Flying* columnist Gordon Baxter does, with "BAXTR" up there, not that far from his home in Beaumont, Texas; thanks to strokes and epilepsy, he is no longer a pilot, but has his share of the air. The FAA's IFR (Instrument Flight Rules) naming system for fixes calls for five or fewer letters that need not make sense; the nearest to BAXTR is PEVET. One wonders if Baxter will now drop the *e* to parade his place upstairs.

HELLO

Its more formal, haughty variant is *hullo*, more common in British English. Almost certainly from the French *holà* and earlier English *holla*, meaning "stop," it has acquired some recent overtones beyond its customary expression of surprise: "Hello, can this be one of those Martian lettuces made of fine-spun glass?" Nowadays, to convey impatience or exasperation, you grace it with an element of considerate stoicism and say "hello," not in greeting but to get things moving again. It can also mean, in hyperbole, *Are you there? Is anybody home? Are you really who you claim to be?* "Hello" will go on accumulating shadings until, perhaps, it no longer serves any purpose as a greeting. "Hell——o" (long pause) seems to have gone already, no longer fusing surprise and announcement as in *Gosh* and *Looky here.*

HOCUS-POCUS

From the seventeenth century, this exploits the phoney Latin phrase *hax pax max Deus adimas* trotted out by itinerant magicians to awe their crowds. In his *Travels into Africa and the Greater Asia* (1634), Sir Thomas Herbert noted that "a Persian hocus pocus performed rare tricks with hands and feet." But clever manual or pedal display faded out, and most magicians by 1800 were mere tricksters, wisecrackers, motormouths. *Hoax* is probably *hocus* anglicized. The phrase in its various manifestations is shot through with weird slanders, from Dr. John Arbuthnot's "Hocus was an old cunning attorney" in *Law Is a Bottomless Pit; or, History of John Bull* (1712) to Charles Macklin's "The law is a sort of hocus-pocus science" (*Love à la Mode,* 1759) and the travesty of consecration formula, "Hoc est corpus," into yet another *hocus-pocus,* what John Richard Green in *A Short History of the English People* (1874) called "a nickname for jugglery."

HOI POLLOI

Best said derisively if you must use it at all, it means the common people seen from above: "the many," "the masses": *hoi,* the, + *polloi,* plural of *polus,* many. The phrase becomes ridiculous only when you write *the hoi polloi*, which means *the the many*, adding an intellectual stutter to a social gimp. Hoity-toity, really, uttered by the same folk who say "the *plebs*" for the same thing.

HOLOCAUST

Not so new, it is a "complete burning," a word used by William Tindale in 1526 ("a greater thing than all the holocausts and sacrifices"). Greek has *holokauston*, from *holos* "whole" (compare *holism* and *hologram*) and *kauein* "to burn" (compare with *caustic* and *cautery*). John Milton was the first author in English to use the word in its widest sense as "utter consumption by fire," in the late seventeenth century. Thereafter, *holocaust* did duty for both nuclear devastation and mass murder; Bishop Ken, in 1711, wrote: "Should general Flame this World consume...An Holocaust for Frontal Sin." In 1833, Leitch Ritchies in *Wandering by the Loire* wrote of Louis VII making "a holocaust of thirteen hundred persons in a church." The word now seems destined to be *The* Holocaust, reserved indefinitely for special use. So does history devour a word and fling it sideways fit for no other, making a monument out of a loan-word. It almost happened to *crusade* and, since no one talks of going on crusades any more, probably has through default.

HONCHO

Term from the Korean war meaning boss, The Man, or big enchilada, it comes from Japanese *hancho* for squad leader and can be used as a verb. "Chief honcho" is sometimes to be heard, but the effect is fractionally vague, squad leader having no exact civilian equivalent. Most users seek to denote almost a CEO when saying *honcho*, which creates an amateurish effect, denoting persons higher in authority than they have ever known, certainly higher than *hancho*.

HONEY

In addition to all its familiar uses, this word, in the gymnasiums of the Bronx, signifies a boxer who can take a punch well, in other words has both resilience and recover power. In other words, the broth of life flows in him/her abundantly, and sweetness converts itself into opportunistic strength.

HONEYMOON

A sixteenth-century word, possibly current much earlier if we judge by the tone, not cynical but realistic, of Richard Huloet in his *Abecedarium Anglico Latinum* (1552): "a term proverbially applied to such as be new married, which will not fall out at the first, but the one loueth the other at the beginning exceedingly, the likelihood of their exceeding love appearing to assuage, the which time the vulgar people call the honey moon." One wonders if body secretions figured in the original metaphor. In his dictionary, Samuel Johnson defined *honeymoon* as "the first month after marriage, when there is nothing but tenderness and pleasure." "Moon" was poetic licence for "month," which imposes fatal waning on love's young dream. Honeysun would have been more tactful.

HOO CHEE MAMA!

"Fourteen years of unrelenting scientific study in advanced aerodynamics," shrills a plane ad in a flying mag, "can be summed up concisely as: Hoo Chee Mama!" It goes on to say "We toyed with the words 'fastest in its class' and '4-place rocket ship,' but we didn't think they conveyed the feeling of speed you get when you fly this aircraft." The ad closes with a pious hope that the plane's performance is bound to wring "some choice words from our competition." I wonder. *Hoo chee mama* must derive eclectically from that fake-Oriental female dance, the *cooch*, common at carnivals and fairs, characterized by what Frank Barton calls "sinuous and often suggestive twisting and shaking of the torso and limbs." Clearly this gobbet of copy-writing, fusing red-hot mama with reptilian hoochie-coochie, aims to find the erotic in the aerodynamic, but what an uncomfortable ride if the dancer's vertical gyrations in any way match the plane's horizontal ones.

HOTTENTOT

If you were a Dutchman, landing at the Cape of Good Hope, the Hottentots would sound like a nation of clickers and clackers, ferocious as they were. All the Dutch could make out in their speech was a series of *hot* and *tot*, so they dubbed the savages *hot-en-tot*; *en* is "and" in Dutch.

HUMBLE PIE

It used to be a simple pie made from the entrails of a deer. Samuel Pepys, in his *Diary* for July 8, 1663, recorded that "Mrs Turner did bring us an umble pie hot out of her oven." *Humble* has nothing to do with being humble, but is a mistaken version of the fourteenth-century word *numbles* ("offal"), from Latin *lumulus*, diminutive of *lumbus* ("loin"), whence our *lumbar*. *Numbles* became *umbles* perhaps because the phrase *a numble* suggested *an*

umble, and the *h* fell upon the front as if thirsting. The expression "eat humble pie," which unites peasant food with remorseful self-regard, came in in the 1830s. Umble pie belongs with tripe, cow's stomach sliced into steaks and fried with onions: another dish of the poor, best buttered and peppered to death as it has no taste otherwise. Where I lived as a boy, the tripe shop was opposite, with all its offal; and it was against this background of "lights" and "wheels" that the list appeared of the team chosen for Saturday's cricket match. You heaved while hoping you'd been chosen to play.

HYPHEN

In Classical Greek, a semicolon was a question mark, and the hyphen was written as a little curve, somewhat like *c* the wrong way up. Before they developed this quaint sign, their word *hyphen* was an adverb evolved from the phrase *hyph' hen*, which meant "under one" or "grouped together." It was so much easier to draw the little squiggle than to write this out. In modern proof correction, an author or a publisher's copy editor will often make such a mark, above and beneath the gap, to reunite severed portions of a word, as in hyphen.

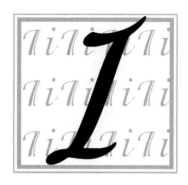

IMPEACH

If you know the Latin word *pes*, for foot, you know the source of two related verbs, *impedire* (to tie the feet together) and *impedicare* (fetter, entangle, ensnare). Of the two inflictions, the latter is perhaps the more familiar, coming as it does from Old French *empecher*, whence modern French's *empêcher*: to block or prevent. Only a casuist would see a difference between the feet tied together and being entangled or ensnared; but I tend to think of impeding as not always successful ("He tried to impede him, but in vain"; "Although impeded, he somehow caught the ferry"), whereas *impeached* is blocked in your tracks, *stopped*. Conceivably, then, a president might be impeded by his past, but not in an absolute sense, whereas one who has been impeached—well, he has been well and truly prevented. Oddly enough, as the twin verbs toured through English, they parted from each other, for different purposes. *Impedire* was clearly a useful verb to the Romans, coming to mean also, in the past participle *impeditus*, hindered, embarrassed, and awkward; a good word to apply to someone burdened with baggage, whereas *impedicare* makes it only into the largest Latin dictionaries. What happened to it was this: Redundantly linked to *impedire*, then wrongly linked to *impetere* (attack, accuse, the source of our *impetuous*), in the fourteenth century it took its meaning from the role of maximum advantage and stayed put into our own day, alive through a happy accident created by someone whose Latin wasn't up to snuff. *Impetere* was weak, *impedicare* was stronger, then strengthened by French *empecher* into having an English sound all of its own. Its use for impede or prevent survived into the seventeenth century, as William Leybourn shows in *Cursus Mathematicus* (1690), writing of "a Ditch of sufficient breadth, and depth, to impeach the assaults of an Enemy." For three hundred years it had also, through a fluke, meant something else, and that's the sense we're saddled with.

My college magazine, alas now defunct, was called the *Imp* and its editor the *Impeditor*, in other words an impeder of his own magazine, though he might also have been thought its main attacker and accuser. Enterprising readers may care to work out, by the way, why the French added a circumflex accent (see) to *empecher* even though no *s* had been dropped. Was there ever a sequence that, over the decades, went *empecher—empescher—empêcher*?

INDRI

Once upon a time, journeying through the forests of what was then Madagascar, the French naturalist Pierre Sonnerat observed a *lemur* with silky fur and short tail, its habitual stance a wound-up crouch, almost like a baseball pitcher taking his job too seriously and risking a compound hernia. It so happened that local observers, in delight or boredom, exclaimed *indri! indri!*, in the earshot of M. Sonnerat. *Indri* is Malagasy for *look!* That is how this demure lemur got its name, thus introduced to what Henry James called the insolence of accident. One wonders if, during extensive travels, M. Sonnerat, when he found out what he had done, might have wanted to change the names of other animals, or even to foist upon certain as yet nameless ones *blurts* of his own.

How would you like a lion called Voilà or an ape called Holy Moly? Somehow the principle, although wrong, seems exciting, close perhaps to our nicknaming people.

What an unfortunate parody M. Sonnerat is of Adam naming the creatures in the garden. In his headlong fashion, the Frenchman evokes worries of other kinds, from onomatopoeia to rumor. Does the hummingbird really *hum*, does the howler monkey really *howl*, does the British cuckoo really seem to beak that word? (Frederick Delius thought it did.) We worry with reason about the anthropomorphic impulse, landing uncritical creatures with names that, under other circumstances, they might have returned to sender. Myself, I wonder if *indri*, fairly distinctive as a noun, is that unfortunate. Officially the lemur's name is *Indri indri*, and the Malagasy republic has not yet got worked up enough to drop the term on account of the *colonialism* embedded in it. One wonders at the state of nature and aboriginal innocence amid which a native population accepted the guesswork of a foreign toff. No doubt because they couldn't be bothered changing their way of drawing attention to something. Entrenched idiom sanctions the invader and vocabulary marches onward, a symphony of flukes.

INFANT

Latin *in-* (not) + *fans* (speaking). In the civil law, a child under the age of seven, so called "*quasi impos fandi*" (lacking the faculty of speech). *Infans* is a noun use of the present participle (source of English *fate*, *fable*, *fame*). *Infantry*, a sixteenth-century word, comes to us via Italian *infante*, whose original meaning of "young person" was jettisoned for "foot soldier." It is unusual to blur the mind a little and think of infantry as incapable of speech or, all under seven years, as the prototype of the holy army of infant inquisitors.

INFIDEL

This vivid if obtuse word has remained close to its etymology, originally directed by Christians at Saracens and Mohammedans because they were "*infideles*," meaning *in* (not) + *fideles* (faithful). They had no faith, or rather they lacked the Christian one, whatever else they professed to believe. You might acquire a similar term of sectarian abuse by purloining the phrase *in camera*, as *incamerate*, to mean someone who lacked a camera. From this root of *infidel* we get *infidelity*, at first an ecclesiastical term, but now seemingly restricted to sexual matters. (Whereas *conversation* used to mean something sexual and *intercourse* mere talk.) A similar word of prejudice, *heathen*, damns the *heath*-dweller for not being a city fellow. *Infidel* takes us to Fidel, of course, over-familiar but perhaps on the ball concerning a man who has stuck to his *creed* (from *credo*, belief).

INK

When the ancient Greeks painted, they sealed colors in with heat, which burned the colored wax into place. *Encauston*, they named the result of this process. In Latin, *encauston* became the name for the purple ink that emperors used to use when signing their names, and then *encauston* became *enque*. So to our *enke* or *inke*. The Greek process, its verb *eqkalein* (*en-*, in, plus *kaiein*, burn) survives to this day as *encaustic*. Purple receded over the centuries and ink now refers to any dark writing fluid. If you used purple ink and were not entitled to it, the penalties were savage.

INVEIGLE

Used by so many still, it means *to blind*, as when Robert Burton in his *Anatomy of Melancholy* (1621) writes "It was Cleopatra's sweet voice and pleasant speech which inveigled Antony." Blinded by her sounds he was; the word is French, from *aveugler*, to blind or delude. Love is not blind until it shuts its eyes.

INVOLUTE

Of this term's mathematical use, nothing here. Its most salient other use goes back to Thomas De Quincey who, in *Suspiria de Profundis* (1845), defined it as "a compound experience incapable of being disentangled." He provided other definitions as well, none as luminous or precise; it is clear that, based partly on his own experience with drugs, recorded in *Confessions of an English Opium Eater* (1856), he was concerned with enigmatic experiences that just would not go away. In proposing to name such experiences, not only reproducing them and devising similar ones, he anticipated comparable tangles in the work of Ionesco, Breton, and Beckett. His extraordinary contribution to modern aesthetic theory consists in his recognition that, as Raymond Queneau said, in an absurd world you live absurdly. So De Quincey invents absurdities of his own that he adds to the absurdities already there in life, realizing that there can be no total, but that, in adding to the absurd you have made your protest even while using the enemy's weapons. Perhaps the most powerful involute in the whole of De Quincey's formidable body of work is one that appears in his essay on Lord Rosse's telescope, in which De Quincey frightens himself almost to death with sketches of what he imagines he discerns on the faces of the heavenly bodies. Ahead of his time, De Quincey was too much for his own, and no doubt too early for us. Yet, as a seminal precursor, he stands out, for brilliant prophetic thinking and daring demonstration. The essence of his involute is, via Latin, something rolled in upon itself, from *involvere* (to roll in, to envelop), like *involvulus*, the caterpillar that wraps itself up in leaves, mentioned by Plautus.

IS

According to *Black's Law Dictionary*, Sixth Edition, "This word, although normally referring to the present, often has a future meaning, but is not synonymous with 'shall have been.' It may have, however, a past signification, as in the sense of 'has been.'" In other words, this word, though normally referring to the present, will not always; nor will it be retrospectively predictive, even though it has been so. With this kind of help, we can all go to law in the vivid present.

ITALICS

In 1501 the celebrated Aldine printing press, revered for its scholarly books, published a special edition of the poet Vergil and handsomely dedicated the work to Italy. The master printer, Aldo Manuzio, had come up with a new slanting font that gave Greek letters a cursive, leaning stance on the page; he now tried it out on Latin, perhaps to his educated, Greek-loving eye making Latin look more like Greek or, to use his word for this particular style, *Italicus* (now denoted in manuscript by underlining). Thus we acquired *italics*, not used for emphasis, however, until the mid-sixteenth century. The reader of Greek, habituated to catching sight of such fugitive-looking items in the line as iota subscript, written beneath a vowel, turning ō into ōi, say (ω into ῳ), gains a sense of onrush not available from

other fonts. The type seems in some haste, even when encum-
bered with enclitics and diacritical marks; but perhaps Greek
does need streamlining a little, being to the uninitiated eye, perhaps, more pictorial than Latin, though not as pictorial as
Chinese. I once asked the Italian fiction writer Italo Calvino if
he wrote in italics; he smiled at this and said he sometimes *spoke*
in them.

PAUL WEST

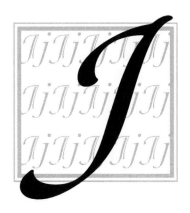

JAFFA

Seaport of west-central Israel constituting with Tel Aviv one municipality. Singularly succulent orange grown here and exported to, among other countries, the United Kingdom, where "jaffa" still serves as the epitome of a superb orange as well as of a perfect maneuver at cricket with bat or ball. Why the orange-cricket connection? It is hard to say, unless you envision a cricket crowd in mid-summer savoring the game while sucking on thick-pelted Jaffas, usually sold wrapped in a noisy tissue paper printed on in two languages and displaying a picture of the harbor.

JANET

A mystery airline owned in part by the military, Janet flies government and military employees from Las Vegas to McCarran airport, Groom Lake, and the heavily secluded Area 51, often suspected of a UFO presence. The airline's name has perplexed many, some of whom have evolved answers of their own, from "Joint Army Navy Employee Transport" and "Joint Air Force Navy Engineering Transport" to "Plaine Jane Transportation," this last the response of several commercial pilots. It has been suggested that "Janet" is merely a random codename to mislead the public, understandable perhaps since Janet is owned partly by a bank in Beverly Hills, partly by the Air Force. "Just Another Non Extraterrestrial Transporter" is another version, wittier somewhat than "Joint Astronautical Nexus Employee Transport." My own guess is that Janet invokes afamous reference book: *Jane's All the World's Aircraft*. The jets, Boeing 737-200s with red stripe along white un-lettered unnumbered body, are there to see, and so are Janet's Beechcraft King Airs (blue and gray stripe along the same anony-mous fuselage). Janet performs a shuttle service (e.g., out at 9:30 A.M., back within an hour). Janet Air Control fre-quencies include "Gold Coast" (118.7 MHz) and "Tonopah Test," "Silver Bow," and "Desert Rock" (all 118.0 MHz). "Dreamland" is yet another codeword, used at Groom Lake/ Area 51. Countless inquisitive souls have studied this zone of military secrecy, famous for its development of the SR 71 Blackbird, and all have halted at the deadly-force-enforced boundary. It may well be that Janet Airlines is no more than a run-of-the-mill aerial bus service (Beckett Air once at Pittsburgh Airport may be more enigmatic especially as it seemed to have no planes and gritted its teeth behind a frosted glass door bearing its name). Rather than some ingeni-ous military prankster at work, a mundane bureaucrat has culled up Janet out of a phone book; or so I conclude, unable to muster much indignation that Janet interiors are ugly—red-dish-orange and navy blue. One *expects* a high-powered military research establishment to be secretive, or, rather, in-different to public concern, much as the diplo-matic corps is. Perhaps, as some say, there really are flying saucers of terrestrial or extraterrestrial origin obeying the hands of the Janet passengers, who leak not a word about their work.

JEEP

The best guess is that a certain four-wheel military vehicle reminded GI's of the odd, springy creature Eugene the Jeep in the "Popeye" comic strip of E. C. Segar. After all, the official army description of the vehicle was G.P., for "General Purpose." The join was easily made. The interesting question is: Would Eugene have made it without the G.P. stimulus or would the G.P. have formed itself into a word without the comic strip? Would echo have worked? Would improvisation have carried the day? We wonder because we rather enjoy this plangent, unofficious blurt of a word, itself almost a traffic signal. I wonder if *jeepers-creepers* (*where'd you get those peepers?*) played any part in such brisk neologism.

JERUSALEM ARTICHOKE

This familiar North American sunflower, *helianthos tuberosus,* has yellow, rayed flowers and edible roots. Euell Gibbons devotes a short chapter to it in *Stalking the Wild Asparagus* and recommends a salad made from the sliced tubers (as large as medium-sized potatoes). He likes to arrange them around a beef roast to cook in the gravy or to pickle them in wine vinegar. The plant has nothing to do with Jerusalem, being a corruption (or promotion) of the Spanish word *girasol,* meaning "turns with the sun." Gibbons confesses himself baffled as to why a tuber-bearing sunflower has been called an artichoke. Indeed, the entire name is an elaborate misnomer, out of slur by folk-etymology, pointlessly calling to mind Jerusalem thorn, Jerusalem cherry, and Jerusalem oak, which may make us discern, however, the Salem in Jerusalem. Holy Salem is another old name, *Hierosolyma.*

JUNKET

It all starts with the Latin word *juncus*, meaning "rush," which becomes prehistoric Germanic *rusk*. With enough rushes, you make what the French used to call a *jonquette* or basket, in which you can take to market a custard made from cream, sugar, and rose water. The more you do this, the more associated with the custard the name of the basket becomes, so you soon have *junket* being fed to children, with no doubt a little gelatin therein to bind it. The image of the basket then took on a new role, being the receptacle in which the goodies of a picnic were carried. So, a basket turns into a custard and lives on as an expense-free outing. My own memories of *junket* are of something watery, like a blancmange with impetigo.

JUVENESCENCE

This was the word T. S. Eliot was groping for when he wrote in *Gerontion*

> In the juvescence of the year
> Came Christ the tiger.

It means to grow up or become young again. In effect, Eliot added to a dead language.

KALAMAZOO

Made famous by a swing number about the wonders of having a girl from there, Kalamazoo is the result of settlers' wit upon seeing gas bubbles at one site in a river close by. Taking an American Indian name for "boiling pot," or so they thought, they named both river and city *Kalamazoo*.

KEISTER

This one is fading, surely, surviving only as a racy-sounding euphemism for buttocks or anus. Its trajectory over the ages has been like this: *kista* (Indo-European), *kiste* (Greek), *cista* (Latin), *kista* (Germanic, unattested), *kista* (Old High German), *Kiste* (German), into Yiddish. Why *ei*, which Germans would pronounce as *eye* whereas *ie* would be *ee*, is unknown, but Americans will often pronounce Steiner as Steener, faintly to unGermanize it, perhaps. *Tush* has replaced it, except as the word for a suitcase that opens up into a counter full of goods (hoboes and street hawkers), a back pocket in pants, and, in the criminal world, a safe or strongbox (cf. German *Kiste* = box), which may imply that a person's strongbox is the rectum, the pickpocket's ultimate greasy dream. Respectable people using the word gain a reputation for raffish bonhomie as if admitting, without being tasteless or too cute, possession of something only a jail could break open. Fear of sodomy spikes this one and anal retention glosses it over. *Box* for vulva sounds oddly angular, perhaps a geometric bow to Pandora.

KETCHUP

One wonders why ketchup, having mutated into *catsup* and *catchup* (which have an unlettered, vulgar sound), hasn't also become *cotsup* or *cutsip*. Malay *kechap* comes from Chinese (Amoy) *koetsiap*, *ketsiap*, meaning the brine of fish; *koe* is minced seafood and *tsiap* brine, sauce, or juice. In Mandarin Chinese this is *chih*. The fishiness seems to have vanished from a sludge mainly tomatoes; it must have tasted very different in south-eastern China or the late seventeenth century when the *New Dictionary of the Canting Crew* (1690) defined it as "a high East-India Sauce." Jonathan Swift writes *catsup* in 1730, but that version together with *catchup* remains largely American, and in the British Isles if you ask for either you will receive the island stare. There it graces the national favorite, baked beans on toast.

KEY

An almost total mystery, deriving from the Anglo-Saxon *caeg*, which rhymes with "bay," while its present pronunciation—*ee*—did not appear until the eighteenth century. Key has no siblings in the other Germanic languages, and may have become involved in a verbal muddle involving quay, *qui*, *keigh*, and *cay*. The astounding thing is that a word so much in use and demand has covered its tracks so well and is actually having not a resurgence but a super-surgence in modern speech: "Costa Rica is key," meaning hugely pertinent. A word with some twenty applications (its dictionary one-third column reads like a war memorial), it may go on to even further uses. It is easy to say, like the forgotten poet Weldon Kees.

KICK THE BUCKET

Late 1700s. To die. Possibly from the bucket that the self-hanged person kicks away at the very last; but not restricted to suicides. Bucket, from Old French *buquet* (balance), was the beam from which slaughtered animals were hung; the dead animals were "kicking the bucket" because their hind feet were hooked to the beam. Other senses for *bucket* are jug, belly, paunch, milk pail, and coal-tub.

KILLINGTON TRAVERSE

One of many shades of white announced by Ralph Lauren for his new line of house paints. Other inscrutable tints include Pocket Watch White and Poncho White, more fathomable ones being Dover Cliffs, Aspen Summit, and Starched Apron. We are in the realm of distinction without difference, one paint varying from another only by virtue of the split hairs drowned in it.

KNICKERS

Anyone who has observed British television knows that the merest mention of this word sends the studio audience (or its canned automatic equivalent) into helpless paroxysms of giggle.

True enough, this is what ladies' underpants were called in the 1880s. In 1882 *The Queen* preferred "flannel knickers in preference to flannel petticoat," while *Home Chat* (1885) plumped for "serge knickers for girls from twelve to sixteen." Women's thighs have come a long way since then, of course, inspired by the cult of legs (*gams* as they used to be called). Actually, it was men who first wore Bermuda-length "knickers," as *The Times* confirmed in 1900 with its "Imperial Yeomanry...in their well-made, loosely-fitting khaki tunics and riding knickers." The name itself, from the concocted Dutch name Diedrich Knickerbocker, Washington Irving's invention for the pretend author of his *History of New York* (1809), recalled the gathered, banded knee-breeches of Dutchmen who settled in New Amsterdam. Many of them were called Knickerbocker. In England, knickers are mentionably unmentionable; in the United States, male golfers wear them. The word sometimes attaches itself to an effeminate male.

KNOCKER-UP

Term bewildering to many a GI stationed in England during World War Two, who identified the word as the label of the impregnator and sought to live up to it (What's wrong with a Yank? Overpaid, over-dressed, and over here: the litany of oppressed native males.). Sometimes the lamplighter (igniting gas lamps along the street), this personage either battered on doors or tapped with a long pole on bedroom windows to wake people up in time for work. Nowadays the knocker-up functions mainly aboard trains, alerting occupants of sleeper compartments to imminent arrival. A rich mythos has gathered about the person of the old-style knocker-up, who indeed knew exactly which husband was missing that day and which variant of the ambiguous phrase "a warm welcome" lay in waiting (either resistance or invitation—"Come on in, flower, and have a bit of a warm."). Thus, the knocker-up—rouser in both senses—stuck by his clients, with an occasional Christmas box of a bottle or some smokes, through thin and thin. An old expression—swift as a lamplighter—survives him; he was fleet of foot, presuming perhaps to awaken everyone at the same instant through sheer speed if undistracted.

KNOTS

Not as simple as it looks, the British expression, "at a rate of knots," is not left blank for someone to fill in the exact number, but actually means "fast." Why so generic an expression should indicate a degree of anything is puzzling, so it must be an abbreviation with "high," say, omitted. In theory anything moving is going at a calculable rate of knots; but, if you want to specify *slowly*, you have (in the United Kingdom anyway) to provide the number; if you don't, initiates will assume that whatever it is that's going at "a rate of knots" is going fast. Perhaps behind this almost covetous codephrase there lies an old-fashioned reverence for sheer speed, so much so that any reference to speed is to high speed. Customarily the expression thrives among the military, to whom accuracy is imperative.

LASAGNA

Literally, if you go back to the Athenian Greeks, *chamberpot pasta*, from their word *lasanon*, more delicately referred to as a night chair. Ever alert for the chance of crude humor, the Romans latched on to this word and, reserving it for large pots of all kinds, cooking and night relief, finessed it into *lasanum*, whence lasagna of the flat pasta and sausages and cheese and who knows what.

LAURA NORDA

This is how Law and Order sounds in uneducated Australian ("strine"), although surely the best Australian speech is superbly melodic, as we have learned from the silken diphthongs and mutated vowels of several Aussie TV presenters. In addition to Australian words and phrases elsewhere in this gathering (*pommy, have a ticket on oneself*, and *on the fang*), it may be helpful to put together *A Little Outback Vocabulary* for use in a tight corner, as follows:

> *Afghan*: a type of cookie
> *bandicoot*: to steal, especially by taking carrots or pota-
> toes from the soil while leaving the tops in place

bark humpy: hut or shanty made of bark (Aborigine word)

belcher chain: puffs of smoke or fire from a chimney or volcano

bluey: red-haired person

chalkie: teacher

chunder: to vomit

cowcocky: man who operates a dairy by himself

dinkum: real, authentic

drack: slovenly, sleazy

drop one's bundle: to panic or despair

dunny: underground passage, cellar; outhouse, privy

esky: portable icebox

fossick: to rummage through someone else's possessions or to hunt for gold

grouse: excellent, splendid

illeywhacker: con man haunting country fairs

jackeroo: youth who works on a sheep station (cf. *jilleroo*)

job: punch, slam

keltie: sheep dog

larrikin: hooligan, yobbo

lilly-pilly: tall flowering tree with edible fruit (*Eugenia smithii*)

lintie: a sprite

milko: milkman

neenish tart: cream-filled almond-flavored pastry with color topping

ocker: boor

off-sider: sidekick, workmate, partner

Old Dart: England

onkus: nasty, wrong; machinery on the fritz

Oz: Aus. (for Australia)

pastoralist: sheep or cattle farmer

point the bone: to hex

saltbush: herb or shrub of genus Atriplex found in arid
    areas

salvo: member of the Salvation Army

sandgroper: native of arid Western Australia

sand shoe: tennis shoe

schoolie: schoolteacher

script: doctor's written prescription

sea wasp: a deadly jellyfish

sheila: woman or girl

sickie: an absentee's pretended illness

skerrick: a scrap or bit

sleep-out: part of a verandah, partitioned off to form a
    bedroom

sling: to tip or bribe; a rake-off

slygrog: liquor sold illegally

slygrogging: drinking the above

snag: sausage

snig: to drag a log along on a chain

snob: shoemaker, cobbler

snout: a grudge

sook: a cry-baby, a shirker

sool: setting a dog to harry sheep

spieler: gambler or swindler

spruiker: barker at carnival

squill candy: sucker

starve the lizards!: exclamation of surprise or dismay

station: sheep- or cattle-ranch

stipe: racecourse steward

stonker: to defeat, baffle (cf. Newfoundland *stonk* for te-
    diously overfed)

stop-up: a night-owl

straight wire: honest, legit

strides: men's pants

sunbakers: sunbathers

sundowner: bum who shows up at sunset, too late to
   work, just in time to eat
swag: traveler's bundle
thingo: thing, thingummy
two-up: illegal gambling game with two coins tossed
tyke: a Roman Catholic
up the pole: daffy
utility: pick-up truck
vee-dub: Volkswagen
washer: washcloth
whacko!: Oh boy
wog: flu, disease
yabbie: freshwater crayfish
zack: sixpence

LEOTARD

After the nineteenth-century French aerialist and trapeze artist Jules Léotard, who devised this close-fitting sheath for the
torso, sometimes having long sleeves, high neck, and ankle- (or
thigh-) length legs. Worn for practice and performance by acro-
bats and dancers. Here is a noun whose plural is utterly unlike
it: *tights*.

LILAC

Dark blue in Sanskrit is *nila*, which poured through Persian as
nil, ending up in *nilak* for bluish. Its further journeys took it
into Arabic (*lilak*), Spanish *lilac*, and the same spelling in early
modern French. The Spanish brought the plant to England in
the sixteenth century, having named it for its purple flowers.

LIMELIGHT

Cynosure or center of attention, *limelights* being stage lights brilliant and severe because lime, calcium oxide, was being heated to the point of incandescence within them. According to Richard Weiner, other lights are *baby*, *junior*, and *peewee*, at one end of the spectrum, and *brute* and *senior* at the other. Others are *mini-brute*, *inky dink* (a small incandescent lamp), and *bazooka*, derived from the armor-piercing weapon of World War Two, called thus for a resemblance to the horn made popular by comedian Bob Burns (1896–1956), who got the name from *bazoo* (slang for nose or mouth), culled from *bazuin*, Dutch for trumpet. The spotlight equipped with a reflector back, the *Birdseye*, was invented by Clarence Birdseye (1886–1956), better known for a technique of fast-freezing food. This is also known as a PAR *light* (parabolic aluminized reflector). *Nookie* is another small light, whereas an *emily* is a *broad*, or a *flood* with only one lamp, hence a *single broad*.

LOAF

In Cockney rhyming slang, this word means *head* from the rhyme with "loaf of bread." It is also a verb, meaning to idle or lounge about (in loafers if you are lucky), or mooch or dawdle (loafers, meaning those who loaf, have ample time for international synonyms). In German a *Landläufer* is a vagabond, running around the landscape. By far the most complex and astounding appearance of *loaf* comes with the Anglo-Saxon words loaf-kneader and loaf-guardian, otherwise known as lady and lord. (See *fiction* for more on kneading.) Loaf or *hlaef* forms the first syllable in *Lammas*, the Anglo-Saxon word for harvest festival, August 1, when bread baked from the season's first ripe grain was blessed. *Loaf-mass* is a winning thought.

LOO

Very British, this, the result of a game-playing pseudo-pragmatism other nations might not relish. Did such a term even exist before 1920? The Old French cry emitted when emptying chamber pots into the street from on high—*gardez l'eau!*—is supposed to have become *gardy loo!*, which sounds no better as English than "gardez l'eau" does as French (it might even mean *keep the water*, which opens up shocking possibilities for that well-known disinfectant, urine, with which the Romans cleaned their teeth). "Beware of the water" needs just a few more words than *gardez l'eau* allows. *Loo* means lavatory or toilet, of course, so see James Joyce's *Ulysses* for a rousing tribute that meets its own Waterloo: "O yes, *mon loup*. How much cost? Waterloo. Water-closet." Or try *Louvre*, for its slatted screens (that might hide a fudged-up jakes). Mispronounced during World War One, *lieux d'aisances*, places of easing or relief (*leeyuh* becoming *loo*), may be the answer. On the other hand, the solution may not be linguistic at all, considering the English habit (formerly) of numbering toilets 100. It was where, to combine two sporting references, you either scored a century or batted a thousand.

LORDOSIS

It sounds like a disease of the aristocracy, one perhaps remediable by insurrection, but it means abnormal forward curvature of the spine, from Greek *lordosis* ("bent backward"), akin to Old English *belyrtan*, Middle High German *lürzen*, both meaning *to deceive*. In the history of these verbs sit the evil twins *lerz* and *lurz*, meaning "left," "to be found on the left," recalling once again the "sinister" mythology of the left-hand side, which makes you lurch leftward and your spine grow crooked, like that of Richard III. Clearly, leftness is to blame for deformity; some evil twists us, having nothing to do with the right-hand side. God must be right-handed, the devil left. How odd that the evil on the left makes the spine grow forward, as if covering its tracks.

LOTHARIO

A friend living in Sweden, but essentially a Parisian, has just called me a Lothario of the soul, which puzzles me as a *lothario* happens to be a frivolous lover and seducer, in our own century at least. In the eighteenth-century play, *The Fair Penitent* by British playwright Nicholas Rowe, the character Lothario (played by the famed David Garrick opposite the Calista of Mrs. Sarah Siddons) is haughty, gallant, and gay (in that time's sense). So this is what my friend meant. Lothario seduces her, an event the play condemns by bringing Lothario to a bad end. In fact, in that libidinous, lax time, *The Fair Penitent* stood out as moralistic. Now I have to find out what souls I have seduced to my evil ways.

LOVE APPLE

The tomato, of course, *pomme d'amour* in French, *Liebesapfel* in German, "love apple" because it resembled an apple proper (some anyway) and supposedly had aphrodisiac properties. *Tomatl* came in later, from Mexico, which was just as well as the Elizabethans had invented a quite different love apple, a peeled one that a lover placed in the armpit at night until it was erotically potent enough, and then handed it over for a new career as a love toy. Tomatoes were too squashy for such abandon and calculation, although the earliest tomatoes were wrinkled and desiccated-looking, deemed poisonous. In fact, once the tomato softened up, the eager lover had merely doubled her or his chances by adding the armpit apple to the *pomme d'amour*.

MANGER

Your eye has not misled you: this is *away in a manger*, not the French verb "to eat," but it might have been; *manger*, the eating or feeding place, comes from Old French *mangeoire*, from Vulgar Latin *manducatoria*, from Latin *manducare* (to chew). *Manger* shows up in English in the alien-looking word *blancmange* (white food, first a savory dish of white meat in a tasty sauce of eggs, cream, rice, sugar, and almonds, that gradually veered off into dessert, sweet and gelatinous, manna for a proper childhood). The skin disease *mange* emanates from this etymology in the fourteenth century and the adjective *mangy* (as of a dog) two hundred years later. One can only marvel at the mills of word grinding small and slow.

MANNA

From Latin which got it from Aramaic *manna*, derived from Hebrew *man*, one of a group of Semitic words specifying a viscous edible substance leaked by a tamarind-type tree of the Sinai desert. Metaphorically this is the long-desired repast or commodity delivered with captivating accuracy. The signal event was, of course, the food miraculously provided the Israelites in the wilderness during their hegira from Egypt. Any spiritual nourishment from heaven qualifies, but notice Jacques Maritain's warning that "It is a deadly error to expect poetry to provide the super-substantial nourishment of man." Not everything provided is *manna*; there has to be an exact desire—books would not have gratified the Israelites, nor jewels, nor music. The tree in question was probably the Eurasian ash, *Fraxinas ornus*, the *mountain* ash from which spears and javelins were made, but which also could be used as a laxative. In any case, it was only the exudate the Israelites received.

MAQUIS

French for scrub or undergrowth, hiding place of the Maquis Resistance fighters who took on the Nazis in World War Two. They hid out in such country, but not exactly in the scrub, which hardly affords enough cover. The word is Italian, by way of Corsica: *macchia*, originally from the Latin *macula*, spot or stain (compare English *immaculate* and *chain* in *chainmail*), but imaginatively reassigned to bush or thicket seen from afar as a spot or stain on a hillside. One soldier in this secret French army was Samuel Beckett, who in his novel *Watt* communicates the atmosphere of the time rather than the landscape. He made a living by picking potatoes. His region was the *départements* of Vaucluse and Isère in the Rhône valley, where he spent two formative years, setting *Watt* in his native Ireland, actually, in order "to get away from war and occupation."

MARCESCENT

You do not need this word until you find it, and then you use a lot of time trying to find an occasion to use it. From

Latin *marcescere*, "to begin to droop" or "to grow feeble," it usually means that something has withered without falling off. There do exist people with such hands, arms, legs, although Roman literature offers a withered vine (Ovid) and a droopy idleness (Livy). This verb distinguishes itself from *marcere* (to wither, to droop, to be feeble) with its *sc* component, which stands for the processive, the inceptive, as elsewhere in such words as *crescent*, *nascent*, and *quiescent*, all states of growing: growth, being born, and quietening down. Perhaps the ideal complement to this verb is composer John Adams's lively piece "What's Wrong with A Withered Hand?" developed from a Southern congregational service. It is perhaps best to think of the marcescent as the bloom that endures on a twig after flowering.

There remains the unanswerable question of why the root *marc-* is the sound that must represent enfeeblement or decay, or *merk-* for the Indo-Europeans. Why *that* one? Hardly imitative. So why?

MARGARINE

The word of Hippolyte Mège-Mouriès, who invented this substance in 1869, basing its name on margaric acid, a term invented in its turn by French biochemist Michel-Eugène Chevreuil for a fatty acid. The first margarine was made from clarified beef fat. Its name was made from the Greek word *margarites*, "pearl," also the source of Margaret and Margot. Both he and Mège-Mouriès were thinking, perhaps dreaming, of the pearly sheen of the crystallized acid. Some pronounce the *g* hard, which would seem correct with a back vowel after it, but most soften it, and a good many say *marge*, beginning in the 1920s.

MARY'S BATH

Martha Barnette identifies several "linguistic sightings of the Blessed Virgin in kitchens," passing from *Lacrimae Christi* ("Tears of Christ"), that sweet dark wine of southern Italy, and the uniquely French (and confident) compliment to a delicate white wine ("It's as if little Jesus peed in my mouth"), to the technique of cooking known as *bain-Marie*, in which a dish is warmed up by being set in a pan of warm water. It is the "exceeding gentleness" of this method that earns it its holy analogy.

MARZIPAN

In the beginning, Arabic *mawthabān*, meaning the king who sits still, was the Saracens' way of deriding a medieval Venetian coin depicting a seated Christ. Then Venice stole its enemy's fire and changed the word into *matapan*, followed in Italy at large by *marzapane* while the coin itself graduated into being a unit of measure. The word entered English in the sixteenth century, creating predictable confusion and culminating as *marchpane*, which endured for three centuries until German *marzipan* took over, itself based on the misconception that *marzapane* meant the same as Latin *marci panis*, St. Mark's bread. Somewhere in this erratic story, a box of a certain size and capacity has been lost, although not without having had its effect on language: It was a box of *confectionery*, weighed and priced according to that Venetian coin. No word better illustrates how fast an association can become central while all other connotations, even denotations, blow away, and Italians end up pricing a sweetmeat by the weight and breadth of a sitting Christ, an odd inversion of the Communion sacrament in its skewed way. The decorative forms on the box echo those into which the ground-almond confection twisted, and its weight ("one tenth of a load") paralleled the coin's status as a ten percent standard tax, as with many other coins circulating their seated king since the Crusades. We have here an initial metaphor enthroned on a coin and then recoiling, as it were, into the gastronomic world of almond paste, egg whites, honey or sugar, sweet-tasting animals and fruits, boxes for candies or rare coins (emptied candy boxes then holding coins), all the sweeter for its transit. Hail, holy secular marzipan, topping so many cakes with a perfect right enclosed in hard icing. I can hardly suppress a Bronx cheer for such a word, out on its own in the violent, unpredictable world, alighting first here, then there, slowly acquiring reputations nobody quite understands even while indulging a sweeter tooth than that of remorse.

A similar bemusement may afflict you if you peer at the Chinese character for *boat*, consisting of three parts:

舟 for *embarkation*,

八 for *eight*,

口 for *mouth*.

It becomes 船 and I ask if the design for boat is not already in the first element, as in the word *emBARKation*? When the part already includes the whole, you wonder at the redundancy.

MASCARA

Anyone applying this substance to eyelashes to thicken them for an evening may not enjoy the etymology that, through Spanish *mascara*, for mask, and Italian *maschera*, returns them to Arabic *maskharah*, buffoon or clown. One of the few poets to mention this cosmetic, Louis MacNeice writes "mascara scrawls a gloss on a torn leaf."

MAUDLIN

This word of pious commemoration honoring a Mary from Magdala on the Sea of Galilee who according to the Bible was present at Christ's crucifixion, has found its way to two colleges: Magdalen College, Oxford, and Magdalene College, Cambridge, both of which pronounce their name as *maudlin*. This Mary, supposedly the first person to meet with Christ after he had risen from the dead, is usually represented in paintings of the Middle Ages as weeping; hence maudlin, coming to be used for excessively sentimental. If, as the story goes, Christ freed her of evil spirits, she had ample reason to weep out of gladness, as at his resurrection; or, in horror, at his crucifixion. "Maudlin" seems a bit hard; what, after all, do we make of those who witness crucifixion, say, with a stiff upper lip or two?

MAVEN

It comes from the Hebrew word for "understanding" and means expert, specialist, connoisseur, agreeably substituting for such polysyllabic vaunts a firm, simple word that parades its own confidence. There are croissant mavens, Tennyson mavens, and *Tonight Show* mavens. They all understand what they dote on.

MAWKISH

Lousy comes from *louse*, and *mawkish* from *mawk*, a seventeenth-century word for maggot, perhaps from the Scandinavian *mathkr*. Perhaps those inclined to use this word will refrain if each time they envisage the burrowing greasy white larva. The word at first meant "without appetite" (not the maggot but the maggot-watcher) or somewhat sickly. In the old days, *maggot* meant a whim or a preposterous fancy, and mawkish came to signify nauseated, put off by the very thought of eating. Then a bridge built itself to "sentimental" and "over-sentimental," closely allying lavish emotion with gastric upset. But how many mawkish things make you really sick? Only metaphorically.

MEDIA

Not Media, the town in northwestern Iran, or the one in Pennsylvania, but the crude plundering of a neuter plural (*medium* its singular form) into a feminine singular. Most usage panels wince at this Bottomic transformation, and even more so at its new plural form *medias*, which evokes a more dignified phrase *in medias res* (into the middle of things), in which *medias* is a feminine accusative. Perhaps all this not exactly superfine categorization will falter one day and vanish, leaving us with discords from the unlettered of our day and forlorn echoes of ancient languages pronounced dead on arrival. Why cannot *media*, the neuter plural for something sometimes neuter and very far from literature, say, remain itself? I wince at *media*, the pseudo-feminine singular spawned by people who don't know a feminine accusative plural from a baboon's nipple, and I somewhat treasure *medium*, the neuter. Besides, are all media so homogeneous that they can be grouped together like soot and peanut butter? I doubt it. What's wrong with "TV broadcasting" and "radio broadcasting"? Alas, I think the very word broadcasting an imminent goner; soon we will no longer know what The Great Broadcast was.

MEERSCHAUM

A smoker and a romantic, you covet a pipe made from foam of the sea, if such a thing might be had. Joshua Sylvester put it graphically in his *Divine Weeks and Works of the Du Bartas* (1598) when he envisioned "Those small white Fish to Venus consecrated, though without Venus' aid they be created of th' Ocean scum." So, you accept a pipe made from petrified foam (*meer*, sea, and *Schaum*, foam), little heeding word of sepiolite, otherwise a tough, white, compact mineral of hydrous magnesium silicate found in the Mediterranean area and also used as a building stone. You are smoking your tobacco in the august presence of *spuma maris* and *halos hakhnē*; Romans and Greeks attend your bowl. It is beside any but the learned point that *meerschaum* was once thought to be a coral compact of mermaids' bones and the beaks of white birds felled by waterspouts. Perhaps the dream never sags, especially if you aim the pipe out over the seething broth of waves and think a white upon it, bleaching as you stare and eyeing the eyes in the foam. A pipe-dream? Yes.

MEGILLAH

Almost always "the whole megillah," denotes something concise and beautiful recited or explained in full. Means song and dance, but, Yiddish from Hebrew for "scroll" or "volume," invokes the Book of Esther read aloud *in toto* at Purim when the deliverance of the Jews from massacre by Haman is celebrated (9:20–22). *Purim* itself derives from *pur*, meaning *lot*, a reference to the lost Haman cast to decide the day for Jewish destruction. When deliverance is far off, perhaps the merest bit of a megillah will suffice, but when, as in recent memory, deliverance has gone by the board, perhaps the whole megillah has uncanny power.

MIGRAINE

Early *mygrame* and *mygrane*, eventually settling down into *megrim*, this heroic word became the eighteenth century's *migraine*, from

French, meaning "half-skull" or "half-head" as in Greek (*hemikra-nia*) and Latin (*hemicrania*). The notion that dominates is the pain of headache in half the head only, plus the bizarre optical phenomenon of seeing with only one eye, or only the top or bottom, the left or right, of something, or, worse, as I can attest, something behind what one is looking at. The word as it stands does little for the sawtooth scintillations of the migraine attack, perhaps because so many people who have a headache credit themselves with a migraine. If the word weren't so popular, perhaps it would have become more accurate, with suffixes for sparklers and spinning cogs. I had migraines regularly until first taking propranolol, the beta-blocker that corrects hypertension, quietens the heart, and stills butterflies in the tummy. To have taken those little blue pills for going on a quarter of a century seems almost too easy a way out of an affliction so famous.

Diluted migraine seems to be gaining ground, even as medication for the real thing improves. An aviation writer, rehearsing the problems of skywriting (find "low-pay part-time pilots able to handle 650-hp taildraggers and fly in formation for four hours straight"), says, "In short, we are describing a never-ending migraine that can only worsen with time. Who in their right mind would take on such an assignment?" No migraineur, for certain.

MISTLETOE

An unsolved mystery, this. A European will have met with the mistle thrush (or missel thrush) whose name reveals its taste for those stalkless, eerie, moon-like berries. Back when it was *mistit-lan* and *mistil*, it was a dung twig spawned by bird droppings. Mistletoe, claims a seventeenth-century essay, "comes onely by the mewting of birds...which feed thereupon and let it passe through their body." The Druids found it a remedy for epilepsy and senile dementia, the ague and the palsy, but only the oak mistletoe. A certain William Bullein, in his *Bulwarke of Defence Against All Sickness and Woundes* (1562), wrote that "The *miseln* groweth…upon the tree through the dounge of byrdes." What an odious catalyst of the kiss, but, the plant being semiparasitic, an ideal emblem for Christmas. The most prosaic view of this poisonous plant is that of American Indians, who used it for toothache. The American mistletoe, says one reference book, rather curtly, does well in zone 7 and farther south. This inimical growth is still linked with the burning of bonfires and ancient sacrificial ceremonies. Was the bird lime made from its crushed berries, smeared sticky on trees to trap birds, also forced on victims of Druidic rituals? Did the compulsory kiss exchange bird lime and so procure not marriage, as myth has it, but mutual suicide after one had spurned the other?

MOSAIC

Truly, word of the Muses, from Greek *mouseion*, which formerly meant "place of the Muses" and has yielded us our own "museum," a doubtful transaction. In Medieval Latin, the word mutated into *musaicus* or *mosaicus* and slipped into English without ever becoming snarled up in the "Mosaic" from Moses. It is worth remembering with some reverence that in the third century B.C. *mouseion* denoted the museum, library, and observatory of Ptolemy Sotor at Alexandria, the pinnacle of Greek civilization. There were nine Muses, who romped Spice Girl–like in springs at the foot of Mount Parnassus, and on Helicon. Was there a Mosaic pecking order? Yes. Kalliope (*kalos* + *ops*, beautiful voice) was alpha, although we do not nowadays think the calliope a classy sound. Second in rank was *Clio*, the Muse of history (*kleio* = make famous), while third was *Erato*, goddess of lyric and erotic poetry. Below this trinity were *Euterpe* (*eu* +

terpo, well-delighting), the patroness of lyric poetry, flautists, and inventor of wind instruments, possibly opera. *Thalia* (tha-leia = blooming) has the name of a Manhattan movie-house, and she balanced joy, comedy, and lyric poetry, thus overlapping with Euterpe. *Melpomene* governed tragedy (*melpomai* = sing) and wore a mask while *Terpsichore* (*terpis* + *choros*, delightful dance) ruled dance. *Polyhymnia* (sacred song) is a combination of *poly* and *hymnos*, many songs) and *Urania*, the Muse of astronomy, from the Greek *ouranos* for heaven, reminds us that the Greeks suffered from no two-cultures dichotomy, but developed a seamless holism. Thus, all the arts are one and remain as one with science and thought. Of all the renderings in music of the Muses, surely the most original and complex is Igor Stravinsky's *Apollon Musagète*, in which an imaginary Apollo looks in on the birth of, creation of, the Muses, which is like the creative process looking in at itself, as it often does. Sometimes this music has a clinical aura, seems a little clipped, which is no doubt Stravinsky trying not to gush when dealing with the sacred mythos of a people who didn't gush either. To have so many illustrious sisters fostering the arts and sciences in complete harmony gives the lie to the squabbles that infest contemporary bureaucratic intervention in the arts. There is, nonetheless, a shallow quality to much Greek poetry; was it top-heavy with monitors and drones?

Looking back over this roll-call of the Muses, a pensive yet not necessarily captious reader may well think some of their assignments, or parts of these, unspecific or even wishy-washy. Euterpe, the well-delighting, kept busy to preclude gossip. Thalia bloomed. They all sang. One thinks of geishas, maybe, certainly not of bluestockinged MFAs in tweeds. Why so many? Were they the pop-singers of their day, savvily promoted to managerial posts in the cultural hierarchy? Or were these the first literary agents, or editors? Trying to endow John Milton with a black Muse, who taught him many sexual tricks in his adolescence (tricks he failed to remember when dealing with his wives later), I incurred the wrath of an English purist who, de-composing in his little album of wrath and envious sorrow, pointed out that no such woman existed. How does he know? Zeus help fiction and its practitioners. If he spares me long enough to write a novel about the Muses, set maybe in a pretty Cambridge college gone to the dogs and infested with beer-fat pedants, I may yet be able to define the salient role that all those who catalytically minister to us enact (*us* being all creators). I am happy that the French title of this novella, *Sporting with Amaryllis*, has come out as *Amaryllis ma muse*. She is the shepherdess in Vergil. When I read from this book in Boston, a high-school teacher of literature told me he had prescribed it for his teenaged students to show them what a Muse could be like to such a poet as Milton. I bowed in homage to this brave and sentient man.

MOUSE

From *mouse*, any number of small rodents: To explore a town with the eager curiosity of a mouse nosing down alleyways and peeking into corners, always on the lookout for hidden marvels, may refer to shopping, but only if it's done with rodentlike verve, appetite, and joyous gusto for exploring. "Okay, you stay here and make the world safe for democracy; I'll mouse the shops." Should not be used when referring to natural wonders. For example, it would be inappropriate to say at a cocktail party: "Have you moused the Grand Canyon yet?" But it would be perfect form, on the same occasion, to observe: "Napoleon—now there was a man who could mouse a whole country." Coinage of Diane Ackerman.

MROK

From French eponymous hero *Jean-Pierre Mroque* (1870–1946), harelipped French shipbuilder, long a resident of Brest, who habitually, when entering a house or a room, emitted a sound most often heard as "mahk," which was his tender way of hailing or greeting either occupants or what they occupied: to intone a certain sound, with a rising or falling inflection, and to denote in the intoner feelings of excruciating delicacy, as if to proclaim: "No one enters this room and house, greets these people with the highly evolved finesse that I do." "Mrok" has overtones of smugness or hubris in spite of the near-monumental refinement evinced in the actual call or cry. Sometimes heard as a bleat, a baby call, or the cry of certain monkeys. Typical use in society: "Mrok as you would be mroked."

MULE

Crime, which often needs to hide itself, is lingo's forge. Cockney rhyming slang deceived the police or unwelcome Irish immigrants to London about what was being said. For example, a look is a *butcher's hook* and then by reduction *a butcher's* (no longer a rhyme as clue) while *bristols* (titty rhyming with soccer team Bristol City) means breasts (the French say *balcon*). The mule of our day, far from the pre-Latin animal known as *mulus* in the Mediterranean zone and the slipper once *mulleus*, red or purple and worn by high-caste Romans, is a risk-taking accomplice who stuffs condoms full of narcotics into a body cavity or swallows them to smuggle them through Customs. Is there a whiff here of the Latin American pack-animal, stubborn and dumb? Mules have also smuggled currency and jewelry. People are more aware of this practice than hitherto thanks to a TV documentary melodramatically tracking the procedure from first swallow (a slow, uncomfortable business) to (within reason) evacuation after arrival. Of course, if the bag bursts into the wall of the intestine, the mule is doomed.

We may well wince at his predicament, seated there in

Economy on the jet winging its way to New York, poring over the school report from the expensive private school to which his profits enable him to send his daughter. She shows promise in languages and art, but has no grasp of math. He worries, but thinks she may become an air hostess someday, little knowing that such a term is no longer in use. Ah yes, the cabin staff, who ply him all the way with food and drink that would kill him, certainly expose him to the law. He starves, dries up, hearing his belly rumble in couvade with the jumbo's huge engines. He has to hold out, maintaining a pleasant smile when he says no, not even a pistachio, no sparkling water, thank you. If they see him at some point blundering up the aisle to the toilet, they have no idea it is over for him, he cannot *contain* himself, a nice young man unaccustomed to air travel and obviously taken short by the lack of oxygen, the vibration, the jet lag, the miserable token food. Meantime his daughter slogs away at her quadratic equations and his wife dreams of a retirement having nothing to do with jail or death: the mule out to pasture.

MUMBO JUMBO

With capital M and J, this is a title conferred upon a priest by certain Mandingo peoples of the Western Sudan, for his being able to protect his village from evil. It can also refer to an object that has supernatural powers over people, and it denotes meaningless activity, obscure incantations, gibberish, and chaos. This is the pagan idea of the misrule revealed by Shakespeare in the person of Falstaff, its more civilized version. From Mandingo *ma-ma-gyo-mbo* (magician who makes the upset spirits of ancestors depart or Makes Grandmother Trouble Go Away). As used in Western society, *mumbo jumbo* is an incomprehensible babble free of evil spirits, more likely to be the product of inferior learning and poor mental discipline.

MUMPS

Once there was a dialect noun, *mump*, that meant grimace or scowl, and its plural for a disease conveyed the distorted face of the sufferer, whose swollen neck glands brought to vivid life the verb *mump*, meaning "sulk." If you had *mumps*, or *the mumps*, you pulled a face, or rather your face pulled you, making you *mumble* (grunt through closed lips). "To keep *mum*" (i.e., silent) is a related expression and the word *mummer*, actor in mime, puts the whole concept into motion again. *Mum* and *mumble*, fourteenth century, preceded *mummer* (fifteenth) and *mump* and *mumps* (sixteenth); it is plain that, for the English, the *mp* formulation had come to denote impeded, contorted, quiet reduction from a state of outward bonhomie to one of glum gurning.

MUMPSIMUS

Have you ever met a *mumpsimus*? He/she has nothing to do with the mumps, but ranks as "a bigoted adherent to an exposed but customary error." Once upon a time, an illiterate priest made an error, a slip of the tongue, at Mass saying for *sumpsimus* ("we have taken") *mumpsimus*. When rebuked and corrected, he answered that he would never take someone else's *sumpsimus* for his very own *mumpsimus*. One suspects Dr. Spooner of Spoonerism fame of holding on to his speech defect, always preferring "a scoop of boy trouts" to "a troop of boy scouts" (see *Spoonerism*).

MUSCLE

As well as sounding like a more appetizing word, *muscle* at its most attractive suggests perhaps only the weight we have put on while pretending to diet. To the Romans, however, those finitely spectatorial people who had a verb for watery eyes, *muscle* was a diminutive of *mus*, for *mouse*, a word best known for its place in a famous bit of Horace: *Parturient montes, nascitur ridiculus mus.* The mountains go into labor, but only a mouse comes out. I don't know how ridiculous a mouse is, per se. Not very, especially (we're told) to elephants. This little mouse of the Romans, *musculus*, seemed to be running about beneath the skin when someone flexed her muscles, I suppose it all depends on how big your muscles are; if huge, then maybe you will have a rat instead. I believe the actual shape of certain muscles played a part in this, in upper arm and calf, so to look like a *musculus* running you had to look something like a *musculus* to begin with. Rome was an observant society, to say the least, although observation is not what it's famous for. Perhaps they sat in the sun a lot, thus exposing their eyes too much to cool winds that blew from the Po Valley. Or was the thing that ailed them what Maurice Merleau-Ponty, that most elegant of French philosophers, called in one of his finest essays "Cézanne's Doubt"? Cézanne, he says, worried that what he painted was in his head and not "out there." Possibly the Romans had vision just blurred enough to make them think a mouse was on the move within, thus enlivening and embellishing something prosaic, as when sticking a lion next to a Christian. Next time you show off your muscles, squint your eyes and guess what's on the trot.

I have now learned that, if you are unlucky enough to be bitten by a black mamba, your leg muscles will ripple and buckle in precisely this "*musculus*" way; but surely the Romans never saw that.

MUSK

Eastern word for an eastern thing, *muska*, Sanskrit for scrotum or testicle, means also "little mouse" and might be compared with *musculus* (the two little mice of the testicles bounding about in the wrinkled fig of the scrotum?). The word is the diminutive of *mus*, like *musculus*, and evokes, as well as *mussel*, the gland from which a male deer secretes musk (it resembles the scrotum). We seem to be living in a closed circuit here of not very far-reaching imagination: mouse-scrotum-muscle/mussel-scrotum again. All the world was scrotators or scrotum spectators. Musk, a word beloved of aftershave purveyors, makes them scrotum-bound and also reels in *muscat*, the name of a grape that supposedly reeks of musk, hence *muscatel*. This is a fourteenth-century word, still going strong, only its oxen having lost out. Nutmeg is another of its relatives, for being musk-flavored.

PAUL WEST

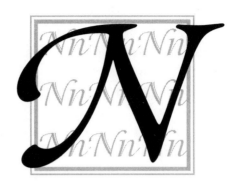

NAILED

Neither finger-nails nor fastening-pin, this adjective appears in the expression "got it nailed," meaning mastered, dominated, beyond question, the certainty deriving no doubt from the fastening-pin idea: Clearly, it isn't going to get away from you now, you've got it where you want it, and your expertise lacks nothing. Not a crucifixion image, one trusts, though "Him" nailed to the cross isn't far away from the fastening-pin idea. Best pun pertaining: "I haven't a *clou*," as in French for *nail*. Catch, seize, grab are not far away. The trapping idea comes from the mid-1700s. And sometimes *nail* means *fuck*.

NASTURTIUM

Prey of the spelling bee and yuppie salad, this peppery some-times acrid flower defies those who spot *nasty* at its front and ig-nore the rest in a flare of vagueness. Its culinary use as a substitute for capers in no way teaches you that the *nas* means "nose" and the rest of the word *twisting* and *puckering*. The Latin *torqueo* means "I twist" or "I torture" (remember Torquemada?). The Roman author and lover of baths Pliny the Elder wrote that the nasturtium "took its name from tormenting the nose." The infinitive *torquēre* bears a long ē, eloquent testimony to the slowness of much torture. Try to say *nasitortium*, the early form of its name, and you get the full dry tweak of its bitter seeds, best sucked by experts and masochists only. What a nasty nosetwister this vivid flower is.

The flower's Greek identity is quite heroic: *tropaeolum majus*, from *tropaion*, meaning trophy. Linnaeus, the supreme taxonomist, found the leaves reminded him of shields used by soldiers in battle, the red and yellow blooms of their blood-stained helmets. From Peru; into Europe in 1686.

NAZI

Since Nazis are still too much with us, late and soon, although little remembered or known about by a new generation, a faint roll-call of their verbal badges seems in order. *Nazi* is scrambled *Nationalzocialist*, first word of Hitler's National Socialist Worker's Party, dominant from 1933. *Flak*, for anti-aircraft fire, came from *FLieger* (flyer), Abwehr (defense), and Kanonen (guns). There is something dumb and wooden about this formation, as if the devising mind assembling "flyer," "defense," and "guns" like someone joining up a train had not been properly alert. Is this any dumber, though, or more wooden than "radio detecting and ranging," which gave us RA+D+A+R for the legendary electronic locating system that now plagues our highways? Wars seem to drive people of all sorts intocrude agglutinative compounds, in all senses. *Gestapo* derives from *Geheime Staatspolizei*, meaning the state secret police, and *Blitz* from the German word (yes, they would have a word for it, just like the Romans for watery eyes) "lightning war": *Blitzkrieg*.

Anyone besotted with this tendency might go on for hours, lamenting the mental set behind the verbal thicket, perhaps resuming with the notorious dive bomber, the Stuka, from *Sturzkampfflugzeug* (Junkers JU 87), first used in the Spanish Civil War and enhanced in the headlong scream of its dive by cardboard sirens affixed to both the plane and its load of bombs. Away with "war-dive-flying-machine"s. What American slang has to teach clotted German is the art of brevity. Winston Churchill's habitual pronunciation of Nazi (Natzi) as *Narzi* renders the word as it might be uttered in Southern England, achieving, I always thought, an almost feral contempt between snarl and roar.

NERVOUS; ULCERSS

If you needed to know the time in Manhattan, you dialed NERVOUS, whatever state you yourself were in; in Los Angeles, you could get the time by dialing ULCERSS. Something bicoastally nerve-wracked in these codes, one dead, the other already doomed, indicates either a sense of humor at work or a pervasive neurasthenia that cankers all it touches. In case you were wondering, the numbers afford no clue: 212 637 8686 and 213 852 3777. I wonder who or what now has either, God help them. In London, you used to dial TIM (rather obviously: no hang-ups there), and Tim became quite a personality in his or her own right. People spoke of dialing TIM as if he, she, were a cat. Perhaps New York is witnessing a retreat from the letter: the new number, 976 1616 (WXY PRS MNO - 1 MNO 1 MNO) yields no word at all; no letters correspond to 1, of course, so the whole thing becomes a jumble, certainly inferior to *Nervous*.

NICE

Never use this word, I was taught, about anything; it's insipid and vacant. How many million times I have disobeyed, not even aware that it originally meant "stupid," from Latin *nescius* for "ignorant." (*Ne* + *science* means not knowing, but *science* means knowing, of course.) After *nice* came into English from Old French, it underwent some sea changes, "ignorant" yielding to "foolish" and "shy," "fastidious" and "refined." The word took a double slide, one leading to "severely accurate or discriminating," the other to "pleasant" or "agreeable," first heard in the latter part of the eighteenth century. Why the shift from "ignorant" to "shy"? Presumably because ignorant people keep quiet, although a recent example cancels this—two graduate students in a University of London seminar kept silent all term, but only because they were afraid, it was revealed, they had uncouth accents and were afraid of being ridiculed. So much for the silence of ignorance. The transit from "shy" to "severely accurate or discriminating" came from shy people's being hard to please. Or so it's said. Our use of *nice* in "a nice distinction," meaning "precise" or "exacting," is perhaps the word's only justifiable use. The rest is social filler. I once knew a girl who couldn't say her Y's and often answered "Nice, ness."

NIGHT HERON

Better known by its nickname, the *shitepoke*, this bird empties its bowels when alarmed; our forefathers were less squeamish than we and rather enjoyed calling a spade a spade, although *night heron* does suggest something august and De Havilland: a good name for an air ambulance, maybe, cruising on top with urgent stretchers aboard.

NIMBY

Responding to a piece I wrote in *The Independent* in 1999 about Belgrade, my sister compressed her comment on NATO bombardments into this acronym. *Not In My Back Yard* is what it means, and she meant Bomb from a great distance if you wish. But there is a world of difference between bombing from Italy and bombing, in theory at least, from three thousand miles away. If the U.S.A. were where Italy is, would there have been any NATO bombings at all? Clausewitz should have thought of *Nimby*; just imagine what it would have been in German.

NOCK

Once the cleft between the buttocks or the upper fore corner of a boom sail or staysail (when cut with a square tack), this is the groove cut across the end of an arrow. Old English *hnocc* meant penis, Middle Dutch *nocke* tip, summit, and Swedish *nocke* pit or peg or end of yardarm. Notching and attaching form the core of all this word's relatives, whether the notch be in the bow itself or the arrow. The diminutive, *nocker*, is either a mountain or an Austrian dumpling rich and light.

NUKE

You have just rented a movie, say that appalling remake of *The Avengers* not even offered to the media for review, and after twenty minutes you look at your companions' aggrieved faces and say "Let's nuke it?" Behind that simple, inert word what a hellfire of disintegration! Talk about using a cannon to kill a gnat. The word has other meanings, to be sure (to destroy, to microwave), but this meaning means *pass up, stop it short*, the disparity of means and target passed into the intensity of rejection. You want to get your disappointment and sense of betrayal into the word. By and large you do not *nuke* people, though you may indeed *snuff* them; nuke is for objects, pastimes, even meals and magazines that have failed to belong in the American dream.

NUN

Epater the bourgeois is one thing; *épater* the veil is quite another, almost a leading sport in Catholic countries, determined to get their own back after so much strict regimen enforced since *infancy* (see *infant*). In Portugal, *barriga de freira*, or "nun's tummy," a sweet egg pudding, will fatten you up for the kill, around the waist anyway. In southern Italy, *zinne de monaca* ("nun's tits") are round Neapolitan cakes topped with icing and a candied cherry, while, if you wish to bite a nun's thigh, try a *coscia de monaca*. It's a plum, clearly full of forbidden erotic delights. Elsewhere, incursions into the private parts and doings of nuns becomes even sterner. In southern Germany, fried homemade noodles tossed into soup or graced with castor sugar and coffee bear the dialect name *nonnafuerzla* for "nun's farts." The French phrase for these, *pets de nonne*, attaches itself to plum-sized fritters deep-fried and coated with fine sugar. The euphemism for this dish is *soupirs de nonne*, "nun's sighs," and, in Latin America, a certain fried yeast cake has the same name (*suspiro de monja*), except when the sex changes and the name changes to the risqué-er "*bolas de fraile*, or "friar's balls." We know this as a *Baptist cake* if we mess with it at all.

NURDLE

This is the quiet, pettifogging accumulation of single runs at cricket, akin to saving pennies, stamp edging, and cigarette butts, although more immediately purposeful—there are times when it pays to garner runs thus. To do so requires a special temperament, a placid minimalism, say, or what the Romans called *fascinatio nugacitatis*, trifling with footling. An associated concept is the verb for batting without ever trying to score runs: *to stonewall*, a New World word among the graces.

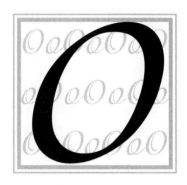

OF

Restricted here to its place in a favored idiom: "too thick of a
haze," in which of course "of" is wholly unnecessary. "Too thick
a haze," perfectly grammatical, seems however, to some speakers,
somehow wimpy and classy. I can see that "too thick of a" appears the epitome of unpretentious rhythm (you would hardly
say, for instance, "too obscure of a haze"). So this peculiar use of
"of" must have something to do with cadence and the dominant
monosyllable of the preceding adjective: a complex phenomenon
involving what I consider rhetorical delay, a way of assimilating
language to its humblest uses. I would never bother to say it
this way, "too———of an" anything, though I grant that *of* rein-
forces the vagueness of the indefinite article, at least until you
realize that we have in this expression a buried noun phrase
such as "sample" or "example." We are really saying "too thick
an example of haze," which sounds academic and fussy, so the
noun phrase falls away, leaving *of* behind. As a novelist,
however, I never shrink from having certain characters shove in
the *of*, mainly in the interests of creating not too learned of a
sound.

The luxuriant maze of American English includes some
bizarre tricks with tiny particles; perhaps these—redundant *of*,

stressed *it*, and omitted *if*—are the real charmed quarks of language, which like some other things is a plasma of extraordinary force. In the long run, language as the people speak it is what propels itself into the next century, leaving brittle rules, barbed-wire boundaries, and empty sentry-boxes far behind, just as English the world over has. The English of 3000, if any, tweaks the heart and shames the mind.

OK

A problem with countless solutions, most of them erratic and frail. The best one is Allen Walker Read's ascription of the great pairing to Eastern imitators of country bumpkins in the early 1800s, who used OK for "Orl korrect." O and K were also the initial letters of *Old Kinderhook*, nickname of President Martin van Buren, born in Old Kinderhook, New York. He used "OK" as a slogan in his 1840 presidential campaign, a year after OK first showed up in print. H. L. Mencken called OK "the most shining and successful Americanism ever invented," he too sub-scribing to Allen Walker Read's *Saturday Review of Literature* so-lution. Martin van Buren's OK Club of supporters won a second term in the White House for the "Red Fox" of Kinder-hook.

OMELET

It is not scrambled egg that has a scrambled word, but this, for-merly "a thin blade," *alemette*, confused with *la melle*, meaning "a thin plate." A plate is not much like a blade, but there it is. *L'alemelle* soon becomes *l'alemette* and eventually *omelette*. Our word has no bearing on eggs whereas incorrectly hearing, mental muddle, and the undisciplined use of language bear extremely on the future of a language. It is as if a nation hired its stevedores to do frescoes. We are lucky to have languages at all, but in part they are not the languages we might have had if we had been properly watched over. There is no doubt something to celebrate in that at your next omelette, when you resist the tang of cold steel and complain about the meager thinness of the blade. *Yolk*, by the way, quite logically comes from Anglo-Saxon *geolca*, yellow. All omelettes to be eaten off the thickest plates around.

ON THE FANG

Australian English for the act of eating or, as they might say, attending to *tucker*. This lupine version is vivid. Compare with the even more generic *on it*, meaning the act of drinking alcoholic liquor.

OOMPH GIRL

Nostalgia-provoking phrase, this, redolent of the sweater-girl movie-star Ann Sheridan, whose *balcon*, as the French say, was prominent, especially when she wore malleable tight wool tops. The sobriquet was coined by press agents in 1939.

OO'S GETTEN CHIP-PAN ON

Filched from an essay by Anthony Burgess (from two, actually, as he repeats the quotation elsewhere), this bit of Northern fog reveals how certain Northern English folk, like my mother, tend to speak Old Norse now and then, "Oo" here meaning *she*, after the Anglo-Saxon word *heo* (all haitches dropped). The line means *She's getting dinner ready*. The *she* is the woman of the house. In my own region, they wouldn't say *Oo* but, I think,

Her or 'Er. Suffice to say, "Oo's getten chip-pan on," which sounds like a question, is not, but a promise of French Fries amid chops, tomatoes, mushrooms, onions, bacon, kidneys and liver. This will not be dinner, but tea, meaning *high tea*, nothing like the demure *afternoon tea* of the South (cucumber and watercress sandwiches with pastries). The question arises, is it possible to make a pig of yourself on afternoon tea, as much as you can on high tea? Only if you trough on all before you, adding toast to finger sandwiches, plastering the pastries with jam, and sweetening the tea with many sugars. Ballasted thus, or by fish and chips consumed with massive helpings of butter on sliced bread, you may venture out among the real people and learn to praise things as "gradely" and "champion" (very French, this), pronouncing *father* as *fayther*, *sleep* as *sleeap*, *road* as *rooad*, and *mister* as *mester*.

ORAL

If dentistry, examinations, and the old speak-sing tradition vanish, *oral* will have only sex to turn to. How odd to find this word fading away, replaced by the admirably specific *verbal*. Some users, with a weakened sense of the word, find all kinds of things verbal that aren't. *Oral* is mouthed, *verbal* has to do with word: These are the things they do not know. The sad thing is, when a society has nothing to say about words (the verbal), it lets the word for it slither away because, thanks to TV perhaps, the only place for the word is the mouth. No more illuminated manuscripts, three-decker novels perused with chronic patience over a weekend, letters highly regarded for their penmanship. Those old scholarship examinations have gone, in which you wrote to impress, maybe to show off, converting every question into a little essay in which to flash your wares. My first such test, at Oliver Cromwell's college,

Cambridge, occupied fifteen papers, roughly half for French, half for English. So much writing while the coal fires purred in November. The others were brisker, especially at Oxford, where you either won or lost on the strength of six hours' writing. Nowadays, students get an interview, yes an *oral* interview only. One conducted in sign language might serve better.

ORANGUTAN

You are an early European traveler or explorer in what is now called Malaysia, and, far from so-called civilization, you become not too particular which bits of the local lingo you pick up and reapply. You hear Malayans of the more densely populated areas, not so thickly treed, calling the inhabitants of the jungle regions by an odd name that nonetheless sticks in your mind. Next thing, you are using the name, *orang-utan*, which means "man of the woods" or manlike ape. The more civilized Malays were being somewhat condescending. If you are Bontius, a seventeenth-century physician who traveled all over the Dutch East Indies, you use the word almost indiscriminately for the big red-haired ape you keep on seeing in the trees. This is a similar goof to that of Pierre Sonnerat in Madagascar (see *indri*), and as with him it has always been too late to put it right.

ORCHID

If you have an inflammation of the testicles, you have orchiditis, and your doctor, infatuated with code, will name it so, knowing that *orkhis* means testicle in Greek. The tuberous roots of the orchid decided this rather rough analogy, and one gets the impression that, rather than hunting around for flawless likenesses, the wilder spirits of the naming impulse wanted something that would enable them to come up with such a phrase as *ballock's grass* for various types of wild orchid. In etymology, the testicle is everywhere. Latin *orchis* went straight into the notebooks of sixteenth- and seventeenth-century botanists, but they replaced the *s* with a *d*. Pliny the Elder has much to answer for, having written "Mirabilis est *orchis* herba, sive serapias, gemina radice testiculis simili." One glance at the last two words and you have his point. A skeptical reader may well conclude that there was more testicle-gazing going on than botanical-biological matching.

ORDEAL

This polite and rather formal word had a harsh beginning as the word for a red-hot iron that a defendant had to carry without flinching (!) in the English courts of another era. This was *ordal*, as was the equivalent test of plunging your hand into boiling water. If you flinched at either, you were found guilty. This was "trial by ordeal." Nowadays, an *ordeal* may indeed be something brutal to undergo or a mere exaggeration of a mild mishap (your umbrella flies inside out during a windy downpour), or the three-hour examination paper on the half-rhyming couplet. An earlier form of *ordal* was the prehistoric Germanic *uzdailjan* (ancestor of German *Urteil*, verdict). Thus did the parceling out of judgment give way to the testing out of the accused. It is as if the severity of the one yielded up the metaphorical "trying experience" made much of as an "ordeal."

ORDINARY

Not so; here's a word that, between the fourteenth and nineteenth centuries, went up like a rocket and stayed polymorphously visible. Latin *ordinarius* meant "following a prescribed course," French for *comme il faut*, "as should be." Its first appearance in English, after *order* from *ordo*, was as a noun meaning "someone with jurisdiction in ecclesiastical cases," and gradually the word mopped up all manner of circumstances and calls, from post, mail, fixed allowance, the priest who visits the condemned cell, and tavern. It was also an eating-house. Today, however, *ordinary* merits no extra, surviving mainly in the phrase *out of the ordinary*, as if all of its various uses have advanced into more specialized idiom while the word, from overuse, has become trite, unrecognizable, and stale (as its name befits). To a Roman Catholic, the Ordinary is the part of the Mass that stays unchanged from one day to another, or a division of the Roman Breviary containing the unchangeable parts of the office other than the Psalms. The ordinary is familiar, to be counted on for being undemanding, as in heraldry it describes the bend and the cross, one of the simplest and commonest insignia (compare an ordinary seaman of the merchant marine). Perhaps an ordinary word for ordinary things is too much to bear.

ORDURE

The poet Geoffrey Chaucer used this word to mean foul language, a phrase that has emerged in the idiom of our own time, though "severe" or "extreme" has replaced "foul." French *ord* gave us another word for *filth*, from the Roman verb *horreo*, meaning to bristle (hence *horridus*). What was horrid made your hair stand on end, much as certain poems made the hair on the back of poet and scholar A. E. Houseman bristle too. *Ordure* has narrowed since Chaucer's day, now restricted to excrement and dung. Offal is not excrement but, literally, the fall-off from a butcher's slab, usually thrown away or tossed to dogs. Offal now means almost garbage in general, possibly because nothing from the carcass gets thrown away any more.

 PAUL WEST

For too long I have tried to explain *ordure* as *or-dur*, French for *hard gold*, but my golden attempt has died at the hands of realists and sentimental coprophobes. This would sadden the late Carl Sagan, an early ally of mine in this endeavor, though we both knew we were asking too much.

OREO

A black whose values and orientation resemble those of whites, based on the popular sandwich cookie with a white cream between round chocolate biscuits; not known the other way around; no such cookie. Afrosaxon.

OUBLIETTE

Abandoned in this, a dungeon with a trapdoor in the ceiling as the only way in or out, you have literally been "forgotten." This is where you put someone to forget them, as we discover from French *oublier*, to forget. The very word conjures up its approximate kindred, from the Black Hole of Calcutta to Poe's "The Cask of Amontillado" and Alexander Dumas's *The Man in the Iron Mask*. This is an almost perfect euphemism because, if you leave someone down there long enough, you forget to forget them. This is not hermetic sealing, of course, which originally depended on the god Hermes's magical power for healing and sealing wounds just as perfectly as we would seal up a jar of preserves. We are accustomed to handling jars which instruct us how to check if the seal is broken, and we wonder just how many wretches have met their end sealed up dry, more or less, under an unmarked lid. By the way, this Hermes is not the messenger of the Greek gods, the dude with the serpent-stick, but Hermes Trismegistus, an Egyptian priest alive at the time of

Moses, confused in the Middle Ages with the other Hermes as a dab hand with science and conjuring, thus earning the name Hermes Thrice-Greatest. A magus three times over. The books of this compound ghost have not come down to us, but he is credited with the shady attribute of "authorship," eventually for his renown in alchemy and benign magic, having confounded many with his trick of "hermetic" sealing. In time, *hermetic* was being read as *alchemical*, and by the 1660s *hermetic* meant "airtight." Complete with grave accent, Hermès also nowadays denotes clothing of unthinkable sleek finesse befitting both the messenger and the magus.

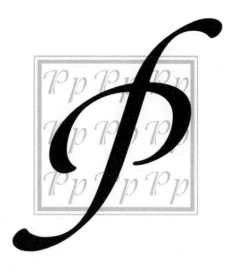

PAINT

Not the usual use, yet predictable, except that the verb is more vivid than one might expect of Air Traffic Controllers, who use *paint* to mean discover a blip on their radar screens. The idiom is oddly suggestive of transferred activity: not the distant airplane "painting" itself merely by being there, but the controller brushing it into being. The passive recipient becomes the depictor in a wholly contrary-sounding dimension, although this type of occurrence renews the old problem cited by the philosopher Bishop Berkeley, who asked if the tree falling in the empty forest made a sound. With no one in the tower, but the radar on, would the blip appear to, for once, paint itself? Such problems hardly concern controllers, or even pilots, but it is encouraging about them both as a breed that the chosen word is almost aesthetic, whereas they (controllers in the main) refer to rain as "attenuation"—it thins the blip out. A controller unable to see a plane's blip once exclaimed over the landline to a colleague, "I ain't paintin' a gumdamned thing out here!"

PANDEMONIUM

John Milton's word for the capital of Hell in *Paradise Lost* (1667). He wrote it "Pandaemonium—*all demons* in Greek—having no idea the word would from the nineteenth century on mean "uproar." So, when, as he also wrote, "All Hell broke loose," all the demons were scattered; it is the disintegration of an infernal city.

PANEGYRIC

The essence of this is public: a formal eulogy in which the praise becomes quite elaborate, part of a known routine. The source is Greek *panegurikos* from *pan* (all) + *agora* (assembly), thus embracing all assemblies or all of an assembly, at least as we understand "all," a word every bit as complex as Empson said it was. From Greek through Latin into French the word came, little modified, bringing a verb *panegyrize* and a noun *panegyrist* we may not need. The flaw in panegyrics is the homogeneous, the monotony, hardly ever varied by a toe of clay, although the American tradition of "roasting" suggests a sceptical model worth emulating on fancier occasions.

PANJANDRUM

Not exactly a tongue-twister, *panjandrum* is one of those concocted words, devised in 1755 by an English playwright and actor Samuel Foote (1720–1777) to test the memory of another actor, Charles Macklin, who had boasted he could remember and say anything said to him. Here is Foote's infliction: "And there were present the Picninnies, and the Joblillies, and the Garyulies, and the Grand Panjandrum himself, with the little round button at top." Note the trap at the end, with definite article omitted. The comedian Johnny Carson once staged such a contest with Jack Webb of *Dragnet* fame, orally stating a series of events virtually impossible to remember and horrendous to say (tongue-twisting), having to do with a burglary, but Jack Webb managed to repeat the whole thing without a slip, a chore requiring stupendous tongue—and lip—control, and a noble memory, especially at the point at which he paused to recapitulate. Our use of *panjandrum* for any officious *poohbah* (see) dates from the nineteenth century.

PANSY

One day a sensitive Frenchman saw a beautiful flower with a thoughtful face and at once named it *pensée*, from *penser*, "to think." This gave us English *pansy*. If the Frenchman had been Blaise Pascal, we might have believed it, but he was not, and this inward-looking member of the viola family has had to grow inauthentically on, at least until the 1920s, when *pansy* became the word for an effeminate gay man. Compare, however, with *pensive*, another thought-ful word of ours, from Latin *pensare*, meaning "to weigh" and also, of course, to ponder, think about.

PARAFFIN

Some words have a delightfully precise etymology, no doubt because in all the world of recorded phenomena they have nothing else to live for. *Paraffin*, devised around 1830 by the German chemist Teichenbach, adds Latin *parum* ("too little") to *affinis* ("related" or having an affinity with). *Paraffin*, in fact, is not closely related to any other known substance, which makes it almost like the Dada movement in literature. First recorded in 1838, *paraffin*, which you smell as kerosene jet fuel at all big airports or when lighting the chimney lamp if you have one, is a Garbo saturated aliphatic hydrocarbon in a series of similar substances, the simplest and most abundant of which is methane or marsh gas.

PARSE

Lawyers have resurrected this dusty relic of the grammar schools, where it meant breaking down a sentence into its component parts of speech, explaining their relation to one another. The Latin phrase for this was, is, *pars orationis*, part of speech, which means not only a piece, a chunk, of a speech, but mainly a functioning unit, like a cog, a distributor head, a spark plug, if language may be said to have such things. It does, and they are known as noun, verb, preposition, adverb, and so forth. President William Clinton famously attended to the meaning of "is," certainly as complex a word as any philosopher ever belabored, and an echo of its paragraph in *Black's Law Dictionary* (see under *is*).

PATTER

Priests have been known to rush things; indeed, one comedian has a routine that guys this habit. A dozen *paternosters* one after the other will foster gabble, which in turn creates the word *patter*, for irreverent mouthing, which in turn gives us *idle patter*, of gossip or prankishness. Often rehearsed, patter seems impromptu but only for its relative obscurity.

PAVILION

Tentlike, and on a breezy night with its side-muslins fluttering, a bit like a rectangular butterfly. Why not? Latin *papilio*, through French *papillon*, gave us this butterfly, whose cocktail-party canopy differs from the shuttered cricket pavilion seen worldwide with front steps and double changing rooms, scoreboard, and wide stable-type doors. Behind all this invention and adaptation remains the ancient Roman who saw a winged creature in a flapping tent.

PENGUIN

A mystery word, it first shows up toward the end of the sixteenth century in a reference to the "great auk." An explorer's narrative of 1582 said "The countrymen call them *Penguins* (which seemeth to be a Welsh name)," and in 1613 John Selden guessed that the word came from Welsh *pen gwyn* for "white head," but surely this reference was to the auk because the like-looking penguin has a black head.

PENICILLIN

Like so many molds, penicillin was there all the time, in the matrix of nature, waiting to be found, and found it was by accident, growing in a neglected Petri dish. The word chosen for it, suitably enough, had lingered in the lexicon since the Romans' *penicillum* (paintbrush), a diminutive of *peniculus* ("brush," itself a diminutive of *penis*). What we call penicillin attracted its name for its spore-bearing brushlike tufts of fine filaments, as a look through any electron microscope will show. *Penis*, by the way, initially meant "tail," whereas the modern idiom "a piece of tail"

refers to a female organ, although indeed "tail" remains a piece of penicillin. Time was, writing was done with a brush that resembled a tiny tail. Sometimes, as Beckett says, the mortal microcosm cannot forgive the relative immortality of the macrocosm, and gets its own back through monotony.

PIP-SQUEAK

Transferred eventually to a small or insignificant person, contemptuously said, this pungent word began as an imitative name for a small shell used by the Germans in World War One. Pip (dot) + squeak. The word has had a remarkably long life thanks to its disparaging swagger, initially intended to dismiss something lethal taken for granted.

PIROPO

How do we manage without this? An extravagant fulsome street compliment uttered in Latin America, mostly by male to female, it approximates a stroke of verbal lightning that persuades the reluctant recipient to hear further overtures. Perhaps. The *piropo* is a bit surreptitious, best done in a stage whisper, almost certainly by a benign stalker, and much more literary in its primitive way than the hardhat whistle from a high girder, emitted by someone to whom all blond girls are Helga. For example, a *piropo* might go like this: "Senora, your bosom is a hot pudding that would melt the indifference of a million men and incinerate the chastity of a hundred-year-old monk." Actually, the word itself, no kidding, is a stunner, more seductive to a word-lover than any *piropo*. It combines fire from Greek *pur* with *oops* for eye. The Greek *piropos* means fiery, golden garnet. It depends what you you want from rhetoric, as from astronomy when you stare at

Betelgeuse. The word *piropo* is worth whispering in its own right: the sound of fire, perhaps able to melt a pillar of cosmic salt.

Those with the leisure and inclination to collect *piropos*, perhaps against a pre-emptive strike by woman akin to the one in Aristophanes's *Lysistrata*, can do worse than consult Professor Alan Dundes's *Parsing through Customs*, essays on folklore from a psychoanalytic point of view, best of all "The Piropo and the Dual Image of Women in the Spanish-speaking World" (with Marcelo M. Suárez-Orozco). We learn from Pitt-Rivers, the anthropologist for whom an Oxford University museum was named, that the word *piropo* means "ruby" and has a similar effect, at least in Andalusia, while Gómez Tabanera says a *piropo* is like a flaming dart a man throws in a state of suspenseful spasm. *Piropeadores*, as such throwers are called, are not always polite or flattering: their inflamed lust has a component of shame and loathing and their *piropos* may express a collectively held male fantasy about women. A note from the sixteenth century says "Beautiful women suffer from the fact that they cannot set foot in the streets without hearing thousands of low words and dishonest signs from thousands of low people, which must sadden and sicken them, if they are virtuous." Now as then, of course. On the other hand, Alan Dundes observes that "In Latin America, women often feel that visiting North American men are inattentive, cold, or unable to praise a woman's beauty, since U.S. men are unfamiliar with the *piropo* tradition."

Some piropos are rather obvious and callow: "Don't get too close to me, I don't have fire insurance," although sometimes embellished with distracting allusion: "Beauty? Michelangelo next to your father is nothing, because I am sure he never in his life made a sculpture as perfect as you." Bolder spirits, with no doubt worse erotic pasts, get a little more candid (or candied): "I would really like to be the tile you step on so I could see your thing." Such imagery is hardly the prelude to an approach by either, exacting from the female retorts either *sinverguenza* (shameless), *atrevido* (bold), or *insolente* (insolent). Such a *piropo* is unlikely to shame a woman into being the walking vagina who accosts the man and humiliates him into non-performance. The following Chaucerian accost comes from Cuba and has to do with pubic hair: "Why don't you show me Fidel's?" This one hails from Buenos Aires: "Don't you want to be the mustard for my hot dog?" Many *piropos* bleat about life with wife or mother, mother-in-law, at the same time extolling the bosom, lauding the *piropeador*'s "sentry" or "flute." Those who go farther afield call "*Como te romperia el culo!*" At least in Buenos Aires they do ("Let me fuck you in the ass"). Some get into biting ("*morderte la conchita*") and many attempt degradation, punning on such a word as *culo*, that means both buttocks and "ugly woman." A *piropo* from Uruguay, addressed to two women walking side by side, yearn-hates to be "the male in the middle." Many *piropos* uttered by a man in a group never reach the women, but the men laugh at the lewd insult, thus reinforcing their so-called manliness. Latin American women feel ambivalent about the *piropo*: fire, purity, regard, milk-bar, sentry, hot dog, flute, the usual male trappings, themselves caught between the cult of virginity and chastity and the male hunger for harlots. Such stresses on both sexes are not unique, but they are more on the surface in Latin America, if only you can overhear the *piropos*, whether you are a woman or an anthropologist.

PLACENTA

A "flat cake," this, of the seventeenth century, from Greek *plakoenta*, accusative form of *plakoeis*, based on *plax* (flat). The phrase *placenta uterina*, "uterine cake," denoting the afterbirth, pays homage to its shape and may be a small joke.

PLIMSOLL LINE

Not a shipping line, but a line painted on ships, the brainchild of British politician and social reformer Sir Samuel Plimsoll (1824–1898), one of those who devised the Merchant Shipping Act of 1876. The line painted on the ship's hull indicated the limits of safe loading. A brand of gym shoes took the line's name and became *plimsolls* after the line running around their rubber welt. Many a child developed *folie de grandeur* at the very thought of chasing around with a safely loaded ocean liner on each foot.

POACH

Both *poaches* go back to the Old French verb *pocher*, "to put in a bag." When you steal something, you pocket it (French *poche* means pocket), and when you poach an egg you trap it in a pocket or bag, so to speak, that enables the white to enclose the yolk in coagulation. You thus *pouch* the egg. This symmetrical, quaint word sends out feelers in all directions, reaching *pock* (plural pox) and pucker, never shifting far from its origin, Frankish *pokka* for bag. It has nothing to do with the *pukka* (correct) in the expression from the British Raj, *pukka sahbib*, for "decent chap."

POBBLE

Singularly affected or precious mode of speech devised at certain British public schools to enable its practitioners to hold forth at length impressively in the absence of any knowledge or discrimination. The sound is that of a bloated, swift gobble, the mouth aimed downward and the tongue thrust forward with its tip lolling just behind the rounded lips. The ideal effect is that of a polysyllabic rumble in which not a single word, beyond an occasional "very" or "wholly," remains identifiable, even though the overall effect is one of stultifying learnedness. Dons with thick Middle European accents did this best, or do; the best I ever heard was Sir Isaiah Berlin, whose dinner conversation was a triumph of erudite phonemes, the scholarship in his case indubitable but its actual presentation, in a series of gargling polyphonic overtures, a bravura barricade. Once a pobbler, always one; it amounts almost to a speech impediment and may always, of course, be complemented by a pipe, a full mouth, ill-fitted dentures, and an utter indifference to the listener comparable to that of Evelyn Waugh's reversed ear trumpet. Quaintly enough, Berlin attended St. Paul's School in Chiswick, London, which doesn't pobble; so clearly he contracted it from a later ethos.

POET

Nothing to do with the arts, this is the Navy's name for a tiny airborne, 1 x 5 inch, expendable jammer that, dropped from a plane, disrupts the signalling system of the aircraft into whose airspace the *Poet* has entered. Since 1986 the U.S. Navy has made 300,000 *Poets*, or seventy daily for twelve years. A similar contraption called FLYRT, for Flying Radar Transmitter, can be launched from a ship. It would be edifying to see the government invest in three hundred thousand real, flesh-and-blood, poets, and never mind whose signalling system they disrupt.

POET

This one deserves to be on its own since its hypothetical Indo-European source is so vivid. Indo-European is not a real language, but scholars have created it from a pattern of inevitabilities found in other languages and worked backward through parallel and word-building, in this instance conjuring up *wekwom-teks*, which means the speech-weaver of texts or songs. We are not far here from epic voice, in *wekwom*, or, in *teks*, from technology, technique, tectonic, and architect. Logic and sensitivity have virtually proved that Indo-Europeans had compound nouns for the way a pious son keeps an aged parent warm, and, probably from Homer and the Rig-Veda, imperishable fame (*klewos ngwzhitom*), strong and holy mind (*is rom menos*), and, noblest of all, the Indo-European poet, the wordsmith weaver, revered in prehistoric Eurasia.

POETRY

An old Aramaic saying claims the word poetry is the sound of water rippling over pebbles, which is perhaps a romantic notion. The poet Rilke said that all things are ripe for poetry, which no doubt includes toothbrushes and pimples. Another view, taken by many dictionaries, is that poetry is what is creative, from the Greek *poiein* (to make), and this is the source of the synonym "maker" for poet. One study of the poet e.e. cummings is entitled *The Magic Maker*. One can see that, if poetry is the most special form of literature, perhaps the most refined and profound, then there is something to be said for sheltering it behind some grandiose epitome such as water rippling over pebbles. It has never yet been dubbed anything like what someone said about the harpsichord, heaven help it: skeletons copulating on a tin roof. There still exists this defensive, protective view of poetry as almost too exquisite for this world, perhaps instigated by poets themselves, more probably by naive readers or bad poets on the prowl. It is interesting to discover that, at writers' colonies, those airy-fairy poets are the ones who get up with the lark and the novelists, who have a daily quota of pages to do, lie abed until noon. The old question, of whether or not certain passages of prose are just as intense, concise, and lyrical as the best poems has never been answered. W. B. Yeats made his choice explicit when selecting Walter Pater's elegant essay on the Mona Lisa as the first entry in his *Oxford Book of Modern Verse 1892-1935* (1936), setting the prose as verse. The result remains startling and suggestive, and one might go farther with the idea, citing Proust and Virginia Woolf, Faulkner and Nabokov, Beckett and Durrell as frequently "poetic" authors. "Only by printing it in *vers libre*," Yeats wrote of Pater's famous passage, "can one show its revolutionary importance. Pater was accustomed to give each sentence a separate page of manuscript, isolating and analysing its rhythm...."

It is worthwhile testing Yeats's Pater (almost like Busoni's Bach) against even the best of Yeats, and asking the usual questions about intensity, originality, cogent phrasemaking, pithy universality, symbolic power. There is no need to make a case for Yeats, but for the following something like respect:

> She is older than the rocks among which she sits;
> like the Vampire, she has been dead many times,
> and learned the secrets of the grave; and has been
> a diver in deep seas, and keeps their fallen day
> about her; and trafficked for strange webs
> with Eastern merchants....

And, if so, what of this?

> She is older than the rocks among which she sits;
> Like the Vampire,
> She has been dead many times,
> And learned the secrets of the grave;
> And has been a diver in deep seas,

And keeps their fallen day about her;
And trafficked for strange webs with Eastern merchants....

In this context it is instructive to remember that poets usually abhor what they consider poetic novels. This bard-in-the manger attitude, which most novelists run into, also spawns the prosaic and commonplace novels written by poets, who keep their best stuff for their poems. One can only deplore a pawnbroking attitude to the novel, or to non-fiction (remembering, say, Carlyle, De Quincey, Ruskin, Pater). A reasonable reader might well decide the difference between poetry and prose, granted equal intensity, is a matter of typography and scansion, syllable-counting and hieratic attitudinizing. *Poiein*'s reach covers several arts, and may simply denote virtuosic acts from the depths of one's being, whatever the art in question. There is versifying and there is poetry; there is, in vast bulk, mercantile and crass fiction all over the landscape, and there is literary fiction designed not to make money but to be beautiful (a harder word to tie down than poetry). Even as a term of abuse, *poesy* has no currency these days, and *poetastry*, sounding almost as archaic, gets rarely said. Poetry cranked out to order or for inferior reasons will always get its comeuppance, but mediocre fiction has no word, whereas cranked-out music, thanks to Paul Hindemith, does. His coinage, *Gebrauchmusik*, by which he meant functional music intended for mass consumption, might well be transferred to novels, at least as a loan word. *Gebrauch*-fiction, revered these days by MBAs who wouldn't know Proustian prose if it bit them in the tail, is too much with us, and one wonders what has happened to all those readers who studied literature in college and made dutiful obeisance to it. Not all the best fiction is poetic, not by any means (Swift, Orwell, Tolstoy, Kafka, Dostoyevsky), but it is surely creative; is not *Gulliver's Travels* as creative as *The Rape of the Lock*? Some fiction is structurally creative, some texturally so, and we should heed such differences, grateful that we have a word to span the disciplines and modes with, that honors, say, Faulkner's *Absalom, Absalom!* along with Mahler's *Resurrection* Symphony, Nabokov's *Speak, Memory,* Alexander Calder's mobiles, and Wallace Stevens's *Harmonium.*

POINSETTIA

Sometimes it doesn't take much (Teddy Roosevelt and teddy bears, minimum; Wrong-Way Corrigan, rather more), and sometimes only a flower. Imagine you are the Honorable Joel Roberts Poinsett of Charleston, South Carolina, statesman, author, congressman, expert on military science, Secretary of War in President Van Buren's cabinet, and Union leader in the Civil War, but you come alive as an icon only when you go off to Mexico on special appointment and there fall for the huge, flamboyant blooms we know only too well. Bringing them home, he gave us *poinsettia.* Can be made smaller for interior placing with chemical dwarfing compounds, or by drenching the soil.

POMMY

Australian slang for a recently arrived Brit, or for a Brit in general, derived from the POHM legend imprinted on the backs of the shirts worn by prisoners being transported to Australia. The legend (a gerund, see, meaning "must be read") meant "Prisoner Of Her/His Majesty." Brits thus referred to, even nonprisoners, tend to take offense at this word for its evocation of apple or Pomeranian, resenting it even more than "Limey," patronizing allusion to the limes consumed aboard old sailing ships to prevent scurvy.

PAUL WEST

POOHBAH

Late 1800s, from Gilbert and Sullivan's *The Mikado*, meaning big shot or honcho, the name probably a combination of two words: one for contempt, the other for defiance. Seen thus, it has an antique ring, like Aladdin, but the complete word has something timelessly authoritative about it.

POONTANG

From many years of engrossed reading experience, I vote this the most frequent graffito word on campus U.S.A. Perhaps it appeals to graffitists as sounding foreign, a blend of *Poona* and Chinese *tong*, but that may be merely wishful thinking from a copyist. To limit the word to black woman seen as a piece of sexual meat is to miss the widening out of the term to denote all women as such. French *putain*, prostitute, has clearly been at work here, but Eric Partridge cites Chinese *poong tai* and *poong kai*, which is a long way from New Orleans Creole. Somehow from the word there emerges revulsion at the female organ, such as one finds in the novels of French author Pascal Quignard; the *poo* of bad smell accompanies the mordant flavor of *tang*. It would be interesting to know if women have fought back with a comparable term of repudiation for the male organ, which is neither nosegay nor Charlotte Russe. I doubt it. The word is common among gays for sexual relations (see *The Lavender Lexicon*). One can only wonder, on the basis of copulation with a colored woman, if *poon* was not at some time *coon*. Certain cunning linguists have been known to acquire a poon-twang.

Deep in the late-nite annals of American bedroom humor, TV host Johnny Carson's guest Zsa-Zsa Gabor, who has brought her cat with her, asks him "Would you like to stroke my pussy?" He answers, "Yes, but only if you get that damned cat off your lap." This detonation is perhaps the best wit an overworked word has yet produced. Obviously we needed another word for vulva or vagina, other than what some call the c-word. It tends to be slang for *woman* but never half so vivid as the related idioms *eatin' stuff* and *table grade*. The pungency and concision of American slang rebukes without even trying attempts by German linguists to remove a thousand words from their lexicon (1998), purging portmanteau compounds from the language, yet describing the proposal in a pamphlet with a many-syllable title. Imagine a German pamphlet called *Table Grade*.

It is to the stand-up comedian Kathy Griffin, she of the erotic gurgling squeal and scabrous candor, that we owe the latest mutation of *pussy*: "pussau," which my spontaneous mind construes more as in Oberammergau or Breslau than as in Hangchow or Golden Bough. It's almost an offensive shriek, no doubt on the brink of becoming a primitive warning or an indignant exclamation after a groper, having done his best, prepares to do his worst. I think too it confers on pussy a way of re-entering polite intercourse (i.e., speech) because it sounds like an old bone a German archeologist has unearthed at some lugubrious crossroads in Bavaria, or indeed like the crossroads itself: Pussau, 7 km. It has already entered our by no means pure idiom as an outcry of sometimes joyful nonsense. Here comes a lovely sunny day. *Pussau!*

POOP

Fits in too many places all at once and patently needed, either for *poop sheet* (its data akin to the *gen* of the RAF) or for being tuckered out, which, in the Royal Navy, was when a ship has taken a wave over the stern (i.e., the poop) and resumes with its rear end dragging from the weight of water. That poop comes from Latin *puppis*, meaning *hull*.

Poop is also a euphemism devised mainly for children, suggestive to them of something that has popped out bidden or unbidden with a p on its end or not: poop or poo. Perhaps the word's use to denote an old person charitably (an old poop) unites the ship's low stern with the usedness of used matter. The word's sound (*poupen* = toot) is an effective clincher, suggesting an enfeebled warning horn. All these meanings come together if you wipe your rear on a poop sheet and walk with lowered stern as if defecating. Perhaps they should be kept apart to forestall offense.

POPINJAY

One of the standbys of educated reproof, *popinjay* goes back to Arabic *babgha*, which made its way through medieval French into Middle English (*papejay, papengay*) as a word for parrot or, in heraldry, parrot or parakeet depicted in green with red legs and beak, and by extension any human overdressed, fulsomely posturing, or given to "senseless volubility." If, as late as the end of the sixteenth century, you wished to indulge in *popinjay* shooting, you fired your arrows at a live parrot tethered atop a pole. Thereafter, the parrot was a fake made of feathers on a frame, with cock, hens, and chicks all to be aimed at from directly underneath at the mast's base. From all this, one deduces the intended fate for any vain, supercilious person: impaled, like one of Vlad's victims, from beneath, whereas Vladimir the Impaler catches them in the front.

POPPYCOCK

A mild-sounding word for humbug or senseless prattle, it has less than mild concepts buried within it, mainly from Dutch (*pappekak*, soft dung) and Middle Dutch (*pap*, for soft food or pap, maybe regurgitated by the father—*pappa*, who personifies food. Hence *pappa-kak* or father-dung, from *kakken*, to defecate, inheriting from Latin *cacare*. *Poppycock* survives as a gentle rebuke, but etymologically damns anyone talking shit.

PORCELAIN

When we sit down to dinner in a swanky restaurant, we perhaps do not realize that the delicate, exquisitely shiny plates we eat from—the porcelain, if we're lucky—have a tricky alias. Delicate, exquisite? It's from the word for a sow's vulva, which the cowry shell supposedly resembles. Who, one wonders, did the fieldwork, spanning farm and kiln? Odd, here, to find almost spurious delicacy mired in pigtracks. There's a vibrant contrast between the hoarse animal and the coral finesse of its internal organs. Perhaps a misplaced fit of gentility happened among all those pig farmers, or a moment of crudity took over a suave designer. The pig's vulva and the cowry (once a unit of currency) have the same translucent sheen, earning perhaps the mellifluous sound of *porcellana* (little sow), easily silkier than *porca* (sow). This is an imported French-Italian discrimination, making one wonder if we have not somehow missed delicate renderings of the foal's mouth or the lamb's backside. Some may find this collision of qualities a little coarse; I prefer to marvel at the fastidious observership that once in a less purblind era attended without prejudice to the private parts of barnyard animals, and snapped up a shell-like gloss wherever it shone.

POSH

In our ears since the beginning of the century, it's one of those words that has become known for not being that well known, and then suddenly they bloom with guidance from a new quarter. *Posh* comes from different sources according to different sleuths, either *posh* (money) from the mid-nineteenth century or *pash*, which was Romany for a half-penny, either from the mid-nineteenth-century word for dandy, or from twentieth-century Cambridge slang: *poosh* for stylish or polished (maybe even this last slurred). The most persuasive because most structured explanation is the acronym for "Port *out*, starboard *home*," a formula for choosing which side of a ship to sail on when going out to India from Britain and returning. Just keep to the north when sailing west-east and east-west. It makes sense, and people even decide their seating in this on transatlantic planes. It still means luxurious, chic, fancy, cozy, swanky, what used to be called "boss" or "keen." Nowadays you would say "posh rules," as it always did.

POSSLQ

Census-speak for Person of Opposite Sex Same Living Quarters (*pssslq* for Person of Same Sex Same Living Quarters). As if it mattered. These acronyms invade us and, perhaps through a phonetic trick inherited from Arabic or Hebrew, while briefly sending the mind blank stimulate it to provide vowel sounds to help us out. Thus, we say *posselcue* or *pisselcue*, remembering perhaps how, in Arabic and Hebrew, the consonantal combination *ktp* or *ktb* provides the spine for the words denoting book, bookstore, and other bookish things. In the same way, what was at first thought the unsayable prefix for books, ISBN, has now matured into *Isbin*, felicitously a pseudo-word combining two bits of the verb *to be*. There is even a guitarist with the same surname. If we become as resourceful as we should, tuning in to the merest hint of sense, adroitly exploiting every twinkle of sayable space, we will soon be dab hands with acronyms, letter jumbles we fill up as they arrive upon us, defying whatever they are supposed to abbreviate in favor of something juicier. ISBN will not mean International Serial Book Number, or some like flummery, but I Swab Blue Noses. American slang will make hay of all of this sooner or later, as ever.

POSTAL

The phenomenon of postal employees going berserk at the office for some real or imagined slight and killing fellow-workers certainly deserves a phrase of its own. Will accountants, Federal Express people, car washers, and waiters eventually follow suit? Part of the irony implicit here is that the sorting and delivery of mail has to it something sedate and cozy, almost a continual hangover from Christmas, so we do not expect violence, least of all from those considered the most introverted of workers. Now, of course, "going postal" is not restricted to postal employees only; the phrase will no doubt stick, but the range of rage will widen. Candidly, one would expect the post office's customers to display a little rage themselves, when the mail gets delivered later and later, misdelivered to streets a mile away, and we have to obey those weird orders given the post office by the FAA about packages weighing more than sixteen ounces. Try to send any packet abroad and prepare to fill out all kinds of forms, even to send a book. The post office is a private concern; so is its paranoia. I for one associate the post office with that quietest of hobbies, stamp-collecting, when you moisten hinges and site the stamp between the dotted lines, handling it with tweezers. Why has our postal service become unhinged? Surely not because Latin *postum*, "placed," described relay riders who sped the mails from "post to post" with wrists uncut. The very idea of mail traveling at speed calls up its opposite, the newly devised phrase "snail mail," which is what has perhaps unhinged postal workers. Compared with the other mails, such as "e" and facsimile, not to mention various express services, the humble snail can only charge more and dream thoughts of ending it all. When the letter has almost the instantaneity of thought, mail becomes no longer mail, but the blatant trudge, designed for letters we hope will never arrive.

POULTICE

You have a boil, and you are little. It is the old days, when Mother told you to be brave (you affronted by such pain coming from the font of bliss), and crammed a soft sludge of bread, meal, or clay, heated wrapped in a bandage or cloth, against the offending area. Such agony for a mere boil. Also called *cataplasm*, which sounds like the collapse of all your plasma. Medieval Latin gave us *pultes*, for pulp or thick paste, a plural actually taken for a singular: *pultes*—*poultice*, meaning *pap*, possibly from Greek *poltos*, meaning of all things *porridge*. It was hot porridge that killed boils. Mother with tears in her eyes, and sometimes, if the deed was a success, pus in her face for her efforts while the child howled. Now there is *Boilease*, which seems to direct the infection back into the body, like a traffic cop enforcing a U-turn, to try elsewhere. The smell of the brown ointment is almost as bad as the poultice's burn.

PREMARIN

That absorbing but inconsistent compilation of drug manufacturers' handouts, *The Physician's Desk Reference*, offers a lengthy presentation of this drug but nowhere explains that its name comes from *Pregnant Mare Urine*, which indeed is the source of this particular estrogen replacement drug. The other drugs Premp-Pro, PremPhase, and Prempac-C also come from the same supply—mares factory-farmed in North Dakota and remotest Alberta, Manitoba, and Saskatchewan. Only the manufacturer, Wyeth-Ayerst, oversees this industry, but much agitated propaganda comments on it, drawing attention to the brutal conditions pregnant mares have to endure, tied up tightly in tiny stalls, obliged to sleep on cold concrete. The horses spend eleven months in their urine-collection harness, sometimes standing in their own feces, with swollen legs from so much standing. Sores oozing with pus go untreated lest the treatment spoil the urine, and, when the horses get ornery, as one farmer reported, a pop on the nose with a shovel calms them down. The rubber cups attached to the mares' urethras have to be held in place by straps, which chafe both legs and belly. Doctors have claimed that premarin should be taken only by women whose normal diet is hay, and certain bumper stickers read "Say neigh to Premarin." Can women be saved only by the humiliation of horses? Swift's rational horses, the Houyhnhnms, would have had much to say about this.

PRICK

Of obscure origin, this word from Low German (compare Dutch *prik*) comes from the sixteenth century, when women used it as an intimate endearment, a habit some people damned: "One word alone hath troubled some, because the immodest maid soothing the young man, calls him her Prick. He who cannot away with this, instead of 'my Prick,' let him write 'my Sweetheart'" (*Colloquies of Erasmus*, 1671). The diminutive is *Prickle*, as little used as the Small condom in Japan. Prick is also used to refer to a detestable person.

PROSE

Once upon a time, "straightforward discourse," which is what some killjoys would still like it to be. The etymology is prosaic, from *provertere* (Latin for "turn forward"), *proversus*, and *prosus* ("direct"). Here we have the source of *verse* and *version*, but not of *prosody*, which has no link with *prose*; Greek *prosoidia* was originally "singing with instrumental backing." Caesar would have appreciated this definition; Cicero probably not, and Petronius not at all.

PROVENCE

Region of southeastern France, on the Mediterranean between the Rhône and Italy, it was Rome's first province in Gaul (a land outside Italy conquered by the Romans but administered by them as a self-contained unit). Latin *provincia* gave French its *province* and Middle English its *provyne*. We can see how the French *e* somewhat mitigated the idea of being a conquered province. Alas that Provence did not, like Soloi, a province of Cilicia (in Greece), supply its conquerors with a badly needed word. The Greek colonists in Soloi evolved a Greek dialect of their own, which so shocked visiting Athenians that they coined the word *soloikismos* for it; the Romans turned it into *soloecismus*, from which English *solecism* developed as a rebuke to provincial uncouthness. No *Provençalisms* so far.

PRUDE

Insistently prim, easily shocked, the prude owes everything to *proud*, once upon a time the same word. *Prude* was clipped from Old French *prudefemme*, meaning a good and honorable woman, but *prude* has long since declined into something critical and narrow. Oddly enough, the nobility of *proud* has survived metaphorically in the phrase *proud flesh*, which denotes the swollen flesh around a healing wound due to granulation tissue (good, gallant, brave), justifiably satisfied with itself and its post-traumatic performance. Uninvolved with surgery, we tend to use *proud* for constrained self-respect.

PTARMIGAN

Sometimes pretentious people get out of their depth, as with this borrowing from Scottish Gaelic *tarmachan*. The *pt* is ignorant embellishment by half-educated people who messed with the word in the seventeenth century, wrongly thinking that the Greek word for wing, *pteron* (compare *pterodactyl*) had some bearing on this chubby, feather-footed type of grouse.

PTOMAINE

Take the Greek verb *piptein*, to fall, and exemplify for yourself a human body that has fallen. If you are an early Italian chemist with a knack for naming, you will call this fallen body *ptomaina*, from the Greek word *ptoma*, corpse. The chemist was intent upon poisons taken from a corpse, and so named pieces of a corpse with his word for decomposing flesh. The interesting thing here is the way the Greeks associated falling with death, surely a rather narrow link.

PUDDING

Botulism is the clue here, derived from Vulgar Latin *botellinus*, a diminutive of *botellus*, meaning "sausage." All puddings once were sausages, which is to say concoctions encased in the fresh-washed intestines or stomachs of butchered animals. Any food cooked in a bag qualified as a pudding (its shape that of the cannonball Christmas pudding). Savory or sweet, it made no difference. As a child I watched at my grandfather's butcher's shop when they fastened one end of a pig's intestines to the tap and flushed the contents away; it was a rough cleansing to be sure, especially when the next filler was one of ground pork. In our own century, pudding came to mean dessert or the sweet portion of the meal, sweeter than steak and kidney pie or shepherd's, for instance. To the English, all dessert is "pudding" in spite of the word's other links, with Yorkshire Pudding, Black Pudding (fat sausage gleaming with olive oil), and Blood Pudding. In my schooldays, the local tripe shop displayed in its window, on shelves of scrubbed white tile, the stomach and intestines ("rops" or ropes) otherwise used for sausages or puddings ("puds") while *bowel* evolved from, of all words, *botellinus*, for which the toxins of botulism were named. I came full circle with a misprinted menu in Jamaica, at the Upper Deck, that read "bowel of salad" (another casing) and promised steaks "barbecued to your own likeness."

PUMPERNICKEL

The world is far from short of people who excel at imitating a fart, and who take great joy in the performance; but there are few words that do this imitation. One is pumpernickel, the sour dark bread of coarse texture, made from rye. The German word comes from New High German *Pumpern*, imitative of the sound plus *Nickel*, or devil, demon, or dwarf, related to yet another German word, *Nix*, meaning sprite. The devil in the bread owes his presence to its supposed indigestibility. Behold the wind machine, runner-up to beans.

PUN

It is not enough to be told that pun comes from *pandigrion*, a late seventeenth-century and early eighteenth-century word meaning *quibble*. Did *pandigrion* slink toward us from Italian *puntiglio* (source of *punctilious*) for "point scored" and quibble? We need to remember that a pun stops time, introducing into the neat Mercator of well-designed lives a clash of criteria. Take one pun that has not yet made its way to the Rialto: "What did Sindbad hear when he said *Open Sesame*? Sindbadinage." Or: "When the Lone Ranger caught cancer, what did his hatchet-throwing side-kick say? *Chemo sabe*." Conflation, the cat eating its own tail, fusion, world made smaller (Borges said you halved the population when you broke all the mirrors): these characterize the aftermath of a pun's being uttered. This is the anomie of which G. S. Kirk speaks in his book on Greek tragedy, when disorder takes over and we crouch, or hunch, emitting that familiar groan of knowledge denied. The groan tells all. You have wounded the company in its most secret heart; they thought all along that language was law-abiding, though numerous homonyms and homophones should have warned them. The pun is a kind of atomic bombardment in which the words survive while the listener's expectations go begging, and his/her intelligence receives a salutary jolt.

PUNKAWALLAH

One of my dictionaries reveals the *punkawallah* in all his glory without identifying him as such, in fact calling him a "servant," which he is. He tugs a cord connected to a fan made of palm frond or cloth hung from the ceiling, and so functions as a human air conditioner, wafting all beneath the *punka* with air whose motion cools. There are tea *wallahs*, and laundry *wallahs*,

PAUL WEST

of course; a *wallah* is a man, a fellow, a chap, closely identified with his trade, but the *punkawallah* can sit down on a comfy rug while plying his arms to a regular rhythm, cooling himself as well as others. He seems almost the epitome of perpetual motion, provided he survives. Hindi *pankha* provides the color in this word, drawing on Sanskrit *paksaka*, fan, from *paksa*, shoulder or wing. In a sense he is flapping his own wing. Old colonial types, returned from India after Independence, can still be heard calling someone, usually of low social status, a *wallah*, when they mean something censorious such as bad egg, scoundrel, cad, ruffian, lazybones. The punkawallah's is a noble trade, a vision of the human as machine.

PUTTY

Not to be confused with soldier's leggings, *puttees*, in World War One, this is a seventeenth-century substance from French *potée* (contents of a pot) and *pot* (pot). It became the term for a powder made from heated tin by jewelers, used to polish with, and a cement made from lime and water, made in a pot and used as a top coat on plaster. Most famous, since the eighteenth century, as a seal on window panes. Windowframer's playdough made from whiting and linseed oil.

QUARK

When the American physicist Murray Gell-Mann discovered a certain particle, he at first thought of calling it *quork*, but then switched to *quark*, a word he'd found in James Joyce's *Finnegans Wake* (1939). Charmed quarks have followed, based on nothing literary at all. The word rhymes not with Ark but with cork. In England, *Quark* is a brand of softened cream cheese.

Those who wish to push farther into quarkdom will find that, much as protons and neutrons compose atomic nuclei, so do quarks make up protons and electrons, and indeed all particles that interact through the strong force, that holds the nucleus together. Quarks have mass and spin, and defy Wolfgang Pauli's exclusion principle: no two particles having half-integral spin can exist in the same state. Quarks have no evident structure and cannot be resolved into anything smaller, though they have generated much banal-looking verbiage. Quarks are compulsively social and cannot be found alone. Gell-Mann's model posited "flavors" of quarks: up, down, and strange, a narrow range of metaphorical suggestion bypassing physical reality (sometimes two or three identical quarks in mesons or baryons have to be in the same quantum state).

Not only that: Quarks cannot be stripped away from the

structures they make up. They behave as though they are free, but something tribal or familial holds them back, and this is the gluon, acquisition or loss of which changes a quark's metaphorical color. The gluon is also the force that binds: The more you try to pull a quark away from its fellows, the stronger becomes the force that binds them together. The quark's abortive motion creates an energy that gluons feed on to create other gluons. While quarks are close together, gluons are weak, and quarks seem about able to get away from one another; but, as the quarks draw farther and farther apart, the gluons get stronger, and the more gluons there are, being swapped about by quarks, the stronger the sheepdog-gluon force. Thus, the more energy that is expended to free a quark, the stronger becomes its bond with its siblings, both quarks and antiquarks. There appears to be no way of isolating a quark, except by language and the purloining of semi-lyrical terms such as "charm" and "bottom" which give the illusion of something explained. Pursuit has now begun of a "top" quark for which nature has allotted a space in its theoretical scheme. Sometimes scientists' cult of whimsical but abstract categories recalls Empson's quasi-mathematical review of complex words. The truth is that, at some point, only a mind can complete reality, and the bit that completes stays mental.

QUINSY

In my childhood, I would hear black-faced miners coming home from shift in their wooden clogs, apologizing to one another for the frailness of their voices—a hoarseness fronting for silicosis, and what we might nowadays call a Mafia voice, high-pitched and dreary. The standard explanation, given with a cough and spit, was "It's me quinsies, duck." Little did they know they were speaking the Greek for "sore throat," from *kunagkhe* (*kuon* + *agkhein*), the word for dog-strangling (dog + strangle). Actually, this word for strangling isn't far removed from *anankhe*, the word for fate that told even the gods what to do. Unless you have a sore throat, *kunagkhe* might be hard to say without another *n*. Gasping dogs preceded gasping humans, though if the Greeks used asbestos as a table napkin I cannot see why. So we get, via medieval Latin *quinancia* and Old French *quinencie*, a word hardly ever used nowadays. One wonders why doctors, who use *coryza* for common cold, have shyed away from *quinsy* for sore throat, at least in the last and present centuries. *Kuon*, by the way, is an eligible sibling of *hound* and *cynic* (a philosopher originally called *kunikos* for his canine sneering or snarling). Some prefer a more prosaic explanation, involving the *Kunosarqe*, Antisthenes's gymnasium or lecture hall.

QUISLING

Vidkun Quisling, leader of the Norwegian fascist party from 1933; his real name was Abraham Lauritz Jonsson. When the Nazis invaded Norway in 1940, he joined forces with them, and in 1942 Hitler installed him as premier. Quisling-Jonsson was shot in 1945 as a traitor, bequeathing to our language his alias as a generic term.

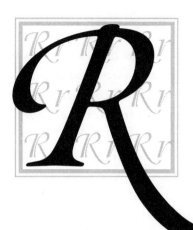

RASPBERRY

Little is known beyond the word's origin in Anglo-Latin *raspes,*
raspis, from the thirteenth century. Four hundred years later,
rasp- acquired *berry.* There seems no doubt, however, that the
raspy element encouraged the devisers of rhyming slang to come
up with *raspberry tart* for an impolite noise made by blowing.
Since then, a raspberry has come into its own, its unsaid complement an echo of the taboo word "fart." The rasping sound
abides, even in the verb *razz,* meaning to tease with such a
noise, once likened to the "the rending of glazed calico." This is
the Bronx Cheer, of course, from a much less rich word-hoard
than Cockney rhyming slang, home of "I should cocoa" (I
should say so), "apples and pears" (stairs), and "Gawd forbids"
(kids). The essence of that slang is stealth, either to outwit the
police or merely to savor the delights of certain privacy, the bliss
of the surreptitious. It is amusing to hear a *raspberry tart* from the
pursed lips of the most secretive people in London town. It almost reads like fastidious delicacy.

REMORSE

This used to be called the "ageynbite of inwit," or the bite-back of conscience, matching Latin *remordeo* exactly: *re* (again or back) + *mordeo* (to bite, as in *mordant*). The past participle of *remordeo* is *remorsus*. The pioneer phrase in French was *remors de conscience* (the rebite of conscience), which fifteenth-century English began to shorten to just *remorse*, which signified the whole process.

RESOUND

Resound is nowhere to be found, but its fussier cousin *resonate* is everywhere. How can a sane society lose the exquisite burden of re-sound, with "s" softened from the "z" sound? To sound again is bliss, to resonate sounds like glue. Can resin be far behind when bureaucrats or yuppies abolish a simple, profound word such as this? Not that long ago, *yes* or *agree* tended to become *homologate*, which was even stupider. Perhaps this is the language of senators and congressmen, elected not to do anything but to wind a thick sludge around their magic and thus install them in indefinable sinecure for life. *Sinecure*, by the way, used to mean an ecclesiastical position without "*cura*," "care," of souls—looking after the spiritual welfare of nobody at all. Pay without work.

RETROTORT

A game attempt by Bernard Cooper to render in tart English the French idea of *l'esprit d'escalier* (the spirit of the staircase), in other words a smart retort that occurs to us too late, as we are going down the stairs after the party is over. Cooper defines his word as "an ideal remark that comes to mind hours, days, or weeks too late." That is stretching the French idea a bit, not so much *d'escalier* as *pensée de passé*, a thought of the past. Cooper's example goes as follows: "That afternoon, a retrotort occurred to Jim; when Natalie had asked him what he wanted for breakfast, he should have said, 'You, on toast.'" Yes, but the nub of the French idea is the torment you feel at being slow in repartee. You want to have told the intransigent Nazi who without distinction calls everyone a communist, "You're just a Narzi old potbelly calling the kettle Red."

RHESUS

Behind *rhesus* looms Rhesus, king of Thrace, who came to help Priam, but, in the very night after he arrived at Troy, was surprised by Diomedes and Odysseus, the former of whom clobbered him, together with a dozen of his companions, while Odysseus took off with his swift horses of famous whiteness. It had been prophesied that, if these horses fed on Trojan fodder, or drank of the Xanthus, Troy would not fall. Now, these things being so, why had his parents called him Rhesus? Son of Eioneus, a Thracian river, and one of the Muses. A lively idea, but not much help there. One phony etymology tells us that *Rhesus* means a leader who will take divine predictions (*hai-res-ei*), but that is "pure desperation," says Emeritus Professor of Classics at Irvine, Brian Reardon. Now, the Greeks didn't name their kings after nothing, or give them meaningless names. Kreon, for example, means "royal" and Oedipus "swell-foot." We have to do with the naming of a child, of course, but *Rhesus* or *Rhesos* tells us nothing at all, nor does Euripides's play *Rhesus* about the Troy episode also recounted in *The Iliad*. If there is a meaning to the name, it has evaporated.

Why does this matter? Because at some point scientists

named a monkey (and a type of blood) for this king. The dictionaries either funk this altogether or use the word "arbitrary." Well, are twentieth-century scientists any less arbitrary than Athenian Greeks? As well call a type of giraffe Clytemnestra or a goat Antigone. Was this a case of lucky dip, with scientists wearied of names that make *some* kind of sense? One doubts it very much after some of the examples here recited: *Warfarin*, *Premarin*, et cetera. Why is there a mystery? Why has no one set down a brief scientific statement to the effect that they were looking for a nonsense word? If *Rhesus* means nothing in Greek, as Professor Reardon says, why call a king that, or a monkey later on? Is this one way of saying that the *rhesus* monkey, or *rhesus* blood, is so enigmatic and inexplicable that only a nonsense word fits? Perhaps history is coming full circle: A *rhesus* monkey was the first monkey to be rocketed into the stratosphere, so perhaps, in a world in which nothing is wasted, some supervening force in the universe will confirm that the monkey's name was not arbitrary but always intended to be so, since King *Rhesus*'s name meant something after all, dubbed simian by an all-seeing providence with no love of dictionaries.

Made desperate by an educational system that often trains us to make sense of life, we may well go back to Rhesus in a mood of obtuse creativity, ransacking the Greek lexicon until it yields "*rhesis*" (saying, speaking, mode of speech) and "*rhesso*" (tear, rend, break, *beat with the feet*). The italics are mine. Surely this king's name is not far from *rhetoric* (rhetor, orator), and Rhesus might be an honorary title, not always given, but nonetheless appropriate, though perhaps not as appropriate, for, say, a baby banging his heels. There is a choice between an honorary oratorical title and a specific allusion to an infant's habit. So far so good. Now, why did the medical profession take that name for a monkey? "Arbitrary," say the dictionaries. Do we leave it at that, or try again? Is this merely a talkative monkey, a rhetorician born? Or does it bang its heels a lot? Baby rhesus monkeys are amenable until they turn cantankerous with maturity. Do they bang their heels then? Is there any connection between King Rhesus and blood? I doubt it, but it is not past the border of human idiosyncrasy for some unremembered primatologist to name a monkey after an expertly talking king, who was gullible nonetheless. Watch this space.

RHUBARB

More and more rarely do people report having had a *rhubarb* (a row) with someone, but the word goes on as a makeshift for actors to mouthe in crowd scenes. No doubt this noisy origin explains the slang use of the term for quarrel or dispute. Whether or not *rhubarb* comes from *Rha*, the ancient Greek name for the River Volga, on whose banks they discovered this plant, the fact remains that, in the coarser villages of the English Midlands, *Rhubarb* serves as the nickname for any fully grown retarded person who comes and goes delivering simple messages with a betrayed, vacant grin. When someone such is at the door, waiting, someone will point and say "Rhubarb," meaning either such and such a person or the arrival of the service.

I wonder if Medieval Latin's *rha barbarum* did not provide the notion that the retarded are somehow barbaric; "foreign rhubarb" alluded to the plant's origin in China and its import into Europe via Russia. As a child, I dreaded it, smothered as it was in sugar and custard. It seemed a bleeding bone, even when chopped up.

RIGMAROLE

Often pronounced *rigamarole*, perhaps because people find a rigor in it, this word used to be *ragman roll*, devised by Scottish nobles who, trying to outwit the English king Edward I, in 1291 bamboozled him with a bundle of miscellaneous papers and signatures masquerading as documents of allegiance. All Edward wanted was Scotland, and the Scottish nobles could hardly refuse; he could seize what he wanted, if he wanted to. Hence this muddled charter thrown together that no one could make sense of it except that it seemed to be a pledge. So *rigmarole* became our word for confusion, gibberish, disjointed nonsense, ever since.

The Scots nobles took their ragman roll from a gambling game, in which players chose a string dangling from a parchment roll that had words written on it: a kind of lucky dip. Perhaps this ragged man was a *raggedy man*, a scarecrow of sorts, a portable mannikin all in tatters.

ROGER (ROGER-DODGER)

Military formula meaning I *understand*; *yes*; *willco*. Derived from the military phonetic alphabet word for "received" or "R." Common Royal Air Force parlance, along with "Tally-ho," an expression vaguely redolent of fox-hunting. A related expression, sometimes sung, invokes "Roger the Lodger, the sod." Roger also means "right" or "right-o" and "fuck."

ROGUE

A must for elephants, of course, but no longer an option for scoundrels or rascals. It still can mean, if you need it to, to defraud, to remove a diseased specimen, to junk unwanted plants. It used to mean beggar or panhandler, from Latin *rogare*, meaning to ask, ask for, to beg.

ROOKIE

Greenhorn, tyro, newcomer, novice, from the British army of the 1800s, it no doubt comes from *recruit* (raw recruit), and the black, rook-hued jacket worn by some British recruits of the time (also *rooky*, *rookey*).

ROSE

Hospital slang for a comatose, dying patient, from the hue and petal-like fragility of such a patient; the term has a sardonic empathy. The first julep was a drink of rosewater (Arabic *julab*); the U.S.A. made it an alcoholic one—1787 records note the landlords of old Virginia spiking their day with a julep at six A.M.

ROTHSCHILD

May evoke money, but it means "red shield." Little Rothschilds played in a garden on the roof because Jewish children weren't allowed to play where other children did. The boys, founding a tradition, went out dressed as girls and brought back bullion: boiled-up precious metal. A quainter, more disturbing foretaste of the Warsaw ghetto would be hard to find.

's

What intimidation the noun works, keeping people from adding a straight *s* to create a plural! Is it misplaced finesse that gives us *heroic's,* or a profound misunderstanding of cases and number? The same happens with verbs, when people write "galvanize's." Perhaps they intend a delicious pause as the noun teeters between singular and plural, the verb croaks a bit before assuming a tense and a number, a person and and intention. Nervousness or shyness might have riddled English with misplaced inverted commas, but it did not, not quite. Is this the last refuge of the uneducated purist who, like Scheherazade, staves off the evil day, the final cry of the grammatic virgin? Or is the intrusive apostrophe a fleck of inhibition as a word better known as a noun gets used as a verb (*debate, type, cook*)? Perhaps it is a clearing of the throat as the word mutates and begins to move; I don't think vice versa applies.

SAD

One of the relinquished tastes of my boyhood was "sad" chocolate cake as made by my mother, breaking all the laws of baking in order to produce something sloppy, soggy, shrunken, and heavy. *Sad* has had an interesting career, all the way from "sad of" (tired of, weary with) and "full." After meaning steadfast or constant in the early 1300s, it evolved into a word for "valiant" or "trustworthy," but it also meant intelligent (full of brains) and came to mean laden with care. In the kitchen, "sad" was aimed at food that seemed too full of itself, from bread that had not risen and cake that began dank. *Sad* comes from the same Indo-European base as *saturate* and *satisfy*, *sate* and *satiate*, with in the background the idea of sufficiency (an early polite way of refusing a second helping was to say "No, thank you, I have had a sufficiency," that startling polysyllabic word stilling all dissent). *Sad* slinks around in the penumbra of the overblown, the bloated, the costive, the heavy, in astonishing demonstration of the body-mind effect: the body choked up with too much experience, or too much fodder. Why did I like my mother's "sad" cake? Because it seemed so much closer to being all icing.

SALIENCE

From the Latin *salire*, to leap, jump, even squirt, a *salience* is what leaps out at you unbidden. It was a vogue word among the Cornell poets in the Seventies, laudably enough insisting that the world is not full of generalities but besieges us with specifics that catch us unawares. Thus, good poems were full of details, not schoolmaster's generalities. Virginia Woolf crouching on her knees in London's Kew Gardens is an example of someone hunting saliences—individual insects, unique blades of grass. God is not vague. Of course, the word, or a relative, had a military vogue and still might: its most notable appearance was in the battle of the Bulge in World War Two, when the Bulge was the salient, so called, the area of the battle line closest to the enemy, in this case a German lunge into the American lines, like a punch into the midriff: hard to repel, even harder to accommodate without retreating. Land war changes all the time, but salients may still happen as armies burst into one another's terrain.

SALTIMBOCCA

A contraction of the Italian *salta in bocca,* and clearly a bit of myth, this dish of veal, ham, and cheese supposedly "jumps into the mouth." Latin *saltare,* to leap, also shows up when we *sauté* something (make it leap in the pan—*sauté* means "jumped"), as when we toss what's cooking. *Saltare* in various forms appears in other words too, from *salmon* to *salacious* and *desultory* and *salient,* which run the gamut from leaping up, leaping onto, leaping about, and leaping out. Most of us don't think of our food as active, but a glance at a menu in any Romance language will disabuse us fast.

SANDWICH

One night in 1762, John Montagu the fourth Earl of Sandwich, a man of ill repute who was also an incompetent and corrupt First Lord of the Admiralty, became so engrossed in one of his all-night gambling sessions that he refused to take a meal break, instead commanding that slices of bread be brought to him with slices of roast beef arranged in between. One-handed, he continued gambling, undeterred, having for all time invented the *sandwich.* One detractor of the sandwich, however (and of the submarine sandwich), has called it a cow sitting between two fields. Some of the best old-fashioned sandwiches in the world one could get at El Viño's on Fleet Street in London, slices cut up into little one-bite triangles with potted meat, fish paste, ham and cheese, bacon and roast beef within. You did not even have to look. The French name for these delights is *dent-de-loup* or "wolf's tooth," honor going to the tooth's shape. The Byronist and historian Peter Quennell used to ply me with these in my salad days, appeasing the wolf with port.

SARCOPHAGUS

Its literal sense veiled by the patina of classical Greek, *sarcophagus* means flesh-eater, from *sarx* (flesh) + *phagein* (eat). It is perhaps hard for us to envision the flesh-devouring coffin or tomb, prettified on the outside but ravenous within. The answer is that the Greek coffin was made from a carnivorous limestone, if such a mineral ever existed. It is one of the most dramatic, clad words, horrifying even if inaccurate, and somehow monstrous to say. When we do use this word, it is with some distance from its true meaning, as if we had said *wardrobe* or *trousers-press*. There could be a limestone that promoted decomposition. One recalls the Nazi limepits. *Sarx* also gives us our *sarcasm*, not exactly a mode of flesh-eating, but able to draw blood.

SARDONIC

Not to be confused with irony, which means the opposite of what one says, *sardonic* is the bitter laugh, supposedly from a Sardinian herb, *Herba Sardonica*, supposed to deform the face of the rash eater. Samuel Beckett in *Watt* takes off on this concept, inventing what he calls the *risus purus*, the laugh laughing at the laugh, negating it in a fit of mental nullity, and along with it sardonic scorn and mockery, sarcasm's open and taunting ridicule, even irony's ambivalence. As the laugh laughs at the laugh, perhaps epitomizing the last laugh, some accommodation seems to have started in which displeasure at human foible melts away into opinionless stoicism.

Those wishing to dig behind the word's relatively settled reputation (*sardonic* seems almost mild, intellectually reputable) may find sarcasm's *sarkazo*, Greek for "tear the flesh." Once upon a time in Sardinia, there was a tradition of biting, savage speech that entailed gnashing of the teeth: the fierce bickering of old salts.

SCHMEAR

The more it changes, the more it remains grease, on the slice, in the palm, butter or soft soap, bribe, and even, by paradoxical inversion, to clobber, to cream, to smear somebody's good name. Best of all, however, is that aggregate vision of the absolute and its demon: *the whole schmear*, without which Manhattan finds you inarticulate. The subtext view of an overloaded bagel ready to clog the arteries of anyone who approaches calls up the deity, whose spit in so many idioms seethes between his teeth in preparatory zeal.

SCRANNY

Among the words my mother taught me were those she herself most needed. This one, meaning insane or crackers, was the one she said she needed most, because her two kids drove her to it, she the concert pianist trying to be a housewife. A milder version of being driven *scranny* was *maddled*, a panic state between harassed and confused; she would often say "I'm *maddled* to death and I'll soon be going *scranny*." Her other words were *slawm*, which meant unctuous displays of affection, and *chavvle*, my favorite of her words meaning to cut cake or bread untidily. Imagine. In between times, we two dictionary-readers and allied crossword-solvers amassed a fair vocabulary of majestic useless-ness—except for crosswords, and she taught me several musical terms for which I had no need, though I have retained *slur* ("arched symbol above or below two notes indicating they must be played legato or rendered as a single syllable") and *rubato tempo*, which she delighted to inform me meant "stolen time," a phrase in which she took enormous pleasure, *maddled* as she al-ways was. *Peu*, she said, was "little" and *leise* "gentle, soft." She also, several times, spelled out to me the essentials of sonata form, which I found as abstract and nebulous as the so-called perfect form of the ideal novel, in which some of my most bour-geois friends believe, unavailingly convinced that the novel is in-extricably linked to the rise and fall of social classes, and to the price of cucumbers. Reading with my mother when I was little, usually stretched out alongside her in front of a coal or electric fire, I picked out with her words of unusual interest, and then we saved them up, almost like Walter Pater recording lovely phrases on visiting card–sized slips of paper, for use in future crossword puzzles; the opportunity rarely came, and there we were, in a rough-and-ready rural village once a Roman settle-ment, stranded with *opsimath*, *heteroclite*, and *yclept*, and other such esoterica (word that had an Erica in it!). We never lost our ver-bal habits or surrendered them to the mere reading of newspa-pers or (in my case) the answering of examination questions. There was a pact or bond beyond the useful, entitling us to mu-tual loftiness in the shadow of our ancestors, amid whose blurts and sound-changes we absentmindedly thrived.

Another word, *throng*, no doubt Norse, was my grandfather's word, but his daughter also used it, and it meant intolerably busy. I still use it, as I do *wittle*, for worry, *jiggered* for worn-out, fatigued, and *crozzle* for frying or roasting food to a black skeet. The unusual part of all this was that my sister and I conversed with her in an unusual idiom we would not normally have used, so it was a bit like talking Inuit to an Inuit, an argot remote from the "correct" English pounded into us in school. These words of my mother's were really Yorkshire words, wetbacks from a boundary only ten miles away. The Norsemen, it seemed, had left more behind them in Yorkshire than in my native Derbyshire, where the Normans had left traces of their own, from Ashby-de-la-Zouch, not far away from my own village, to Frecheville, up the road. My mother spoke Norse in Gaul.

There were other Derbyshire words (some of them from over the borders in Yorkshire or Nottinghamshire) I never heard my maternal grandfather use and certainly not my mother, who thought them vulgar. *Snap* was food (sometimes *snaps*) and *maungy* was cantankerously miserable. *Nesh* was hyper-sensitive (my mother deplored any attack on sensitivity, she a true daughter of Chopin and Schumann). *Mardarse* was a "mardy arse," a crybaby pest, and a *ladlass* was an effeminate boy. With such taboo words she had no truck and flinched if I, a verbal holist, ever descended into using them. She came from a wealthy, highly educated family (two brothers brilliant scientists) and she had married "down," when she tied the knot with my father, her childhood sweetheart, the lover of history. English, she always felt, had to be kept up, and that meant both using language correctly and keeping it decent. Actually, she kept it *docent*, which means teaching; she taught me to read by four years, then conned me into reading a book on grammar, a subject, she claimed, close to musical theory and harmony. No wonder I felt at home among the highbrow examiners of my teens and the philology professors who doted on Old Norse.

SCRAWM

A more disheveled form of *scramble*, meaning to fidget about when you should be sitting still, and so doing in the untidiest, noisiest manner possible. Little boys in preliminary to fisticuffs indulge in the *scrawm*, moving from *scramble* to *scrum* and *scrimmage* in no time.

SCREW

Deep source, a Latin word for *sow* (*scrofa*), source of *scrofula*, once deemed a pig disease only. By the Middle Ages, *scrofa* had widened its range to include the pig's curly, corkscrew tail, and, by mistaken association with Vulgar Latin *scrobis* (the word for *ditch*, *trench*, and *cunt*) the slot or groove incised across the head of a carpenter's screw. It already looks, in the eighteenth century, as if the pig's corkscrew member and tail, the echo of *scrobis*, and human obviousness, are going to introduce screw for copulate. It comes in, but from Old French *escroe*, deriving from Latin or prehistoric West German. Perhaps because we enjoy the inevitability of patterns, we might relish the pig-disease and screwhead gash that give us screw for copulate, but sometimes language goes its own way, maybe the long way around, as here, going back to Latin and French to receive a word, *scrofa*, it already had, but only, it seems, lingered on the brink of, unable to sexualize in human terms the precolloquial hints present in the porcine and the screw. Perhaps the pay-off is the huge variety of expressions using *screw*, already just about devoid of offensive taint, from *screw around* and *screwball* to *screw up* and *screw you*. Perhaps the sound of the word suits; its connotations are almost a diaspora, from turnkey to clusterfuck.

SCREW THE POOCH

Word books tend to stay away from this bestiality-afflicted phrase, which has always entertained me. Does it mean that, through some inadvertence, someone thrust his organ into a dog? Or did he do it out of defiance? The astronaut who fouls up the mission and most of all its recovery haunts *The Right Stuff*: He "screwed the pooch," they say, and that's why he doesn't get the big ceremony, the best medal, and Jackie K. I fancy some devious willfulness gets him on the wrong track, tantamount to screwing the pooch when all he intended to do was walk the dog. Is this a vision of humans at their most erratic, not at their most perverse? My childhood was full of stories about obtuse Derbyshire bachelors prowling the night meadows with stools to help them swyve the cows. What these fellows were after, out in the moonlight, only Nature knows, but they put me in mind of someone searching human experience for something that most probably isn't there at all. Behold once again the old Faustian want.

SCUZZ

Grunge or mung, provoking nausea even if it's only an unappetizing young woman (skag or skank). Scuzz food—junk food such as popcorn, potato chips, and sugared cereal—sooner or later scuzzes out just about everyone, but not as much as if someone used an obsolete hunk of slang. As William Safire says, "Slanguists are scuzzed out at the squared-out weirdos who still use grossed-out." Perhaps this word comes from *scum* and *fuzz* combined, or *scum* and *disgust*, *scust* yielding *scuzz*. Or *scum* and *gross*.

SERENDIPITY

Coined in 1754 by English writer Horace Walpole (1717–1797), who had read a popular romance entitled *The Three Princes of Serendip*, whose leading characters, as Walpole put it, "were always making discoveries, by accidents and sagacity, of things they were not in quest of." *Serendip*, by the way, is an old name for Ceylon, now called Sri Lanka. Even science needed this word, for its faculty of making happy inadvertent finds, such as *penicillin* (see).

SHAG

Without the least concern for my own feelings, a former girl friend used to tell me how she, a BOAC stewardess then, and a certain senior pilot used to *shag* using a garden swing. She would swing toward him, legs splayed wide, and impale herself on his erection where he stood between the uprights. It struck me as a fine guarantee of injury and introduced me, in the flesh, to the absurd I'd been reading about. Of course, *shag* is sexual in British eighteenth-century English and in American slang of the 1930s. Now a laborious film called *The Spy Who Shagged Me* has awakened American speakers to the other meaning again: not leave fast or "book," nor chase nor fab, groovy, but fuck. I see no harm in acquiring another old synonym; it's like running into a syphilitic friend in the exercise room. It's all right if shag the cormorant doesn't mind. I've heard *shag off*, utterly in line with shag as *scram*, akin to *sod off* and *bog off* and *bugger off*, though these—anal, coprophilic, and anal again—are slower goes. Shag used also to be *shag ass*, and I begin to detect something shady even in the shag parties of 1960s teenagers, there to fondle one another and experiment carnally.

SHAMBOLIC

An amateur worldbuilder created this, relying not so much on the idea of *shambles* as a meat market, a butcher's shop, or a row of meatsellers' stalls, as on the scene of complete disorder or ruin that follows the evisceration of a meat animal. Latin *scamnum* gave the diminutive *scamellum*, for "little bench," and Old English *sc(e)amel* (table) yielded Middle English *shamel*: table for display or sale of meat. To the general idea of disorder or ruin, carnage or bloodshed is not necessary, although earlier it was. *Shambles* happens to be a plural noun of almost biblical enormity akin to a vision of chaos. So, someone who in his unlearned way has heard *symbolic* perpetrates an echo and comes up with the firm-sounding *shambolic*: "What's it like in there, then? Shambolic. People and stuff all over the place, everything smashed, the people too." Actually, *shambolic* often serves as a euphemism for *untidy*, as *smashed* for *drunk*.

SHIBBOLETH

See Judges 12:6 for the story of how the Gileadites managed to pick out Ephraimite intruders at the Jordan Fords. A captain ordered one such intruder into his tent and told him to say the Gileadite word *shibboleth* (an ear of corn). Unable to pronounce the test word properly, the spy came out with *"Sibboleth"* and was promptly executed. A similar thing happened with Japanese infiltrators in World War Two, the test words being such as "Llewellyn," "lollipop," "lollapalooza," and "Kalamazoo." Fascinatingly enough, the Japanese, who were pretending to be Chinese, could not say *l* but pronounced it as *r*, whereas the Chinese cannot say *r*, pronouncing it as *l*. Something usefully circular here, a double jeopardy; the Japanese spy cannot physically say *l*, or tactically say *r*, because the Chinese cannot say *r*, and has only *l* to go back to, which defeats him. So his presumed silence condemns him. This is much subtler than those basic baseball questions posed during the Battle of the Bulge when Germans disguised as Americans tried to bluff their way through the American lines. Even bad questions worked: "What do they call the Brooklyn Dodgers?"

SHINOLA

Theoretically, if *shit* did not exist, neither would Shinola, having nothing to alliterate with. But it does, eminent among such formulae of caustic differentiation as *not know one's ass from a hole in the ground* or *not know one's ass from one's elbow* (why? does this liken coccyx to elbow?). Shinola, a brand of shoe polish, coming in brown and other hues, oddly evokes the bribery and extortion of *payola* and reminds us also of *Pianola* and *Victrola*; the suffix *-ola* denotes something automatic and inexorable and gives a Thirties flavor to more recent doings and brand names.

SHIT

From a prehistoric Germanic base *skit*, deriving from Indo-European *skheid* (split, divide, separate), whence English *schism* and *schist*. This is a fourteenth-century word, descended from Old English *shite*; the noun form, *shit*, is first noted in the sixteenth century. The substance runs the gamut of its spectrum, from outright revulsion to a strange neutral inclusiveness (*get my shit together*, meaning my *stuff*) to voluptuous doting. The poet Edward Field has a coprophilic poem, and millions have described their drugs as "good shit," in which phrase even voluptuous loathing has yielded to paradoxical gloating with the metaphor shoved so far beyond its original gist that we have almost a denatured word, tinged with abstractly registered bravado. Like other monosyllables, overworked and trite (from Latin *tritus*, worn), this one supposedly puts unsqueamish people at ease, invoking a lowest common denominator for those reluctant to sing the national anthem.

SHVANTZ

One day there will come along a euphemism that, while limning the lewd, seems to offer itself up on a different plane: that of verbal delectation. Compared with *dick, schlong, johnson,* and *willy,* and so many more, *shvantz* offers something almost serene and glowing, perhaps recalling Weinberger's *Schwanda the Bagpiper,* or the elegant skater's curve cut on the water by Sibelius's swan. This applies equally to such variants as *schvantz, schvanz, schwantz, schwanz, schvontz, shvonce,* and *shvuntz.* The hilarious contortion envisaged in the new idiom *step on the (your) shvantz,* displacing *step on it* and *step on the gas,* evokes what used to be called the anatomical impossibility: go fuck yourself. Add to this innovation the military version of the phrase, meaning to blunder, commit a snafu, and you gain some idea of the verbal Laocoön that someone cussing can become entangled with. It has been said that, without the Jewish passion for reading, there would no longer be any serious literary culture left in the United States. By a similar token, without Yiddish, there would be a dearth of saliva-spraying, mildly obliterative words and phrases of condemnation. Moral: Those who read know what and how to damn.

SILHOUETTE

Done in black on white or the reverse, this image or design in just one hue and tone was the way the eighteenth and nineteenth centuries made portraits, in cut-out or paint. The word also denotes outlines or shadows of definitive sharpness. This much is clear, so to speak, but the rest is not so much fuzzy as perhaps overembellished. It is worth remembering, though, that the French phrase *à la silhouette* refers to an object deliberately marred or made incomplete, something of unlasting value.

One view of silhouette says that the word derives from the name Etienne de Silhouette (1709–1767), Comptroller-General of France from March to November 1759, a short enough career made even shorter, in the mass, by his frequent absences from his bureau. This career has attracted to it the word "evanescent," and no wonder. What Etienne went away to do was cut out paper shadow portraits, fast-named for him. Indeed, another of the meanings of the phrase *a la silhouette* was *on the cheap*. While taking pay for doing little besides boosting the land tax on the estates of the nobility and planning to abolish government pensions, he made inexpensive replicas of his friends and acquaintances. There is an interesting boomerang effect here: A man's name attaches itself to the products of his hobby, then slides out into the national idiom only to appear behind him to recall (and memorialize) his cheap, erratic ways. Silhouettes, no matter how nightmarishly evocative they can seem, also leave something to be desired—something missing, and this is true of Silhouette's personal performance: an imperfect man satirically recalled by an imperfect art. He might have played truant in order to produce art of mesmerising perfection, but he did not.

Did he invent the silhouette, then? It is likely that Stone Age peoples beat him to it in cave murals in France and Spain, filling in outlines with flat color.

SINCERE

Brought to me by my uncommon dentist, an ebulliently cheerful man, *sincere*, meaning unaffected, natural, unfeigned, true, harks back to Indo-European *ker-*, a thick primordial stew in which the goddess Ceres (of agriculture) meddles with a growing boy *korwo* (Greek *kouros*). So, you have both the growth of fruits and the crescent boy. I am not sure that, buried in all this, there isn't a hint of child molestation or, to put a finer point on it, timely seduction (remember how young the character Juliet is: twelve or thirteen). There's an overlay, too, of a young girl, so perhaps this is merely Ceres striding abroad amid the crops, under the fruit trees especially, with a young human on either hand, divinely gloating at the *foison* (old word for plenty) in her grasp. It is the supreme image of fertility, imaged upside down in the pupil of the eye, and reduced. Words that crop up from this noble stew are *cereal*, *creare* (to bring forth, create), *procreate*, *crescere* (to grow, increase), *crescendo*, *crescent*, *crew*, *accrue*, *concrete*, *decrease*, *increase*, and *recruit*, plus many words having to do with purity and cleanliness, lack of stain. After some pondering, one fits "*syn + Ceres*" (together with Ceres) into fertile unpretension, a trust in nature's potency. Ceres's sidekicks are the fruits of the earth, as André Gide called them in *Les Nourritures Terrestres*. If someone is as sincere as nature, as Ceres, then you can trust them outright. This is a generous view, to be sure, but nobody trusts someone who trusts nobody.

SIREN

Irresistible glamour puss (to use an old terminology) or sea nymph, this word was destined to travel far. In Greek myth, *Seirenes* sat on rocks and lured impressionable mariners to disaster with their sweet singing. Latin turned the word into *sirena*, and it made its way into English via Old French as *sereine*. Having paused without much purpose, in 1819 the word appeared on an acoustical instrument devised by Cagniard de la Tour, which made musical sounds and also measured the frequency of sound waves. From the 1870s on, it was this device that inspired the sirens that warned, as eventually in World War Two, when the alarm was an undulating bleat, the "All Clear" a sustained single mid-pitch note. *Siren* may be coming back in its old sense since a 1994 movie ironically and pleasurably full of them, called *Sirens*. Odysseus and his crew, ears crammed with wax, are nowhere to be seen in this opus, single-mindedly sailing past creatures half-woman, half-bird. Odysseus even had himself lashed to the mast to keep him where he belonged. Sad that so potent a legend should have fallen victim to an air-raid warning as common on Iwo Jima as in wartime London.

SIRLOIN

Did some English king, carried away by carnivorous relish, knight a tender piece of meat? Henry VII, James I, and Charles II have all been credited with this bit of meaty flummery. Sirloin is older than any of them, though, from French *surloigne*, meaning part of the loin in front of the rump. The spelling "sir," first noted in the eighteenth century, possibly came from the bogus story of Sir Loin, which has a Shakespearean touch.

SKEAT

My military time while stationed on the Isle of Man led to a paltry word-hoard, but certain words remain, among them *skeat*, which has nothing to do with what you shoot at. In Manx it means an astute, sly watcher of the human pageant, a snoop, even a spy. *Coosh* is to warm yourself in front of an open fire by opening up your body in a receptive array or dish, a posture of complete surrender to the life-giving warmth. *Tredaloor* means much the same as Arabic *inshallah*, as Allah wishes, or *c'est la vie*—life is as it is, take it or leave it, literally. Perhaps three words per island is enough, so my haul from Newfoundland is inadequate, amounting to one word only: *lunch*, which you can use for any meal of the day, calling it "a lunch."

SKIVE

Twentieth-century British military slang for gold-bricking, the word generated *skiver* for one who skives. It's really the same verb as the little-used eschew, which means dodge or evade. Its parabola has contorted charms, from prehistoric Germanic *skeukhwaz*, Vulgar Latin's *skivare*, and Old French's *eschiver* or *eschuer*. Eschew means doing without something whereas skive means not doing what you're supposed to do, an exercise without which the military would crumble.

SLATHER

An orphan, this, attracting few lexicographers, to neither guess nor explicate. It has to be a combination of *lather* and *slop*, meaning you apply too much. It may have come in with only the aerosol can, but deployers of the shaving brush, especially those inclined to let the foam sit awhile and soak the beard, may have larded the soap on, either on themselves or shavees in the Sweeney chair. I detect in its use an element of voluptuous joy, even in its plural applications as in *slathers of money* or *peanut butter*. Slang, this, brimming with onomatopoeia.

SLOB

Late nineteenth-century word for a messy, pudgy, unwantable adult, *slob* suggests the disorderly and slovenly person who inevitably becomes a butt or victim. In the original Anglo-Irish, the word had affectionate overtones, often referring to a peaceable, stout, lethargic child. *Slow as cousloppe* goes the medieval idiom (cowslop), with *slop* not far from *slob*. Who would deign to pour it? Only a slob, drawn to a congruous natural element.

SLEDGE

Sledge of sledgehammer fame was once a word in its own right, meaning heavy hammer, from prehistoric German *slakh*, hit. Related to English *slaughter*. The snow vehicle came from Middle Dutch, as did *sleigh*, whereas *sled* came from Middle Low German. These are ancient sliding words. The Australian use of *sledge*—disturbing or unsettling a batsman with taunts and commentary—began in the 1970s. Perhaps it is a sledgehammer technique and is thought of as such, most of all in boxing.

SLOPS

Slops, the poet and critic William Empson told us before coming to dinner, was all he could eat; so we prepared him some soup and stew, both of which he cooled by filling his mouth and then squirting the mouthful back into his soup plate. That is one version of *slops*; Empson was awaiting his National Health teeth from England. Another *slops*, the accumulated nightsoil of several chamberpots dumped into an enamel bucket primed with Izal disinfectant, has to be dumped into the outdoor toilet or into the street. Empson, of course, was correct, as someone so linguistically scrupulous would be, resorting to an expression for watery, insubstantial invalid food. The *slops* bucket has a polite counterpart in the *slop basin*, the bowl into which tea leaves and coffee grounds, not to mention cocoa crust and Horlicks nodules, are emptied at table or after being scraped loose. A Lancashire *slopstone* is a concave block of soft stone to be found where washing or washing-up is done. Imaginably, only third-world countries have *slops* buckets even as they aspire to the slop basin.

SLUSH

From the sound of, as with its close relatives *slosh* and *sludge*, though sludge is slower. Squelching or splashing whereas *sludge* sucks and squeaks. Perhaps this word came in from early modern Danish (*slus* for sleet) and Norwegian (*slusk* for slushy) rather than from local weather observation. *Slush fund*, oddly enough, a nineteenth-century word, derives from the use of *slush* for grease that is a by-product of cooking in a ship's galley. Imagine the black depths of that congealed lard used to grease people's palms; it's money, of course.

SNITE

Not polite, not now, but once upon a time it was, from being Old English *snytan*, to blow the nose, akin to Old Norse *snyta*. The dialect meaning is to blow the nose without benefit of handkerchief, which is to say either between finger and thumb or by pressing one nostril closed with a finger. This practice, familiar from the behavior of athletes, is also part of the repertoire expected of fictional anti-heroes, among whom figure those of Samuel Beckett (the sort of characters who, when asked to produce their papers, fumble out bits of toilet wipe). There is a double snite developed mainly by boxers and fencers, people whose hands are hampered, and this is not hard to witness, if you can keep calm.

SNOB

This word has widened out like a fan, first meaning "shoemaker," then, in the Cambridge of the late eighteenth century, the students' term for a townie (as distinct from a gownie), extending in the early nineteenth century to include the common folk. "The nobs have lost their dirty seats," crowed *The Lincoln Herald* on July 22, 1831, "the honest snobs have got 'em." Thus was social revolution proclaimed. The next meaning was *a blatantly vulgar person*, but William Thackeray clinched things in his *Book of Snobs* (1848), when he used the word for someone "vulgarly aping his social superiors." None of this seems familiar to us, who do not consider snobbish those who aspire to refinement. Our sense of snob is of someone who disdains, for social or intellectual reasons, arrogantly or affectedly. Whence *snob?* We do not know, though one suggestion is that it stands for *sine nobilitate*, "lacking nobility"; but what about the world before Latin? *Some Nasty Old Bugger* doesn't quite make it, although *Seen Naked Over Banisters* might work, and *Syphilis Natural On Behind* works briefly, evincing an undergraduate pettiness. *Snobs*, by the way, is an English children's game, requiring the sudden picking up of earthenware pieces with one hand, a curious simile for upstart advance.

SNOOP

Dutch *snoepen* means to eat on the sly, which we have all done from time to time, except for the American novelist who, equipped with sandwiches, journeyed from Buffalo to Manhattan by train, but felt too intimidated to open them up during the trip, and so arrived in New York with a rumbling tummy. Our current sense of prying into the affairs of others, mostly by prowling about, seems to have left out the food element, which suggests that the snooper's true repast is dirt.

SNUFF

Snuff it is a late nineteenth-century phrase for "die," but *snuff* movies, which depict a murder, belong to our own time only of course. English boasts three *snuffs*, all connected to a prehistoric German base, *snuf*, the sound of air noisily entering a nose. The powdered tobacco inhaled comes from Dutch *snuf*, taken in turn from Middle Dutch *snuffen*, to sniff or snuffle, whence our own *sniffle*. *Snivel* belongs to this same constellation of sounds and attitudes. *Snuff out*, regarding candles, came in the fifteenth century from *snuff*, meaning "burnt candlewick" in the shadow of the obsolete verb *snot*: to put out a candle or blow the nose. John Ayto goes so far as to suggest "a perceived resemblance between an extinguished candlewick and a piece of nasal mucus." These are all sniffy-sounding words, to be sure (see also *snite*), and one wonders at so keen an eye upon matters mucous when there was so much else to peer at. Yet perhaps not: In poor light, one might not be overwhelmed by a panoply of visual delights, and flop to the lowest common denominator. One eighteenth-century cynic spoke of a certain pleasure: watching the English talk and listening to them eat.

SODA

A common and somewhat refreshing word, whether you have to deal with fountains, siphons, or swimming pools, *soda* shows up all over the place, originating perhaps with Latin *sodanum* (samphire, glasswort). A samphire-gatherer appears in *King Lear*, clinging to a cliff in blinded Gloucester's articulate babble:

create

254   Paul West

The crows and choughs that wing the midway air
Show scarce so gross as beetles; halfway down
Hangs one that gathers samphire, dreadful trade!
Methinks he seems no bigger than his head...(IV.vi.12)

This is brilliant, utterly modern writing, cut from raw experience and mastered vertigo. If you wanted soda, you burned *samphire* and so were able to make glass. *Samphire* was also regarded as a nostrum against headaches, and it has been suggested that *sodanum* came from Arabic *suda* for headache, itself derived from *sada*, meaning "split," and thus evocative of migraine's "half-headed" effects. The word *sodium* was coined by the indefatigable Sir Humphry Davy (see *aluminum*) from soda in 1807.

SOMMELIER

Now the waiter in a restaurant put in charge of wines and their service, always equipped with a light chain of office recalling his earlier, less palmy days as a driver of pack animals or a court official charged with transportation of supplies. From Old Provençal *saumalier*, pack animal driver. A sumpter.

SPIN

To a cricketer, spin is the complementary opposite of pace, the slow bowler versus the fast. To a political flack, spin is a doctrinaire tilt given to what used to be a fact. To a pool player, spin is English (they invented it), but it has nothing to do with a pitcher's curve ball (whose physics turn out to be quite different, having to do with air pressure and humidity and pitching stance). All of this creates interest, reminding us that *spin* is maybe the Jungian, subjective aspect of ball (or fact)

management. There is the plain, undeviating ball, and the ball that does tricks. Perhaps, somewhere, there is a politician, or a press agent, who delivers the goods spinless. What interests me is that *spin* has come to do duty for what we used to call *expressionism*: How you feel about something is more important to you than how it actually is. Perhaps people never used *expressionism* in talk, unless they were hidebound academics: Now *spin* is in, an unobtrusive simple word promising much; there might be a bit more sympathy for expressionist art, say *Dr. Caligari's Cabinet* or Edvard Munch, the Norwegian painter. There may well be no such thing as the truth in the spectrum of preference. I mean, for instance, here is a TV book show on C-SPAN, but the author has used in her book the Latin tag *et al.* (Al was always showing up, we used to joke), and the host doesn't know it means "and others," is short for *et alii.* She, however, is trying to cite a book by André Maurois, author of *The Silences of Colonel Bramble,* but she calls him "Marot," not even Maurras or Malraux. And I wondered, when I saw this, if it mattered: Shall we not go down to oblivion with just as much panache with our heads full of junk, as vacant of fact, as we would with first-rate educations lovingly remembered in remorseless detail? Neither the severe interviewer (no fiction on this show) nor the eager respondent was trying for spin, but spin there was, in the sense of distortion. I suddenly thought, yes, there it is: So long as you feel emotionally about something, it doesn't matter if you've got it wrong. Spin away. We are an histrionic species, dead unless we emote. I think spin is newspeak for slant, or even doublethink. Boyhood memories, which often save me and see me through hard assents, take me back to the famous spin bowler, Tom Goddard of Gloucestershire, who all his life marinated his spinning finger—the one he twitched the ball with—in alum, to harden and safeguard it. The batsmen always knew he was going to spin the ball, but not which way it would revolve when released.

SPOONERISM

Warden of New College, Oxford, the Reverend Mr. William Spooner (1844–1930) had a habit of reversing the initial letters of all he said, thus achieving "the town drain" (down train, i.e., from London to Oxford), "hush my brat" (brush my hat), and "scoop of boy trouts" for "troop of boy scouts." He is sometimes also credited with remarking to some members of his college, when he caught them bathing naked in the Isis and they flung towels over their loins, "Well, gentlemen, most people know *me* by my face." But could he have *said* it thus? No serendipitous wit awaited him this time. There is something Joycean about Spooner, and their felicities are often similar, in both men perhaps the result of one side of the brain interfering with another, enforcing on both an almost inchoate sentence structure proving, according to some modern theories about the compositions of nuns, that neither would die of Parkinson's disease (the more complex your sentences, the better off you are).

SQUIRREL

This fellow is really a "shadow-tail" from Greek *skia* (shadow) + *oura* (tail), a combination that well depicts his characteristic lollop beneath his quiff.

STENTORIAN

Not as much used nowadays as in the nineteenth century, it may revive with the surgical use of *stent* (from Greek *stenos*, narrow). The stent is a coil that keeps an artery open, slid in during angioplasty. *Stentor* is a loud-voiced herald in *The Iliad* (Greek *stenein*, to groan or moan). I like to think of all the wide-open blood vessels that, instead of whimpering, whoosh with stentorian roar. Said only of the voice. Fanatics may ponder the use of the suffix *t* to denote instrumentality or the use of something to make something right, no doubt derived from -ent as in *instrument* (Latin *instruere, instruens,* for "prepare," "equip."). *Stentor,* an aquatic trumpet-shaped microorganism, blows the same trumpet as the *Iliad*'s herald, though much tinier. It nonetheless has cilia around its oral cavity. Doomed forerunner of the blow-job.

STIGMA

In Ancient Greek this was a tattoo mark, in Latin (as one dictionary says) it was a brand imposed on slaves or a cut inflicted by an unskillful barber. The plural form, *stigmata,* has mostly religious or mystical force. *Stigma* can be social or anti-social, but, until long after the Romans, not biological, in which realm it designates a puncture, a pore or spot such as a respiratory spiracle or an eyespot, or botanical, where it refers to the apex of a pistil upon which pollen is deposited. Its strongest use among us, perhaps, is the verb *stigmatize,* which means to brand with ignominy. Additionally, this overworked word may be a birthmark (a nevus) or a mark burned into the skin of an ancient criminal. The source of it all is the Greek verb *stizein,* to prick or tattoo.

STONE THE CROWS!

An expression of shock or surprise, mainly Australian, though it can be heard at racecourses and sports grounds in the north of England as fortune fails to smile on a horse or someone endeavoring to catch a ball. An element of exasperation emerges.

PAUL WEST

STRIDE

In piano jazz, it is alternating treble and bass, according to pre-set patterns or preferences that rapidly emerge as a personal style. Oddly enough, not listed in the Glossary of Gunther Schuller's otherwise excellent *The Swing Era: The Development of Jazz, 1930–1945*, though he does mention an Earl Hines number, *Stride Right*, played with a Johnny Hodges–led group in 1966. Stride piano, wrote Albert Goldman, is "Harlem's version of ragtime." Severe contrast rules this art in which twin resources are far apart.

STROPPY

A barbering image misapplied? A strop is that old Sweeney Todd favorite, the widish belt of leather canvas-backed that hones your cutthroat razor before the chair swings and drops you into the cellar. Can *stroppy*, which means bad-tempered, dif-ficult to cope with, have anything to do with stropping a nasty disposition to slicing point? Surely *stroppy* implies abrasiveness whereas a strop just about guarantees no friction. I think the im-age is not a comment on the razor but on the stropper; someone stroppy hones his temper to a further pitch, and indeed needs some stropping to smooth him out.

STUMPS

Not a club for amputees, this denotes the two sets of upright wooden dowels that form the basis of a cricket match. The man with the ball tries to knock them over while the batsman defends them. *Stumps* is the term for close of play, when the players leave the field and the two umpires uproot the stumps and lay them on the pitch, to be collected by ground staff. Atop each trio of stumps sit two *bails*, light lathed trimmings that settle into grooves cut in the top end. Over the years, these little wooden trinkets have tended to blow off, and the one substance to hold them firmly in place without making them immovable by the ball has been held to be raspberry jam.

For a tiny thing, *bail* has a large etymology, coming either from Latin *bajulus* (carrier or cross-beam) or from *baille*, meaning "enclosed court" (cf. Old Bailey), which in the thirteenth century meant the outer walls of a castle, in the nineteenth a bar separating stable stalls, to this day in the narrowest, slightest sense remaining a cross-bar or -beam in two pieces.

SUBJUNCTIVE

This "mood" of "joining under" has always intrigued me, almost as much as the sound changes of a verb such as *fero, ferrere, tuli, latum* (see *thunk*). The whole idea of a mood's invading verb form appealed to the nascent expressionist in me, especially the impact of verbs that insist or demand, that wish fervently or wholly dread, almost as if, while the external world remained horrific, the matrix of language became gentler, accommodating the shift: "I wish I were"; "Would that I were." The subjunctive is a subordinated form, deriving from a Greek idea called *taktike enklisis*, "tactical subordination." It is as if the sentence has dropped its voice in the mood of subordination. English subjunctives are rather sloppy, but other languages reveal how severe emotion or rampant hypothesis can slur the physical bearing of a verb. The subjunctive betrays the presence of worry, whether about something's being true or something emotionally demanding, as with desire, doubt, and will. In "God bless you," *bless* is subjunctive, like *write* in "I insist that he write to me." Not that you would know it from the verb form, which carries

PAUL WEST

within it a little social marker we never see and sometimes miss but which checks us a tad, imperious as carbon-dating.

SURPLICE

Clergy in the Middle Ages found their churches too cold for repeated services, so they wore fur coats under their robes of office. Thus today's *surplice*, from Latin *superpellicum* (*super*, over + *pellicia*, fur coat), remains an overgarment in name only. We may recall the canard that has high court English judges wearing garter belts and bras under their ceremonial silks. Perhaps, before central heating, these judges themselves sported a fur coat underneath in those frigid courts of law.

SWELP

Cockney for "so help" (me), akin to universal "snot" for "it's not" and "snice," which needs no gloss. Abbreviators like aviators have to be careful, as in "Snow good complaining, snot nice."

SWIVET

Here rings the death-knell of the word-lover: etymology unknown. I guess the dither it implies depends on a swivel that keeps you mentally spinning around, at no rest, just as if you are being *swyved* (Old English) or fucked.

SWOT

Term of schoolboy abuse, a derivative of *sweat*, applied to a student or pupil who works too much, hits the books too hard. Only a nation such as the English, who in my day used to impose at least three hours' homework on you, would need such a word. The French, who do even more homework, have several words for the complaint or condition, from *bûcheur* (*-euse*) and *bosseur* (*-euse*) to the verbs *potasser* and *bachoter*. I became a swot only at university, or rather I swotted hard without being found out by my schoolmates; I loved books so. In fact, one of my grammar school reports characterized me as "a boy of ability and intelligence who does not concentrate or work hard." Around the same time I was adjudged too slow for Latin, too ungifted for Art, and so, as I enjoy reporting, was relegated to Shop and thus, liberated by a scholarship, went off to Oxford as a fully qualified carpenter. I was a secret swot.

SYPHILIS

In 1530, an enterprising Veronese doctor, Girolamo Fracastoro, published a long poem about Syphilus, an imaginary shepherd who, after various misdemeanors including indifference to Apollo, contracted "the French Disease" or *Morbus Gallicus* then ravaging Europe. As the poem says,

> ...he who wrought this outrage was the first
> To feel his body ache, when sore accursed.
> And for his ulcers and their torturing,
> No longer would a tossing, hard couch bring
> Him sleep. With joints apart and flesh erased,
> Thus was the shepherd flailed and thus debased.
> And after him this malady we call
> *Syphilis.*

In the long run, the shepherd is made well with a nostrum made from the guaiacum tree, an actual remedy of the time. The story of poor Syphilus caught on, even though Dr. Fracastoro "did not write for fame," but rather to improve people's morals and, as we perhaps still say, raise their consciousness. *Syphilis Sive de Morbo Gallico* (Syphilis Or the French Disease) remained a popular tract, in whose presence everyone forgot that the name *Syphilus* actually meant "friend to swine."

Although Syphilus was the first person to contract the dreaded disease, at least according to Dr. Fracastoro, the doctor did not use syphilis as the disease's name until 1546, in a work entitled *De Contagione* (Concerning Contagion). The word *Syphilis* in the title of his earlier book referred not to the disease but to Syphilus the pig-lover himself, and his doings.

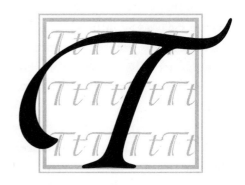

TATTOO

Close the bars said this ancient call: *taptoe*, from close the beer tap, when *toe* meant *close*. The same word, tap, also appears in taps, sounded just after the bar-closing tattoo. In 1644, a certain Colonel Hutchinson instructed his garrison at Nottingham, England, "If anyone shall bee found tiplinge or drinkinge in any Taverne, inne or Alehouse after the hourse of nyne of the clock at night, when Tap Too beates, he shall pay 2s 6d." Tattoo as a skin adornment, however, comes from Polynesian by way of Captain Cook.

TEA

1660, nosy old Samuel Pepys notes in his diary: "I did send for a cup of *tee* (a China drink) of which I never had drank before." Tea, as it was called, after the sailors' and traders' *tay* (as distinguished from the suaver word *ch'a* of the cultivated Mandarin speaker), was first served in England at Garway's Coffee House. First mentioned in the Far East around A.D. 350, *tea* was just the drink to keep wild youths away from hard liquor, so the Buddhists espoused it, but not until the seventeenth century was tea grown in Java, where the Dutch discovered it and carried it off to Europe. A *cuppa cha* can still be heard in England, a country in which tea's magical properties have never seemed to wane. Variants abound, but one of the most famous is *sergeant-major tea*, made so thick and sweet with either of two varieties of canned condensed milk that, it's said, the spoon stands up straight. Afternoon tea, by the way, is a light repast, tea with crumpets or finger sandwiches of watercress with biscuits (cookies), whereas *high tea*, often confused with afternoon tea (perhaps through a mix-up with the Oxbridge college's High Table), is a hearty northern hot meal with, for instance, liver and tomatoes, bacon and kidneys, eggs and chops, with fried or roast potatoes and onions: nothing fey about it, with bread and butter, no pastries.

THUNK

Even lexicons of slang omit this one, perhaps maintaining grammatical propriety when all else is crumbling. It is understandable that speakers, just as they invent slang, grow impatient with certain forms of certain verbs, ascending from the mere mistake of *went* (I *should have/of went*) to the innovation of *thunk* because the correct past participle seems insipid. Something robust and forceful surfaces in these maneuvers, and some of it sticks, amusingly so when you consider the stance of the amateur grammarian, flailing around with word-forms like some old Anglo-Saxon, yet never going quite so far as the Roman who first cooked up the forms of the verb to carry, bear, or bring: *fero, ferre, tuli, latum*, in which case *fero* has become mixed up with (or usefully complemented by) another verb, *tollo*, so that *tuli* was originally *tetuli*, and *latum* was unsayable doomed *tlatum*. *Tollo* ended up meaning "to take up," with eventual forms that ran like this: *tollo, tollere, sustuli, sublatum*. How fascinating to see this Coliseum of verbs in which one, too feeble and unattractive to stand alone as it is, helps itself to another of kindred meaning, only to have that other one disown itself, so to speak, and evolve new forms postoperatively to those pirated. Such is the motion of an undead language, evolution fidgeting about to make a way through. The 1998 edition of the OED admitted *snuck* to the canon of received English, which I suppose means that anyone who thinks a weak verb isn't strong enough (that old distinction) can change things around. So, instead of weak *sneak, sneaked, sneaked,* we will now have *sneak, snuck, snuck* (or, Zeus help us, even *snaught*). The essence of a strong verb was that it could mutate its own vowels (*drive, drove, driven,* even in up-to-date English). It is almost as if the strong verb got an erection and had an orgasm, forever banishing the weakling's *ed* ending. I like this onslaught on the rules and traditions, though I find *thunk* braver than *snuck*; at root, there is a yearning for a more emphatic, more chromatic English, with greater variety of phonemes and less monotony, although foreigners, already dismayed by the strong verbs (as we, by the French irregulars, say), will lament the groundswell toward root mutancy.

What force, I wonder, lies behind what I found in *The Los Angeles Times Review of Books*: "philosophy texts weaved together." Is there an aversion to burly "woven"? Does the new wimpiness demand, or prefer, the sapping of strong verbs into weak? Try saying *weaved*, then say *woven*. With nothing but weak verbs and their incessant -ed endings, English is going to sound as monotonous as modern Greek.

TITCH

In the 1860s, Arthur Orton returned from Australia claiming to be the rightful heir to an English baronetcy, his true name Roger Tichborne, formerly lost at sea. A famous *cause célèbre* en-

PAUL WEST

sued, and a tiny music-hall comedian, Harry Relph (1868–1928), looking somewhat like him impersonated him on stage as "The Titchborne Claimant." In this way, Relph became known as "Little Tich," a phrase that soon overtook many small persons, although not until the 1950s achieving non-slang standing (tich, or titch), from which titchy formed itself. A standard though mild term of abuse for the diminutive, "Little Titch" survives to this day.

TOAD

It has no known siblings in any other Indo-European language and so seems to have come out of unusual circumstances hardly widespread. Where did all the other toads and toads get to? A toady was a sycophant, an attendant who assisted itinerant quack doctors and pretended to eat a (poisonous) toad. The quack then administered the fake remedy and saved his sidekick's life. This toad-eating flunkey came to personify servility and dependency, as well as obsequious praise. Toadstools, stool-like, were so-called for their poisonous link, fungus to toad. The toady will do just about anything to gratify his patron or anyone else with loot and fame.

TOAST

In the British Tatler for June 4, 1709, the Irish playwright Richard Steele reported in his fulsome, antic way that a certain gentleman had scooped up a cupful of a famous beauty's bathwater and drunk her health in it. Toasted her, in fact. At which, one of his elegant companions, "a gay fellow, half-fuddled," observed that he didn't care for the liquor but would have the toast, meaning the paragon soaking in it. What is going on here?

Toast comes from the French verb *toster*, to parch, presumably from Latin *torrere*, *tostum*, meaning to roast, burn, or parch. From this verb we get *torrid*. Our *toast* comes from the old habit of dropping into your drink a piece of spiced or toasted bread, usually in ale or wine. So the half-fuddled, gay fellow was making a highly accurate metaphor: offering a toast to a toast; perhaps she was as torrid, even in the drink, as the smidgen of toast in his glass. Not reggae chanting, or a synonym for cool, tits, tubular, *this* toast is what you say when someone is used up, burned out, finito, raw material available for further spoliation by just about anybody: "He was toast." The conjured-up image of someone charred and dried, and therefore brittle, breakable, has a forlorn touch close to the French *épuisé*, in which a dried-up well skulks.

TOOTS

Although rather baffled by this word, commentators on it write confidently about it, citing uses by Raymond Chandler ("tootsie-wootsies") and Art Buchwald, breezily invoking games with a child's toes and the view of a dear woman as one's babe or doll. It makes more sense to summon up Yiddish *zees tushele* (sweet bottom), so that *toots* figures as a version of *tush*, *tushie*, etc. Perhaps the *z* of *zees* has wafted into the pronunciation of *tush*: tuzh, tootz, and so forth. People are not obliged to assign all the noises they notice to the correct visual outlines of the words they hear. *Toots* tends to disparage the woman addressed, never mind how affectionate the word sounds; there's a challenge to it, a scintilla of defiance, a take-it-or-leave-it insouciance. If she objects to being addressed thus, the word seems to imply, the speaker can always move on. A similar word, though not a mode of address, is *poopsie*, which I discovered at the College of William and Mary in Virginia, when I asked someone about a candlelight march of nubile young women all in nightdresses only to be told they were "poopsies." A *poopsie*, then, is one who marches thus, victim of glassy banality, apple of the eye to those whose wet dreams have a paramilitary aura.

TORQUE

Torque is *twist*, from collars, necklaces, and armbands to the twisting techniques of Torquemada, the Spanish Grand Inquisitor (1420?–1498). It is also the moment of a force, from Latin *torquere*, to twist. If you are flying a piston-engined plane, and the propeller is rotating clockwise as you look at it, the plane will veer leftward, and you will have to push right rudder to keep on track. In the United Kingdom on the other hand, since propellers there, on British planes at least, go anti-clockwise as you look at them while piloting, the veer is rightward, and you push left rudder. There is *torque* in *tort*, *extort*, *torture*, *contort*, *retort*, *tortuous*, *distorted*, and *torment*. It is in part what you try to impart to a cork in a bottle or a rusted-in screw.

Reasonably, U.S. Air Force slang includes *torqued*, which means hot and bothered, upset, pissed off, twisted out of true, like the plane tugged to the left when all it wants is to go straight, as in "straighten up and fly right." Can't be done unless you feed in some right rudder.

TORTELLINI

The diminutive of Late Latin *torta*, for small round loaf, is *tortella*, whose diminutive is *tortellino*. Make an alimentary paste of pasta dough, roll it into a cylinder lined with savory fillers, cheese or meat, then slice off coiled rounds and boil them. Legend has it that a Bolognese innkeeper once spied on

Venus through a peephole and fixed his adoring gaze on her bellybutton, whose chubby pasta replica he then set to work to make. What would he have done if she had turned her back, as in *tournedos à la Rossini*, created at the composer's request by a Parisian restaurant: *tourner* (turn) + *dos* (back). Why turn? Either because beef filets cook too fast on one side or because Rossini's original design for the dish (fatwrapped tenderloin on fried bread topped with *pâté* and a truffle sauce) so horrified the proprietor that Rossini offered to turn his back in order not to embarrass the chef. I wonder about both versions.

TREASURE

One of our most fascinating, festive words, this is really Greek *thesauros*, meaning hoard or wealth, familiar to us from the word-hoard called *thesaurus*, perhaps the finest treasure-house of all. It is also an endearment still used, having an antique magnificent aura. Why the Greeks came up with this word, we do not know, but the Romans, quicker to metaphor than the clear-headed Greeks, quickly adapted it as *thesaurus* to treasuries of thought, words, gods.

TRIKINI

One of ignorance's finest leaps, based on the mistaken idea that the *bi* in *bikini* is Greek for two, this is the word for a woman's bathing suit with two top pieces. Or, mythologically speaking, was it based on the aberrant notion of a three-breasted woman unseen even on highly radiated Bikini atoll where fish climbed trees? You never know. You have always to reckon with the likes of Rebecca Romijn-Stamos who, in *The Palm Beach Post*, admitted, "I just wore a monokini—a bikini attached down the middle with a tiny strip. I didn't find that very flattering. And if you have any bosom at all, bandeau tops are deadly." Now chew on that.

TRILBY

My father wore several of these and he called them his trilbies, never his hats. He didn't know his headgear had been named for Trilby O'Ferrall, heroine of George du Maurier's 1894 novel *Trilby*. Trilby O'Ferrall, an artist's model living in Paris, came under the spell of Svengali and became famous for her exquisite, sexy feet (in the early twentieth century, "trilbies" was the slang word for feet). In the stage play, Trilby wore a soft felt hat, dented with the heel of the hand from front to back along the top, and this style caught on, until somebody discovered the alternative way of pushing the hat's top outward to fullest extent, making of it almost a bowler.

TRIUMPHALISM

I first heard this word on the radio, used by an Irish priest to denote—well, what? When asked, he could not define the word, although he was responding to its connotations. He had been describing a procession of Irish Protestants marching over a bridge and wanted to express people parading with all the pomp of victory without having yet triumphed: all the swank of what Keats would call a proleptic victory, one celebrated before won. Since then I have heard the word used in connection with (again) Northern Ireland and also with Serbia. Perhaps *triumphalism* restricts itself to fratricidal violence, an empty, overbearing display of jubilation in the absence of any triumph whatever, and as such voluptuously negative. Perhaps, too, it is the showing-off of those not accustomed to winning, on the occasion of neither winning nor losing, but putting a brave face on stalemate.

TULIP

It looks folded, and it is, compressed multifoliate, from obsolete French *tulipan*, honoring Turkish *tulbend*, and Persian *dulband*, their way of saying turban. How swathed it is. In Middle Eastern countries, it's a term of opprobrium for an effeminate male. The so-called black tulip is really dark purple, but there does exist a cash prize for the person creating the first true black. There must be lethal competition among wannabe black-tulipeers, a long way from the demure rivalry over roses in the film *Mrs. Miniver*.

TUMBLEHOME

Used mainly about the sides of a ship, this is the curvature of a hull, or a fuselage, a cockpit cover, as it tapers from the widest breadth upward and inward. In a sense, the contour "tumbles home" upward and inward in a dwindling slope. The name has an almost sentimental overtone, suggesting, perhaps, the coziness of enclosure achieved by the completed curve, igloo- or shelter-like. Seen from within, the curving material comes close and aims at a point above your head; seen from outside, it goes away from you, shutting you out. It seems at the heart of all aerodynamics, where teardrop and sphere come together.

TUXEDO

No longer familiar, perhaps, as a swing number made famous by Gene Krupa and his Orchestra (perhaps an early avatar of Arthur Honegger's own locomotive tone-poem, *Pacific 231*), *Tuxedo Junction* mechanizes an old Indian people, the P'tuksit, who lived along the western shore of the Hudson River. The name of this subtribe of the Delawares means "wolf-footed" or "round-footed." It was not a name of their own coining, but a slander foisted upon them by enemies who had found them easy meat in hand-to-hand combat, easily knocking them over. English colonists in the area soon converted P'tuksit to *Tucksito* (no loss to these maligned Indians), and actually named this part of New York State after them. Hence *Tuxedo*, which became the wealthy resort town Tuxedo Park. In 1886, Griswold Lorillard went to an annual ball in an English dinner jacket without tails. The tuxedo was born, and the big junction that brought the nobs to Tuxedo Park to play became famous, not least for the huge tromboning grunts and rending shrieks of wheels as ponderous locomotives steamed their way in and turned.

TWADDLE

Those who, as the dictionary puts it, prate or talk foolishly, or indeed write thus, may not know that *twaddle* probably comes from Scandinavian, akin to Old Norse *thvaetta*, meaning to wash or babble. *Thva* repeated becomes *thvaetta*, from Common Germanic *thwahan*, meaning *to bathe*. What we have here is the mental equivalent of someone washing out his socks or his mouth, and taking his time about it. The rhythm of the washer-woman coincides here with that of the motormouth. Emergent dirt is the trivia.

TWIT

Still a verb meaning "to taunt," *twit* means fool or butt. Some relishers of the word link it to *twat* (vagina), which combined with *twirp* or *twerp* to make a term for a contemptibly trivial person. *Twat* is not so fierce a barbarism as calling someone of either sex a *cunt*, however, and one can only marvel at the male sexism that thought up such a term of abuse. In *Vanity of Vanities*, an "improving" text of 1660, one sentence reads as follows: "They talked of his having a cardinal's hat, they'd send him as soon an old nun's twat." Perhaps Robert Browning found himself dazed by the punctuation, for he wrote in *Pippa Passes* (1841): "Sing to the bats' sleek sisterhoods full complines with gallantry, Then owls and bats, cowls and twats, monks and nuns, in a cloister's moods, adjourn to the oak-stump pantry." He thought *twat* was some item of a nun's apparel. This was the flub that antagonized James Murray, father of the *Oxford English Dictionary*, but we have to take Browning as we find him, misconstruing while inspired. In the scuffles of my boyhood, *twatting* (for reasons yet unknown to me) meant to thrust screwed-up silver paper (*the crab*) from a chocolate bar down the back of the collar of the person sitting in front of you at school or the movies. Since the advent of *Monty Python's Flying Circus*, *twit* has become a vogue word, thanks to their incessant use of it in the sense of *nitwit*.

TYCOON

A trumped-up Japanese title, *taikun* was a word used to magnify the role of the shogun or military commander of the country, especially when he was addressing foreigners, the point being to suggest that he was more potent and important than the emperor himself. The word meant emperor or great prince, borrowed from the Chinese *t'ai kiuen* (Great prince). After the word entered English in the middle of the nineteenth century, it increasingly came to denote a person of high rank, but its present reference to movers and shakers in the world of finance begins only after 1918. F. Scott Fitzgerald's tycoon was by no means the last.

UGLY

Just listen to this word's source, and the words related to it: *ug-gligr*, *ugr*, *ugga*, almost the spittle-thick, syrupy-throated Turkish gurgle of the vowel-gobbling Turkish judge in *Midnight Express*. In fact, *uggligr*, *ugr*, and *ugga* are Old Norse, source of our own less deterring words for fear and fearsome. The word first meant hideous or horrible, certainly in the thirteenth century; by the next century it had acquired the supplementary meaning of awful to look at. This is perhaps an access of sensitivity, implying degrees of recoil, from outright horror to aesthetic flinching. In the early 1930s, with a new spelling, *ugli*, it landed on a new Jamaican citrus fruit, a hybrid of grapefruit and tangerine with an off-putting loose wrinkled yellow rind.

ULLAGE

This word, revived by space science, comes from the fifteenth century, denoting the amount of space left in a bottle or barrel, descended from Latin *oculus* ("eye") in the sense of bunghole in a barrel. It was the void you could see and estimate through the eyehole. As *oculus* launched out into French, becoming *oeil*, it developed a verb form, *ouiller*, meaning to fill up a barrel to the bunghole (tamp it, top it off). Hence French *ouillage*, yielding via Anglo-Norman *ulliage* the word we now know from its use about the fuel tanks of rockets.

UNIQUE

Slowly losing out to those who think there can be degrees of it, *unique* means one and only, like nothing else, not even in the faintest amount (compare with *paraffin*). Many think it means special, out of the ordinary, but it should be kept for the purpose the Romans devised it for, as *unicus*, the only one of its kind, unparalleled, or as the Greeks put it, *hapax legomenon*.* Perhaps materialistic democracy has blunted people's responses, convincing them that the unique does not exist, but only the unusual, whereas of course every blade of grass, every snowflake, is unique, a fact that no one lives long enough to prove. So sometimes the *unique* has to be taken on trust as a Platonic form wafting about among commonplace things. "Very unique" and "completely unique" are redundant expressions that bother purists such as me and almost no one else.

UPSTART

Some words have to go back to front in order to survive, much as *wops* had to become *wasp*. An upstart is one who has started up, but gone too high, leaping, springing, vaulting, and *start-up* he was called, as in Shakespeare's *Much Ado about Nothing*

---

*A word or form that occurs only once in the recorded corpus of a language, often referred to as *hapax* (= "a thing said only once").

(1599): "That young start-up hath all the glory of my overthrow," says Don Juan. Reversed, that *upstart* is still with us, among the upchucks and the upfucks.

URANIUM

Not so new, *uranium* goes back to 1781, when the English–German astronomer Sir William Herschel designated Uranus a planet ("a wandering star") and chose for it the name of the Greek sky god *Ouranos*. Eight years later, Martin Klaproth, a German chemist, discovered element 92, which he named to honor Herschel and his planet. Some dictionaries still describe this basis of the atom bomb as "A rare, heavy, white metallic element, having no important uses." Actually, during the nineteenth century uranium was used medically in many ways, against ringworm and birthmarks, for instance, and in the production of exquisitely tinted glass, an entire (radioactive) set being given to Queen Victoria. The metal occurs in several minerals, including pitchblende and carnotite, and yields the isotope U 238 from which plutonium can emerge.

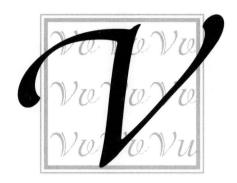

VERNACULAR

When Jack Valenti described the swearing-in of Lyndon B. Johnson as president aboard Air Force One in the presence of JFK's corpse, he used the phrase "contagious patriotism." He was not using the vernacular, but calling upon the resources of his vocabulary to convey the exquisite pain of that occasion. Latin *vernaculus*, meaning "native" or "domestic," comes from *verna*, its word for "slave born at home, in other words born into household slavery." So vernacular literature, as we sometimes patronizingly call it when referring to Europe in the late thirteenth century, was writing not in Latin but in the local patois, the native dialects. One assumes that slaves were read to rather than reading for themselves. The word has a poignant twist.

VISIT

This one puzzles Brits visiting the U.S. more than vice versa because the narrow English meaning is part of the voluminous American one. In England, *visit* means go and see, as does Latin's *visitare*, whereas in the U.S. *visit* encompasses a whole bevy of social doings, mainly sitting down and having a real good jaw about everything, and this leads to some unusual uses of the word. "We had a real good visit" means more than *go see*, implying a truly satisfying exchange of news and opinions. The epitome of aloof visit is the French novelist Raymond Roussel, wealthy and eccentric, who sailed all the way to India, to *see* it, then turned around and went back, having seen it. The American version almost suggests nothing held back, but incessant chat until all participating minds have been emptied out. The Indo-European base is *woid, weid, wid*, and some siblings of *visit* are *revise, envy, survey, video, view, visa, visage, visible, vision, visor, visual, vista, wise*, and *wit*. Once, when the poet William Empson had the office next to mine, he told me he was going off to visit another poet, Wallace Stevens. "You will find him changed," I said; Stevens had died some years earlier. I never heard any more about this *visit*, but I sensed Empson implied something quite American—this *visit* would be copious, convivial, and magical.

Of course, the most startling aspect of this verb is *visit with*, comparable to *converse with*, whereas the British use restricts itself to transitive verb plus object; no interfering prepositions. To an American ear, *visit with* sounds like a complete deed, whereas merely to visit someone—that odd blend of hauteur and distance—seems ultramontane.

WANK

Not found in polite dictionaries, this word for masturbation has extended its reach into *wanker*, one who practices what used dramatically to be called self-defilement. A *wanker*, broadly used, is a person of acute spiritual inanition, concerned only with lazy private gratification. Actually, *wanker* has been around since the late nineteenth century, always the word for jerk-off, and owing something to a dialect word, *wank*, a violent blow (to one's meat, et cetera). Perhaps akin to *wankle*, meaning unsteady (Old English *wancol*). The *wan* component recalls schoolboy myths about masturbation, principally that it made you deathly pale and hollowed out your spine. Wise boys kept their yield in huge stone jars beneath their beds at least until manhood, when such vessels might be passed on to weaklings who needed them to boast about: hence a freemasonry of sperm (or spunk).

Note Anthony Burgess's comment in *One Man's Chorus* (1998): "When I was told, untruthfully, that I was still 'wanking,' I assumed that this meant masturbating, but it has developed the meaning of lazing, refusing to work."

WARFARIN

Deadly to rats as D-Con, and possibly to humans in the wrong doses or potentiated by other drugs, this anticoagulant takes part of its name from the foundation that sponsored it: Wisconsin Alumni Research Foundation, the remainder from coum*arin*. People put on this drug (a common brand name is Coumadin) have often been on parenteral heparin beforehand, the drug made from the plant coltsfoot. Coumarin (from *coumarou*) is a toxic white crystalline lactone with an odor of new-mown hay, found in the tonka bean and clover and used in perfumery and soap. Anyone taking warfarin may well marvel at the usefulness of something that may make rats nostalgic for a field of new-mown hay while making them bleed to death. An illicit yearning forms in some patients, who wish all their drugs were cryptic acronyms indicating provenance and financing. The pill-taker in the street can only wonder why warfarin ever needed coumarin if not for intensified blood-thinning. That same pill-taker will never eye a box of D-Con without feeling something for the rat. No one has ever remarked on any aroma of new-mown hay emanating from the daily dose.

WASISTDAS

Reputedly said by a German visitor to Paris in the days of horse carriages, who kept on looking behind him through the little window provided in the cab's rear. The cabbie promptly named this window the *wasistdas* to honor his fare's repeated question "*Was ist das?*" It has not caught on, but it deserves a run even as a spyhole in a rubberneck's pimpmobile.

WEDGIE

Supposed impolite for an approximately wedge-shaped hunk of undercloth trapped between the buttocks, doomed to emerge, when tugged, less pristine than when it snuck in, but one of the hazards of moving about when clad. The contortions of people trying to dislodge a wedgie without touching it in public are a joy to watch: women seem more agile, sometimes advancing one knee, then the other, or doing a backwards sashay of the buttock, as if trying to produce a dimple, whereas men have the temerity to pluck away, but as if removing a smut or a feather, sometimes even delivering the offending gash and its contents a bash with the fist. The tighter your clothes fit, the fewer wedgies you will have since they feed on ripples, blebs, and overlaps.

WEIRD

Ridiculing the country's legal system, one comedian cites the case of Lorena Bobbitt, who cut off her husband's penis and threw it away. The authorities detained her in a mental hospital for six weeks to see if she did anything weird. He means extraordinary or uncanny; but the old sense of *weird*, when it was *wyrd*, had to do with destiny and fate. *Wyrd* things were ordained by the force called *wyrd*. And so, medievally speaking, what Mrs. Bobbitt did was perhaps inevitable, and she was merely a pawn. *Wyrd* comes from an obsolete Old English verb, *worth*, meaning "to become, to come to be," kin of German *werden*. Thus the weird sisters in *Macbeth*, with whom Mrs. Bobbitt perhaps makes a fourth, are the exponents of fate rather than its reporters. In this, they resemble the Scandinavian norns and the famous three Greek fates: Clotho, who spins; Lachesis, who allots; and Atropos who snips. An odd thing about the Greek gods and fates is that a well-known force called *Anangke*, or necessity, operated above them and in spite of them, going its own inexplicable way while those other forces and personages tried to go theirs, all calling the shots for baffled humans. *Wyrd* was always weird.

WENCH

Always a touch derisive, this, perhaps because it is a jocular verb as well (males go wenching); Middle English *wenche*, short for *wenchel*, child, comes from Old English *wencel* deriving from Old High German *wanchal*, which meant unsteady, someone committed to the verb *wankon*, to stagger, to totter, to flicker, almost as if, long before them, someone had envisioned the characteristic gait of a woman in high heels, especially one unaccustomed, whose ankles turn to rubber. This word has a robust, down-to-earth flavor not complimentary to women since it regards them smugly as sex toys.

As the following old Midlands song suggests:

> I know a clacksome wench, and she is clacksome,
> Oh how clacksome she.
> I will her placket drench.

WHORE

The *wh* first appeared in the sixteenth century where unadorned *c*, *k*, and *q* had served before, from Indo-European *qar*, Latin *carus*, for "dear" (source of *charity* and *caress*), Old Irish *caraim*, meaning "I love," and Latvian *kars*, "randy" or "greedy." There is

no heart of gold in this formula, but along with the rapacity goes a certain professional bonhomie. So, fused, we have lust, money, and good cheer. Prehistoric German had *khoron*, which yielded German *hure*. Pronunciation varies a good deal, sometimes "hooah," sometimes "hor," but never as far a reach as, say, Texas's "spa" for *spy*.

WIDGET

Variant of *gadget*, usually a small contraption affixed to something else, although often limited to a small cylindrical container for sending messages along pneumatic tubes. Its most mythic presence consists in its being the name of any hypothetical contrivance, as yet undesigned, that touts the standard output of a company. A theoretical prototype. Something Platonic gives the *widget* an appealing, fictional flair. It is not yet the name of an aircraft, although it seems it should be.

WIGGY

You are wiggy when your head is overworked and performs as if unconnected to the body, as may happen with a *wig*, just as unconnected. Crazy or strange will serve as meanings, but *wiggy* is unlikely ever to lose its connotations of jive talk, free rap, bugging someone, excellent or neat, exciting, intoxicating, ecstasy. Like the word *ass* ("The country needs his ass"), *wiggy* is a *synecdoche*, meaning a part stands for the whole or the whole for a part ("Here comes the law" as a cop approaches), from Greek *sun* (with) + *ekdekhesthai* (to take up with another, or to take one thing for another). In British English, a *wigging* is a telling-off, with *wig* from shortened *periwig* (the sort of telling-off a bewigged judge might deliver).

WIMP

This word was born around 1920, but not in popular use until the 1960s. Perhaps it derives from *whimper* or from an obsolete term for a woman (*wimp*). A feeble, inconsequential person is the clear meaning, but, oddly enough, since the word became a fashionable slur, its underground meanings have surfaced as if to explain it. They do not, neither the acronym for "Weakly Interacting Massive Particle" nor, from cyberspace, "Windows/ icon/mouse/pointer." At this rate, either "Why is Mother paralyzed?" or "Wet idiots must pray." Perhaps the word is best read as an incentive to undoers of acronyms, who will strive for majestic idiomatic fluency and shocking relevance.

Lovers of curiosa will relish the facts that *Wimpy* was the name of a chain of British coffee-shops and the nickname of the Wellington bomber used in World War Two.

WODGE

People tend to use this word not so much to be precise about an object or some stuff as to convey their feelings about either. A wodge is a shapeless, unrecognizable lump of something, screwed-up gluey wallpaper, papier-mâché, decayed cheeses, foul compost removed from a dog's bowel. Burlier than *wedge*, and evoking both *stodge* and *podge*, it makes the user an amateur expressionist, intent more on feelings than on accurate depiction, and, as such, supplies an important need: saying *wodge* somehow saps the thing or stuff envisaged of its *wodginess* and confers a sense of control where all is blur and blob, seep and viscous rot.

WOOLGATHERING

Doubtful if this practice, in the literal sense, goes on much outside New Zealand. It's a back formation from *wood-gathering* and

denotes wool tufts shed from sheep and found snagged on bushes, but also vagrant flights of fancy, thought that goes nowhere. People are often accused of this, but more often accuse themselves although not with cogent vehemence. "I was wool-gathering" is one of those rueful, semi-joyful admissions tantamount to relishing the sensation of still being alive.

WUSS

Can it truly be a fusion of *wimp* and *pussy*, or an abbreviated *pussy-wussy*? This denotes a weak or pitifully lenient person, the word suggesting cowardice and seepage all in one, as well as echoing *worse-worst*, mostly teenagers citing for contempt. *Wuss out*, an increasingly popular form, means to give up out of spiritual inanition or plain old gutlessness.

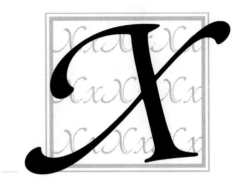

X-RAY

It was 1895 and the German physicist Wilhelm Konrad von Roentgen was busily passing currents of electricity through various gases sealed in a vacuum tube. All of a sudden, he found that radiation was going right through things opaque to normal light. He had discovered *something*, much in the manner of Varèse the composer who, asked when he experimented, replied that he did so *before* he began to compose. "What did you think," a friend asked Roentgen, "when the radiation passed through?" "I didn't think," he answered, "I experimented." His discovery he named *X-strahlen*, the X denoting the unknown nature of the rays. X has come to stand for other things than the unknown: lewd, obscene, or pornographic movies; to delete something; as XX to betray, as used by the novelist John O'Hara; marking the spot, and, as X—, profoundly inferior. Recently of course, we have the *X-Files*, a series also devoted to the unknown, but in dark green darkness such as only Seattle knows, amid which enigmatic discontinuity masquerades as cosmic enigma. Illiterates, we might remind ourselves, sign themselves with X. In the Middle Ages, a row of X's stood for kisses, though of course not ending a letter by an illiterate; the X here stood for St. Andrew's cross, and people pledged themselves to be honorable in his name. You kissed your signature to make it firm. As Diane Ackerman points out in *A Natural History of Love*, "It used to be fashionable in Spain to close formal letters with QBSP (*Que Besa Su Pies*, 'Who kisses your feet?') or QBSM (*Que Besa Su Mano*, 'Who kisses your hand?')." The lore of kissing is endless. In my boyhood, you signed a letter BOLTOP (Better on lips than on paper) and SWALK (Signed with a loving kiss). These were only two of the formulas, and probably still are.

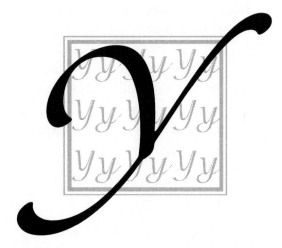

YAPP

A bookbinding in which soft leather overlaps the page, protecting the edge, giving the book (often a Bible or a prayer book) a luxurious feel, perhaps summoning up the idea that a book's pages should be wholly encased in similar leather, with the edges of the yapp actually meeting like hands in the Indian greeting, *namaste*. A man called Yapp invented this binding.

YENTA

Copious motormouth, often female, possibly taken from Italian *gentile* or French *gentille*, "nice" or "gracious," but more certainly abstracted from an officious, funny character Yente Telebende, denizen of a regular column in the New York City Yiddish newspaper *The Jewish Daily Forward*.

YES-MAN

From the early 1900s, but still current, always referring to fawning and ceremonious subordinate, brown-nosing, ass-licking, first appearing in a 1913 drawing by the sports cartoonist T. A. Dorgan, depicting a bunch of newspapermen, each one placarded yes-man and blatantly agreeing with his boss. I suspect this word is mostly written these days, rather than uttered, perhaps because, written, it has the sting of an ancient curse revived but slid out in silence to reward him in this world and damn him in the next. The essence of being a yes-man, surely, is never to be known as such.

YO

This is crude, usually an interrogative greeting, a caricature of *you* (*you there*), as one epitome of machismo hails another. Not often heard in galleries of art or chamber music concert halls, it reaffirms the caller's masculinity, even if unanswered, and (presumably) warns the hearer not to respond if unable to do so in a deep and complicitous enough rumble. Military in tone, or redneck.

I sometimes wonder if British *yokel*, for country bumpkin, an alternative word for woodpecker, does not sit in this coarse summons's background, recalling us to *gowk* for cuckoo, half-wit. In this case, *yo* is clearly insulting. In the North of England, *yo* is common for *you*, especially in the accusative and vocative. In upstate New York, as *The Ithaca Journal* makes evident, the word is both blurt of pain, an entreaty of some familiarity, and a mumble from the heart: " 'I came down the steps and my brother raises his head and says, 'Yo, sis, help me, I've been shot.' "

YOMP

Advancing toward Port Stanley over white grass and fiddle-dee in the barren foothills of the Falkland Islands, British soldiers, carrying 120 pounds of equipment in front of them and on their backs, evidently felt the need for a word that conveyed the peculiar gait required to advance eastward from Goose Green, so they came up with *yomp*, perhaps a relative of *tromp*. Something dutiful and ungainly emerges from this word, far from *romp*, but you never know where military humor will send you next. The best example I ever heard was by Clive of India (1725–1774), who encrypted "I have taken Sind," a province of India, to the Latin *peccavi* ("I have sinned"). I would have promoted him on the spot despite his territorial greed.

ZED

Last letter of the alphabet in English-speaking countries that do not call it *zee*, this is the term of abuse that Shakespeare used in *King Lear*: "Thou whoreson Zed, thou unnecessary letter" (II.ii.69, 1605). Nineteenth-century children often called it *izzard* or *uzzard*. As to Shakespeare's contention of the "unnecessary," he surely meant voiced *s* as in *exercise*. A certain Mulcaster in 1582 had already complained that "so manie zeds in our tung are herd, and so few sene." The letter Z, as we are told at the end of the political movie so entitled, in Greek means "is alive." If letters began as pictures (A as the horns of an ox, B a two-chambered shelter, H a fence, L a whip, and G a camel), Z seems to have depicted a sword and a shield, but it might just as well have been a cobra or a plant. Why does Z come last in our alphabet? It did not always, sixth for the Greeks, but dropped by the Romans, who eventually had to bring it back and so stuck it on the end. Z too is the trademark of the masked avenger Zorro, incised in the skin or clothes of his enemies.

ZIPANGU

Marco Polo's name for Japan.

ZOOT SUIT

This was a man's suit of a style popular in the early 1940s, with full-legged, tight-cuffed pants and a long jacket with wide lapels and broad thickly padded shoulders. A rhyming formation with suit. Shown to flamboyant advantage in the movie *Zoot Suit* (1981). The phrase was coined by American clothier and band-leader Harold C. Fox, born in 1910.

ZYMURGIST

From Greek *zume* (leaven) + *-urgist* (as in metallurgist): one who works with yeast, a brewer. *Brewer's Dictionary of Phrase and Fable* quaintly ends with this word and the final gloss: "Brewer, the last word in dictionaries." A *zymurgist*, like a cleaning-lady and an exterminator, a drug-dealer and a gold prospector, traffics in dust.

Acknowledgments

The following people have offered suggestions or proffered books invaluable to my word-collecting habit, and grateful thanks are due. Any errors made here are mine, not theirs: Diane Ackerman, Michael Bergstein, Bill Carini, Marcia and Sam Fink, Sheila Forster and Professor William Forster, OBE, Tanis and Christopher Furst, Jeanne Mackin, Bradford Morrow, Chris Nash, Diane Orcutt, Jim Orcutt, Steve Poleskie, Janette Reardon, Bryan Reardon, George Rhoads, the late Carl Sagan, Marah Stets, Marcelle Lapow Toor, and Mildred Noden West.

Martha Barnette's *Ladyfingers and Nun's Tummies*, a joyous work by a real classical scholar, has fed me well, as has her *A Garden of Words*. Karen Elizabeth Gordon's *The Disheveled Dictionary* is a "curious caper" indeed, like her *Paris Out of Hand*, *Torn Wings and Faux Pas*, *The Ravenous Muse*, and *The New Well-Tempered Sentence*, all of them almanacs of honed high wordplay. Diana Wells's *100 Flowers* is just as learned and has given steady pleasure and knowledge. Robert L. Chapman's *American Slang* (unabridged) is invaluable and decently detailed, offering as it does another language. Margaret Moore's *Understanding British English* helped me to remember. Wilfred Funk's *Word Origins* provided many an excellent starting point and John Ayto's *Dictionary of Word Origins* is a delightful classic, crisp and learned. I have resorted to many other books, but mainly those named, and a bevy of dictionaries, best of all *Webster*, the *American Heritage* with its invaluable Indo-European supplement, and the *Oxford English*. I thank all toilers in this delightful vineyard for being so various and committed. Poring over some of them many years ago got me started, infected, newly elated by this oddly spacefaring, backwards quest. My gratitude to Cornell University and Charles W. Jermy, Jr., Associate Dean of Continuing Education, for the opportunity to try out some of these ideas and words on a large, responsive summer audience. Any errors in the book are the result of sheer ignorance on my part.